The Romans in Central Europe

THE ROMANS
IN
CENTRAL EUROPE

Herbert Schutz

Yale University Press

New Haven and London

1985

Designed by Mary Carruthers and set in Monophoto Baskerville
Printed in Great Britain by Butler & Tanner Ltd, Frome and London.

Library of Congress Catalog Card Number 84-052245

ISBN 0-300-03200-5

Contents

Illustration Acknowledgements

Augsburg, Römisches Museum, Plate 7b; Fig. 112. Augst, Römermuseum, Plate 6c; Figs. 2, 86, 89, 133, 139, 156. Bad Deutsch Altenburg, Museum Carnuntinum, Figs. 67, 98, 100, 120. Bad Homburg/Taunus, Saalburg Museum, Figs. 18–25, 114, 115. Basel, Historisches Museum, Figs. 11, 47. Berlin, Bildarchiv, Preußischer Kulturbesitz, Plates 6a, 6b. Bonn, Rheinisches Museum, Plate 7c; Figs. 53, 54. Bregenz, Vorarlberger Landesmuseum, Fig. 55. Bremen, Landesmuseum, Figs. 9, 33, 34. Darmstadt, Hessisches Landesmuseum, Plate 1a; Figs. 58, 121. Freiburg, Museum für Ur- und Frühgeschichte, Plates 4c, 5c, 5d, 8b; Figs. 4, 5, 41, 46, 66, 81–83, 85, 127, 128. Graz, Steiermärkisches Landesmuseum, Joanneum, Figs. 48, 102, 103. Heidelberg, Kurpfälzisches Museum, Fig. 79. Innsbruck, Tiroler Landesmuseum, Fig. 101. Karlsruhe, Badisches Landesmuseum, Figs. 50, 51, 77. Klagenfurt, Landesmuseum für Kärnten, Plate 1b; Figs. 70, 73, 74, 118, 119. Köln, Römisch-Germanisches Museum, Plates 1c, 1d, 4a, 4b, 5b, 7d, 8a, 8c; Figs. 52, 78, 84, 91, 96, 104. Ladenburg, Lobdengaumuseum, Fig. 1. Mainz, Mittelrheinisches Landesmuseum, Plate 7a; Figs. 84, 90, 130, 132, 141, 149. Mainz, Römisch-Germanisches Zentralmuseum, Figs. 93, 61, 76, 92, 95, 97. Münster, Westfälisches Museum für Archäologie, Figs. 7, 8, 12, 43–45, 124, 131, 135. München, Prähistorische Staatssammlung, Figs. 13, 39, 72, 122, 138, 143, 147, 165. Monza, Tesoro del Duomo, Fig. 42. Nürnberg, Germanisches Nationalmuseum, Fig. 17. Obernburg/Main, Römerhaus, Fig. 64. Petronell, Freilichtmuseum, Figs. 32, 60. Regensburg, Städtisches Museum, Figs. 93, 99. Rottweil, Stadtmuseum, Plate 3a. Speyer, Historisches Museum der Pfalz, Figs. 16, 123, 125, 126, 129, 155. Straubing, Gäubodenmuseum, Plate 5a; Figs. 14, 136, 137, 142, 144–146. Stuttgart, Württembergisches Landesmuseum, Lapidarium; Figs. 56, 59, 63, 65, 80. Trier, Bischöfliches Dom- und Diözesanmuseum; Plates 2a, 2b, 2c, 2d. Trier, Rheinisches Landesmuseum; Plates 3b, 3c; Figs. 87, 108–111, 117, 151, 152, 158, 162. Wien, Kunsthistorisches Museum; Figs. 6, 40, 68, 69, 116, 140. Wiesbaden, Sammlung Nassauischer Altertümer; Figs. 10, 15, 62, 71, 75, 134, 148. Xanten, Freilichtmuseum; Fig. 31. Map p. 91; Westfälisches Museum für Archäologie, Münster.

Author's photos, Plates 1a, 1c, 4b, 4c, 5d; Figs. 3–5, 10, 18–32, 35–38, 46, 57, 60, 62, 64, 66, 81–83, 85, 88, 91, 94, 96, 103, 105, 106, 113, 127, 128, 153, 154, 157, 159–161, 163, 164.

Foreword

It is the intention of this book to place the centuries of Roman occupation north of the Alps into their early historic context. It continues the overview of central European cultural history begun in the earlier volume, *The Prehistory of Germanic Europe*. The discussion of the Roman presence is necessarily restricted to those parts of central Europe actually occupied by Rome and organized as the provinces of *Germania inferior* and *superior*, *Raetia*, *Noricum* and *Pannonia superior*. The treatment of the latter, however, and of the so-called *Germania libera* is incidental.

While the earlier book had to be based exclusively on the analysis and evaluation of archeological evidence, the discussion of the many aspects of Roman provincial culture can draw on written records as well as on the material evidence provided by archeology. This evidence alone could suffice to indicate that a complete and brilliantly developed material culture had imposed itself on a receding indigenous culture. The written records contribute details of specific events, of techniques in the arts and crafts and the names of people, places and things. Much of the historical documentation concerning such topics as techniques, religion, society and the economy is, of course, not exclusive to the central European provinces and applies to other regions of the Roman Empire as well. From that point of view, the book provides illustrations of the forms which Roman provincial culture took in the former Roman provinces along the Rhine and Danube. Over the years, the accumulated archeological evidence has assumed vast proportions, so that it is possible to deal only with representative illustrations of some aspects of this evidence and no claim to completeness can be made, especially in view of the amount of new material coming to light under the ongoing pressures of salvage archeology.

As might be expected, the military arrival of the Romans in central Europe brought a disruption to the cultural development of the area. Military campaigns into the interior and attempts at romanizing the Germanic populations disrupted social structures and tribal links. Less than three hundred years later new tribal groups and retinues, headed by personalities benefiting from acquired leadership principles, would in turn contribute their part to the destabilization of the Empire. Yet in those Celtic areas actually occupied by Rome and incorporated into the Empire there was continuity in some established aspects of the cultural inventory. There is material evidence that the everyday culture of the native population was affected only marginally by romanization. The natives had little to contribute to Roman arts and crafts that stands out in its stylistic individuality, which is not to say that romanized craftsmen had not learned the techniques involved in the production of works in stone, paintings, mosaics, pottery, glasswares and metal objects.

The cosmopolitan sophistication of the new urban culture and its reflection on the estates was new to the area and is best represented by the suggestive power of imperious monumentality inherent in Roman architecture. As in previous periods, the culture-carrying tribal elites, whether Celtic or Germanic, were well prepared to accept the new ways in order to participate in the religious, political, economic and cultural life of the new order. Throughout the Roman period the question of actual native participation in the 'High Culture' of the northern provinces remains open. Life of the 'pagans' in the *pagus*, the simple folk of the countryside, was only marginally affected by the urban culture introduced by Rome, partly because the multiculturalism of the Empire made the survival of indigenous forms possible. This was particularly true for religion, where the Roman interpretation of native divinities promoted their survival far into Roman, even early Christian, times, after the search for religious constancy had transformed a religious life centered on cults to one of personal mystical experiences with ethical content. The Empire itself survived in a religious form.

Some elements of continuity notwithstanding, the Roman period constitutes a significant change in the cultural development of central Europe. During the early period of the Roman occupation a new people with new materials, new forms, new methods, new concerns and new interests brought to an end the formerly brilliant Celtic La Tène period. During the Roman Imperial period the tribal structures of the Germanic peoples crystallized against Rome's northern borders. In the prolonged clashes with the more simply structured tribal societies from beyond the frontier, the organized Roman state with its complex institutions was forced to seek the support of these same tribal units to fight other threats from within and without. The Germanic kingdoms which arose in the western part of the Roman Empire saw themselves as heirs and preservers of Rome and during too many centuries to come the Empire and the world of forms which it represented were to remain the frame of reference for future northern kingdoms and empires.

In preparing this book I have met with the kind cooperation of many directors and curators of museums and archives. Once again I thank Dr O. Höckmann, Römisch-Germanisches Zentralmuseum Mainz; Dr B. Heukemes, Kurpfälzisches Museum der Stadt Heidelberg; Dr H. Hellenkemper, Römisch-Germanisches Museum, Köln; Dr J. Garbsch, Museum für Vor- und Frühgeschichte, München; Dr Boosen, Westfälisches Museum fur Archäologie, Münster; especially Mr Dangel-Reese, Museum für Vor- und Frühgeschichte der Stadt Freiburg; Dr W. Weber, Bischöfliches Dom- und Diözesanmuseum, Trier as well as Dr W. Binsfeld, Rheinisches Landesmuseum, Trier and to the many others in Germany, Austria, Switzerland and Italy who permitted me to photograph or who supplied the photographs for this book.

I owe thanks for the continuing interest and support of my university and to Mrs Joyce Lucey for typing most of the manuscript and to my colleague Prof. F.R. Skilton for placing his computer expertise at my disposal in preparing the subject index. I would like to take this opportunity to express sincere thanks to my readers for their selfless assistance: to Mrs Libby Klekowski of Amherst, Massachusetts, who read the manuscript for American orthography; to Mrs Mary Bell, Librarian at the Albright Knox Gallery, Buffalo and to Mrs Margaret Grove, Reference Librarian at Brock University, St Catharines, who read the galleys.

I wish to make special acknowledgement to Mr John Nicoll, Editor, Yale University Press, London, for his interest in this volume and to Miss Mary Carruthers for the skill and accuracy with which she prepared this book for publication.

I owe special gratitude to the members of my immediate family who cheerfully accompanied me over thousands of kilometers, at times over difficult terrain, and who listened to my seemingly endless lectures on the subject with patient interest. For making his knowledge of micro-computers available to me I owe my son Christopher a special expression of gratitude and I dedicate this book to him.

H. Schutz   March 1985.
Brock University
St Catharines, Ontario,
Canada.

1. The Military Setting

Before Caesar arrived in Gaul in 58 BC the Celtic Helvetii engaged in almost daily strife with their neighbors situated north[1] of the Rhine between Lake Constance and Basel and south of the river Main, the old Celtic core area from which the Helvetii had come. This area was occupied by members of a tribal confederation called the Suebi, a collective term which appears at different times throughout central Europe. In 58 BC Caesar first encountered them on the Upper Rhine; later, before 38 BC, the Ubii on the Middle Rhine complained of Suebian harassment. Still later, c. AD 100, they are known east of the Elbe in the North German Plain where Tacitus included them among the Nerthus people of the western Baltic Sea. Caesar listed the following member tribes in the Suebian army confronting him:[2] the Harudes, a people associated with the Cimbri, on whose native territory in Jutland two Celtic ceremonial wagons have been found;[3] the Marcomanni, then located south of the Main in that fallow border territory termed a 'Mark' which had been vacated by the Helvetii,[4] and was now occupied by those Suebi who in the first century BC came to be identified as the Marcomanni;[5] the Triboci, Nemetes and Vangiones, tribes of undecided origin, of which the Triboci and Nemetes are known only by their Celtic names, while it is held that the Vangiones (derived from *vanga*, field, forested meadow),[6] located further north on population maps, were Germanic. These three appear to be heavily, if not totally, celticized, a factor which may explain why they remained on the left side of the Rhine, to become completely romanized in the end.

Roman involvement in the affairs of the north-western Alps stems from Rome's alliance of 121 BC with the Celtic tribe of the Aedui, 'brothers of the Roman people,' located west of the Rhône in central Gaul. Towards the middle of the last century BC the struggle for supremacy between these Aedui and their eastern neighbors, the Sequani, upset the stability of the area,[7] when some time between 70–65 BC the Sequani appealed to the Suebi for assistance against the Aedui. Under their capable leader Ariovistus, the Suebi, deemed invincible by the Gauls, entered the conflict on the side of the Sequani, who though now victorious over the Aedui, promptly regretted the invitation which they had extended to Ariovistus when he claimed, in return for services rendered, one-third of the Sequarian territory on which to settle other arrivals from across the Rhine. In protest, the Sequani reconciled themselves with the Aedui and presented a common front against the Suebi, who quickly defeated the alliance in 61 BC and now exacted another third of Sequarian territory as compensation. Over Aeduan protestations in Rome, Ariovistus was recognized by the Roman

Senate as *rex et amicus populi Romani*, King and friend of the people of Rome, on the advice of Caesar, named consul in 59 BC.[8] Caesar thought it advisable to conclude such a formal relationship with Ariovistus, even if it meant recognizing the new status quo in an area that was quickly becoming a Roman sphere of interest. It is significant that the title bestowed on Ariovistus was not worded *rex Germanorum*.

The pressure from the Suebi induced the Helvetii to set out towards the Atlantic. This migration would have brought them through the Roman province of *Narbonensis*. The permission to do so was refused by Caesar, who had assumed the provincial command over the entire area in 59 BC and in 58 BC the role of defender of a molested Gaul. A decisive battle at Bibracte in 58 BC not only forced the Helvetii to turn back but enabled Caesar to see himself installed in the lands of the Aedui as their protector, having delivered them of the Helvetii. He also found himself favorably positioned against the Suebi, whose immediate neighbor he had now become. It was not a characteristic of Caesar's to stumble into situations but to manipulate them to his advantage. It is reasonable to assume that he was preparing and following some well planned options. To remove Ariovistus and the Suebian peril from Rome's borders would be a more difficult task, since Ariovistus enjoyed the protection of Rome very much at Caesar's own instigation.[9] How was he to reverse his position, wage decisive war on the Suebi and not incur the censure of the Senate? Caesar most likely presented his campaigns and their necessity as defensive and precautionary actions on the edge of civilization. Caesar recognized his opportunity to strain relations with Ariovistus when the latter continued to attract reinforcements to settle in the newly conquered territory west of the Rhine.[10] Caesar requested that Ariovistus should not

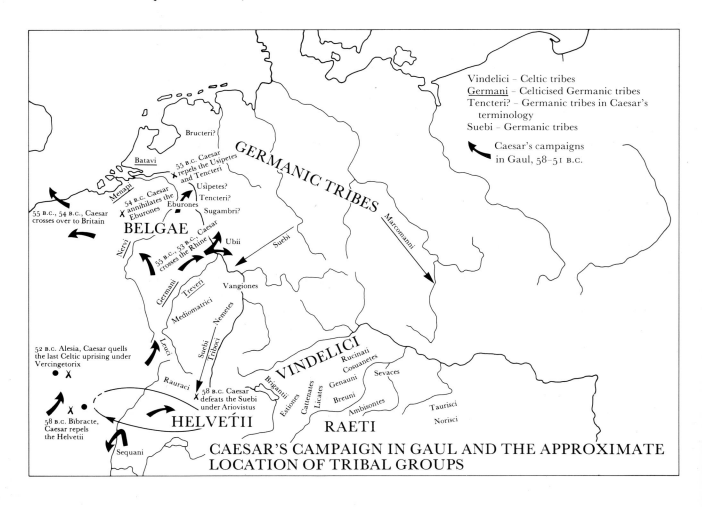

CAESAR'S CAMPAIGN IN GAUL AND THE APPROXIMATE LOCATION OF TRIBAL GROUPS

1 Funerary ware of the Neckar Suebians, hand formed and imported from the ancestral Elbian lands. It contained ashes and gifts and was closed with a lid. The hole is thought to have allowed the soul to escape. (Second quarter of first century AD. (Lobdengau-museum, Ladenburg)

continue with this resettlement. Ariovistus, proclaimed King by the Roman Senate, recognized as such when King Voccio of *Noricum* gave him his daughter's hand in marriage,[11] and commanding a victorious force thought to be invincible, suggested to Caesar that he was meddling in strictly internal affairs, that he, Ariovistus, had been invited by the Gauls[12] and that Caesar's assumption of the role of protector of the Gauls was no more than a pretext to oust the Suebi from their newly acquired lands. Caesar had circulated alarming reports emphasizing the vast military power of Ariovistus—he suggests at least 100,000 warriors—and the threat this force constituted to the security of the Roman frontiers. Ariovistus' position was probably much less important and less threatening than Caesar would have it believed.[13] To secure his rear Caesar had treated the Helvetii benevolently. Too weak to face Caesar's legions, Ariovistus had resorted to skillful negotiations which did nothing to compromise his prestige as leader of a mighty force. Initially the Roman legions had fallen into panic when ordered to advance on the Suebi. Caesar was proud to relate how he rose to the occasion, shamed them and then convinced them to the point of enthusiasm for the inevitable successful outcome of the impending battle.[14] The actual place of this engagement has not been located, though a number of sites between modern Besançon and Mulhouse in Alsace have been suggested. This battle resulted in a crushing defeat of the Suebi which ended in their complete withdrawal from the left bank of the Rhine, except for the Triboci, Nemetes and Vangiones. Hereafter the Suebi came to be known for their harassment of various tribal groups east of the Rhine (Fig. 1). It must have given the Gauls cause to wonder though, why Caesar did not withdraw from the area and leave the Gauls to govern themselves.[15] Instead he set out upon the systematic annexation of Gaul by means of an extensive encirclement of the interior which, by the end of 57 BC, he believed to have concluded. Not until after the fall of Alesia in 52 BC was the conquest of Gaul a fact.

In all of his campaigns Caesar succeeded in rallying local sympathizers to his cause, so that he could count on the Gaulish aristocracy and their best fighters to swell the ranks of his auxiliaries. It was in this manner that the horsemen of the Treveri became his cavalry, and were used to such good effect against the Gauls,[16] a circumstance which has been taken to mean that the Treveri were at least a mixture of Celts and Germani. Caesar had a high opinion of his mounted infantry.[17] Thus he reports how 800 horsemen of the Usipetes and Tencteri, tribes located on the Middle Rhine, set to fight his own Roman cavalry of 5000 horses. Harassed by the Suebi, these two tribes—Caesar suggests 430,000 people—had crossed the Rhine in 56–55 BC, and had come into conflict with Caesar, who used the occasion to arrest their leaders and destroy their encampment.[18] The bloodbath was of such horrendous proportions that when word reached the Roman Senate, Caesar's old opponent Cato moved that Caesar be handed over to the Germani for his perfidy.[19] While the name Tencteri is Germanic, the Usipetes—the well-mounted ones[20]—were Celts. Caesar had pursued them across the Rhine.[21] To do so, he threw a bridge across the river, rejecting an offer of boats made by the Ubii. That there were mixed feelings about the new allegiance to Rome is perhaps indicated by the action of the Treveri,[22] who in 54 BC instigated a revolt among the Eburones[23] and then sought to establish links with the trans-rhenish tribes. Caesar's absence in Britain in 55 and 54 BC and the repeated requisitions, the plundering and the compulsory levies of auxiliary troops among the tribes, helped stir up a revolt led by Ambiorix,[24] who was chief among the Eburones, a Germanic tribe which had crossed the Rhine quite early. In the early winter of 54 BC, the Eburones ambushed and destroyed fifteen Roman cohorts, the equivalent of one and a half legions.[25] This success encouraged other rebellions in northern Gaul.[26] Caesar quelled these one by one, encircling the Eburones until he had isolated them completely and then descending upon them with avenging judgment, he annihilated them almost completely, a feat he reports with some satisfaction.[27] From his strategic point of view, a Belgic alliance with any of the Germani had to be crushed in the bud. In retrospect, had Caesar not done so, especially in view of the uprising led by Vercingetorix, his accomplishments in Gaul would all have been placed in the balance. The northern frontier had been established and with only minor adjustments, such as the settlement of the trans-rhenish Ubii onto the land left vacant by the Eburones, the Rhine came to be the dividing line between a regressing Celtic and an evolving Germanic culture.

Already in Caesar's time the Ubii enjoyed a preferred status in that Caesar considered them to have been once, by Germanic standards, a considerable and prosperous nation, somewhat more civilized than the other tribes, owing to their proximity to Gaul which had induced them to adopt Gaulish ways.[28] The Ubii had sent envoys to Caesar, had entered into alliance with him, had given hostages and had asked Caesar for a show of strength against the Suebi, to whom they owed tribute and who continued to harass them.[29] They even offered Caesar boats in which to cross the Rhine, as mentioned above, an offer Caesar refused not only because of the risk involved when crossing in boats but also because he felt it beneath his dignity as a commander, preferring to construct a bridge instead, a technological feat bound to impress.[30] For eighteen days he stayed on the right side of the Rhine as part of a demonstration of Roman skills and military strength.[31] His second crossing into Ubiian territory was occasioned by the revolt of 53 BC when the Treveri had received reinforcements from the Suebi further to the east. The Ubii's protestations of non-involvement in the revolt were accepted by Caesar.[32] In his commentaries he referred to their political unit as a state[33] led by chiefs and a council and presented them generally as willing and submissive allies of Rome. A people which could be credited with statehood and administrative institutions with diplomatic skills, which engaged

2 Bronze coin showing Augustus and Agrippa from *Augusta Raurica*. (Römermuseum Augst)

3 *Tropaeum Alpium*, partial reconstruction of a monument erected in 9 BC and dedicated to Augustus to commemorate the conquest of the Alps. Located at La Turbie on the heights above Monaco. Original height 50 m.

in trade and was willing to learn from more advanced neighbors could not be termed barbaric. With such a progressive people Rome could enter into relations of friendship. Soon afterwards they were entrusted with the protection of the section of the Rhine near modern Cologne. Their gradual crossing of the Rhine was brought to its logical conclusion when, in 38 BC, Marcus V. Agrippa, the closest friend of Augustus (Fig. 2), resettled them in the depopulated lands of the Eburones.[34] That the Ubii were celticized Germani is not in doubt.[35] Their center, the *Oppidum Ubiorum*, a settlement with considerable administrative self-determination, was to evolve quickly into one of the key cities of the Roman Empire, a brilliant center of Roman provincial culture on the Lower Rhine, and ultimately into the modern city of Cologne. Its role in the Roman Empire will be discussed below.

Though Caesar's conquest of Gaul was not to be completed until 51 BC, the Rhine frontier had been defined. However, the readiness of the Belgae to call in raiding parties from across the Rhine persisted into the Augustan period. In 25 BC some Roman merchants had been ambushed and killed, which necessitated a punitive expedition. Repeated Germanic incursions are documented until 16 BC, including in that year an invasion by the Germanic Sugambri, Tencteri and Usipetes which wiped out the *legio V alaudae*,[36] which was such a severe blow to Roman self-esteem that Augustus himself came to Gaul, from 16 to 13 BC, in order to supervise personally the reorganization of the province. One measure taken was the stationing of at least five legions along the Rhine, drawn from the Rhône and Saône. Another, was the establishment of a border with forts at *Vetera*, opposite the entrance of the river Lippe into the Rhine and at *Mogontiacum* opposite the confluence of the Main and Rhine.

5

4 Republican and Augustan silver coins from Dangstetten. The fort at Dangstetten was abandoned in 9 BC. (Museum für Ur- und Frühgeschichte, Freiburg)

5 Augustus Cameo, showing a victorious *imperator*, perhaps Tiberius, stepping from his chariot, welcomed by Augustus and Roma. Detail lower left shows elevation of a victory standard with cowering captive barbarians. (Kunsthistorisches Museum, Vienna)

Events in Gaul must have impressed on Rome that a more direct route to the Rhine was necessary than the detour via the Rhône valley allowed. The need for short lines of communication made the conquest of the Alps an immediate objective and by 25 BC all the Alpine passes were under Roman control. Between 25–16 BC a disposition was prepared which allowed the stepsons of Augustus, Tiberius in Gaul and in the western Alps, and Drusus in the central Alps, to launch the decisive pincer campaigns into the lands north of the Alps in the spring of 15 BC. The preparations involved gaining control over the southern Alps in 16 BC, as indicated on the *Tropaeum Alpium* set up in 7/6 BC which celebrates the conquest of the Alps and names forty-five tribes which were incorporated into the Empire (Fig. 3); the building of a road complete with protective towers and military camps from Como via Chur and Basel into the Alsace; and the raising of the *legio XXI rapax* from among the young men of the area, thereby also reducing the danger of attack from the subjected Alpine tribes in the rear. A *castrum*, a legion fortress, was established at Dangstetten (Fig. 4), just across the Rhine, by the *legio XIX* (Fig. 6) from where the area could be controlled and from where the attack on the Celtic lands north of the Alps could be launched.[37] The Celtic Vindelici were beaten following their defeat in a naval engagement on *Lacus Venetus*, the modern Lake Constance. One more great battle took place on August 1, 15 BC and the momentum of the attack carried the Romans to the Danube.[38] That same year the *Regnum Noricum* was absorbed peacefully into the Roman Empire as a client state.[39] Five years later Rome gained control over *Pannonia* and the Upper Danube became the demarcation line towards the north.[40] In Germany there is no evidence that fortified posts on the Danube controlled strategic points before the reign of Tiberius. The southward pressure of northern peoples was still many years off. With the submission of the last tribes in the western Alps the old passes linking an area of the Upper Rhine and Italy had been secured (Fig. 5).

It is likely that the Romans' ability to visualize the geographical features of central

6 Bronze platelet of *legio XIX*, *cohors III* from Dangstetten. (Museum für Ur- und Frühgeschichte, Freiburg)

Europe is not reflected in the linear conception of the Roman marching maps. It cannot have required reconnaissance to reveal to them that the Upper Rhine and the Upper Danube forced an inconvenient detour on east–west traffic. It is also likely that even before reaching the Danube the Romans had heard of a north–south amber route and of a great river flowing northward into the sea.[41] Surely what applied to the explorers of North America can be expected to apply to the Roman merchants active in central Europe. At first this information may not have been realized to be strategic intelligence; however, the subsequent campaigns waged by Roman generals, intent on stabilizing the populations of central Europe, suggest that the Roman field commanders, especially Drusus and Tiberius, did look upon the North Sea coast and the Danube as well as the Elbe and the Rhine as perimeters of their actions. The need to subdue central Europe to the Elbe would have recommended itself as a natural consequence, once it was appreciated that the converging Rhine and Danube frontiers would act as a funnel towards the south-west and thereby intensify the known population pressures then developing in the Germanic hinterland.

Events beyond the northern frontiers during the next forty years are interesting in themselves and of enough significance for the development of central European history to warrant an account in some detail. The reorganization of the realm instituted by Augustus in 27 BC divided the Empire into Imperial and Senatorial Provinces.[42] To the Emperor fell the unpacified, militarized border provinces. These had a military administration whose task it was to provide a protective buffer zone and to promote a process of consolidation, acculturation and gradual romanization.[43] In 27 BC the future provinces of *Germania superior* and *Germania inferior* to the left of the Upper and Lower Rhine were still military operational zones in which the defensive role had been assigned largely to the border tribes settled on the left bank of the Rhine. By 12 BC the Batavi, Caninefates and Ubii held the line along the Lower Rhine while the Vangiones, Nemetes and Triboci held it along the Upper Rhine, in position to discourage other trans-rhenish tribes from attempting a crossing.[44] At the same time Augustus introduced the concept of designating a principal city as a permanent and cultural center upon which all attention in the province would be focused.[45] The *Oppidum Ubiorum* was to become such a center. During this period the Roman presence in the area generally was kept to an operational minimum. Whether the territories to the left of the Rhine were considered secure or whether the demonstrations of population pressures on the right bank of the Rhine, such as those posed by the Sugambri, needed a show of strength which then gradually committed the Roman military command to ever deeper penetration of the interior, the year 12 BC marked a decisive departure from Augustus' policy of consolidation to one of expansion and control.[46] The dangers and difficulties facing any military operation in the areas east of the Rhine, already pointed out by Caesar, shaped Roman policy into one of sporadic punitive incursions into the interior. Now Augustus ordered an aggressive approach to stabilizing the Rhine frontier. Until this point it appears as if Rome had only peaceful intentions, inclined to make use of military power only as a show of dissuasion in order to impress upon the people east of the Rhine the uncompromising might of the Roman legions, and that it had no intentions of engaging in territorial expansion beyond established frontiers.[47]

All of this changed with the appointment of Drusus to Gaul and of Tiberius to the eastern Alps. Tiberius' subjugation of the area east of *Noricum* to the knee of the Danube—*Pannonia*—had been largely completed by 11 BC and finalized by 9 BC. Drusus assumed control of Gaul and promptly set out to regulate conditions along the Rhine border which now ceased to be a purely defensive line. The forts along the Rhine, many of them located at a point where a river from the east entered the Rhine, now became operational bases for the campaigns launched against the interior.[48] These campaigns necessitated the presence of a much greater number of Romans, so that it was only from now on that the romanization of the area began to intensify quickly. It is possible that conditions forced an expansionist policy on the military commanders. The absence of roads, the damp climate, an inhospitable nature

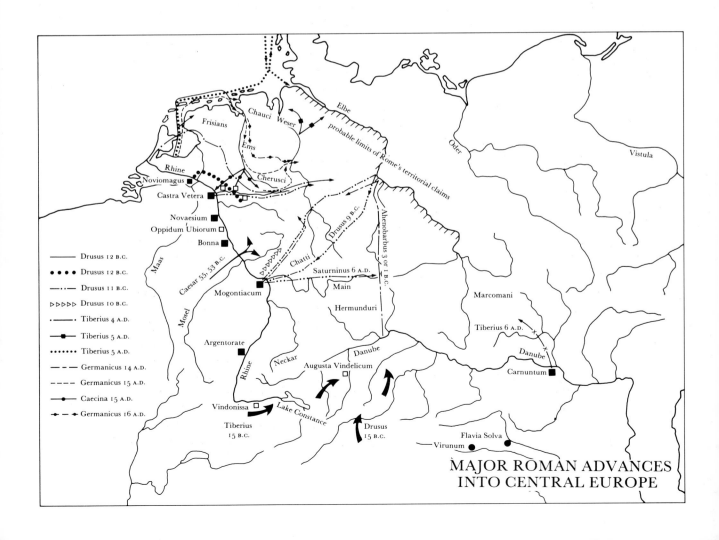

MAJOR ROMAN ADVANCES
INTO CENTRAL EUROPE

of vast forests, mountains, moors and swamps, the absence of allies and the shifting populations frustrated Roman attempts to gain control of the country and to secure their supply lines since the natives could easily remove themselves with guerrilla hit-and-run tactics. Confrontations had to become campaigns of encirclement which involved combined operations by sea, river and land, in which the army struck out eastward and the navy had to penetrate inland from the north by sailing up river, bringing reinforcements and supplies, and thereby taking the tribes in the rear. The river Elbe then presented itself as a natural eastern line of demarcation. To see the possibility of an extension of this line to the Danube in *Pannonia* was only a matter of time, especially since it would remove the inconvenient Rhine–Danube frontier. However, whether or not an Elbe–Danube frontier was Augustan policy, his field commanders made the Elbe the eastern limit of their operations.

In 12 BC Drusus headed north[49] into the land of the Usipetes to intercept tribal elements, which Dio Cassius called Celts, and thereby prevented them from withdrawing to the east bank of the Rhine.[50] Drusus returned along the right bank of the Rhine, ravaging the lands of the Cherusci. The entire expedition had been designed to intimidate the tribes to the east of the Lower Rhine and to determine sites for future bases of operations. Later that same year he imposed Roman 'protection' on the coastal Frisians. The losses suffered by his naval forces in a North Sea storm prevented him from bringing the coastal Chauci further east into the Roman sphere. In the end these coastal tribes became loyal friends of Rome, even during the extensive uprising of AD 9. By the end of that year Drusus had established a foothold on the Frisian coast from which to conduct future naval operations, had explored the region of the river Lippe, an area that was to see much Roman activity in future years, and had established a chain of earthwork forts to link *Vetera* with *Mogontiacum*, the nerve center on the Rhine, in order to supervise the comings and goings along the Rhine. To make it possible for the Rhine fleet to sail directly into the North Sea he had a canal built—the *Fossa Druisiana*—from the river Vecht to the Zuider Zee and into the North Sea.[51] The activity which the Romans were able to generate indicates something of the efficiency of the Roman administration. This alone must have impressed the local populations. When Drusus launched his attack in the following year against the Usipetes, Sugambri and Cherusci, he found that the Sugambri had moved south to attack the Chatti. Taking advantage of their absence he pushed straight through their territory and that of the Chatti as well, to reach the Weser river. Because of the late time in the year and supply problems, not to mention a bad omen, Drusus was forced to retire under severe attacks from those tribes which had avoided his advance.[52] Though he established and provisioned two outposts, the army moved into winter quarters west of the Rhine. The year 10 BC was devoted to subjugating the area contained by the rivers Main, Lahn and Weser, the land of the Chatti in fact. For the Romans, operating from their bases along the Lower Rhine, it was a year of consolidation and preparation. Base camps were erected along the river Lippe (Fig. 7) and along the other routes to allow a deep penetration of the interior in 9 BC. That year the campaign struck out from *Mogontiacum* against the Chatti north of the Main, against the Marcomanni, now located on the Upper Main, and, veering northwards, defeated the Cherusci. Drusus halted his advance somewhere on the great westward bulge of the Elbe.[53] On his return to the Main by a more direct southerly route, his horse fell on him, crushing his leg. He died of gangrene thirty days later on September 14, 9 BC at the age of twenty-seven. Upon

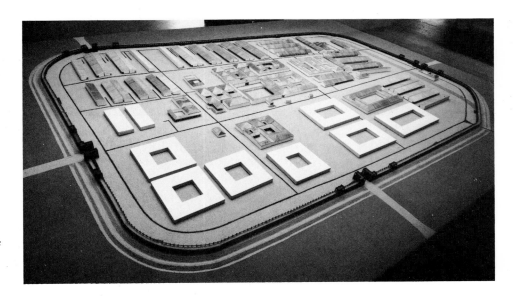

7 Model of the fortified encampment at Haltern on the river Lippe, before AD 9. (Westfälisches Museum für Archäologie, Münster)

receiving the news of the accident Tiberius rushed to his brother's side, travelling an incredible 200 Roman miles (296 km) in twenty-four hours.[54]

Augustus turned the supreme command in the north over to Tiberius, the conqueror of *Pannonia* and *Illyricum*, who the following year made a show of Roman strength throughout the land. Since he met with no opposition, it would appear that the tribes were ready to accept the Roman presence among them. Only the reluctant Sugambri and some Suebic allies were forcibly resettled west of the Rhine, after their leaders who had been imprisoned by Augustus[55] took their own lives so as not to tie the hands of their people. This tribe too assumed frontier duties. The Marsi occupied the vacated land. Drusus' campaign to the Elbe and his encounter with the Suebic Marcomanni may have contributed to the crystallization of the confederation of the Marcomanni who soon after 8 BC had moved from their territories in the Central Highlands into Bohemia. Their leader Maroboduus had been educated in Rome and had received military training in the legions. Under him the first organized Germanic 'state' came into being, consisting of a federation of tribes—Rugii, Lugii, Goths, Langobardes, Semnones and Marcomanni—extending from the Baltic Sea to the Danube,[56] an extensive area east of the Elbe and of the Roman sphere of operations.

It is possible, though the archaeological evidence is not extensive, that by the middle of the last decade BC many Roman army posts were scattered about the interior, especially along the rivers leading into the interior and at other strategic points, not only as winter quarters but as bases for an army of occupation.[57] By 7 BC Tiberius had completed his campaigns and the new territories of *Germania* generally are assumed to have been secured in the course of five or six years as a new province of the Empire.[58] It must be assumed that the Romans tried to tie the tribal leaders to Rome. Their sons often grew up in Rome as hostages. In spite of Tiberius' voluntary exile to Rhodes in 6 BC, the legions must have continued to make their presence felt in the province. Thus between 6 BC and AD 7 the Elbe was reached again by L. Domitius Ahenobarbus, who may have set out from the Danube in *Raetia*, crossed the Elbe, set up an altar to honor Augustus,[59] concluded friendship treaties with the trans-elbian tribes, apparently laid out roadways of beams—the *pontes longi*—in the northern fashion, and then left for the Rhine. By 2 BC Ahenobarbus moved the

Hermunduri into the area formerly occupied by the Marcomanni. The Hermunduri remained trusted clients of Rome until the second century, adding greatly to the stability of the region of the Upper Main.[60] As commander on the Rhine, Ahenobarbus was less successful in that his attempts to repatriate the Cherusci embroiled him with their neighbors. An unsuccessful war lasting three years was waged by his successor Marcus Vinicius sometime between 6 and 1 BC.[61] The information is very incomplete.

Prior to AD 9, probably during the governorship of Marcus Vinicius under whose control the inner organization of the new area was proceeding perhaps too quickly, an altar dedicated to Rome and Augustus—the *Ara Roma et Augustus*—was set up at the *Oppidum Ubiorum*, making it the cultic capital of the new *Provincia Germania*, just as the *Ara Roma et Augustus* at *Lugdunum*, modern Lyon, was the cultic center of Gaul.[62] It was the duty of the provincial tribes to tend it on a rotating basis. The consolidation of the area as a province was proceeding perhaps even more quickly than that of Gaul. Under the various field commanders the Rhine and Danube ceased to have any resemblance to frontiers. Trained to command mobile forces, they carried the frontier with them. This in itself suggests that the situation in the province was unsettled and ambivalent, neither free nor subjugated.[63]

Tiberius returned from exile in AD 4 as co-regent and supreme commander to resume his command in the north. A new phase was to begin with his arrival. As if to make certain that the province was indeed pacified, he launched two massive campaigns, the first in AD 4 against the Cherusci whom he took under Roman 'protection', the other a co-ordinated campaign in which naval units sailed up the Elbe to meet a force striking cross-country from the west, thereby confirming the Elbe frontier as a reality.[64] The arrival of this Roman force on the Elbe was a reminder to all of Roman suzerainty over the area. It was on this occasion in AD 5 that his ships explored the coast northwards to the tip of Jutland. The joint operation between navy and army evidently had been intended to overcome obstacles of terrain and to establish an operational base on the Middle Elbe. Again the river system provided a convenient network of access routes by means of which reinforcements and supplies could be transported more easily to the theater of operations. According to the historian Caius Velleius Paterculus, an avid admirer of Tiberius who had served in Tiberius' Pannonian army, all *Germania* had been overrun by Roman armies, its people subjugated and dominated by Roman troops.[65]

In the absence of lasting fortifications and roads in the interior it is not clear what form this subjugation would have taken. The submission which the Romans urged the tribes to accept may have meant no more than establishing dependency agreements between Augustus and the leaders of the east-rhenish tribes, guaranteed by the surrender of hostages to Rome, the service of the sons of the nobility with the legions and the granting of Roman citizenship to the most prominent members of the tribal communities.[66] Maroboduus of the Marcomanni and Arminius of the Cherusci would be illustrations of such practices, which in turn may imply that Rome was pursuing a policy of drawing the tribal leadership into a close system of checks and balances under Roman control, which assumed the characteristics of a Roman overlordship with the tribes of the province, based not on the actual presence of permanent garrisoned fortifications but on understandings. Dio Cassius states that the Romans exercised actual control over only a few isolated districts rather than over the entire country.[67] These understandings were probably rather one-sided in that Rome expected its provisions from the tribes and enlisted the young men in the auxiliary formations, in return for 'protection'. It appears fairly certain that Arminius and some of the Cherusci saw service in the army of the Lower Rhine during the campaigns of AD 4–6.[68] Under the terms they were 'free', provided they also saw themselves as loyal subjects of the Empire and once under the 'protection' of the Empire any protestation of independence was interpreted as rebellion meriting ruthless suppression.[69] Such loose arrangements would account for the annual intimidating show of strength by Roman forces, designed to reaffirm tribal loyalties. It would account also for the total collapse of Roman control over the province after the events of AD 9. It is known that Rome was not committed to honor any agreement with any of the 'uncivilized' tribes if a situation arose from which Rome might profit.

Such a situation must have loomed before the Roman command when ten or twelve years earlier Ahenobarbus had led his military expedition to the Elbe and back. That Ahenobarbus had originally been *legatus* of *Illyricum*, which, incidentally, was the southern end of the amber trade routes reaching from the north through Bohemia,[70] may be immaterial, but his Danube-Elbe-Rhine campaign implies at least a growing awareness of a direct link between the Elbe and the Danube. During earlier periods the Elbe had been part of a north-south trade route, so that if the Romans did not know of this initially, the local merchants trading with the north would soon have informed them of the great salt sea to the north from where the amber came.

By AD 6, with the Roman fleet actually coming up the Elbe and a commander-in-chief who knew the northern and southern legs of the route, the Elbe-Danube link may have become a keenly felt need if for no other than strategic reasons. The Dacians were increasing their pressure on the Middle Danube. Marcus Vinicius had crossed the Danube in 9 BC and had beaten them. Locating the frontier in Bohemia would make campaigns of encirclement against the Dacians possible too. During the next two centuries both the Marcomanni and the Dacians would be serious sources of conflict for Rome. Though much is conjecture, in the year AD 6 according to Tacitus, Tiberius assembled twelve legions and units of auxilliaries to carry out a pincer movement designed to bring Bohemia under Roman control. The obstacle to the plan and its intended victim was the budding federation of the Marcomanni, a source of concern to the Roman command in *Noricum* and *Pannonia*.[71] The intended campaign was expected to break up the coalition. Events were to prove this expansion of the Empire premature.

A two-pronged attack, one advancing from *Germania*, the other from *Pannonia*, was to take the Marcomanni from the front and from the rear. Tiberius himself took command of the legions stationed in *Pannonia*, assembling them at *Carnuntum*, a site originally in *Noricum* that was to become one of the key centers on the Danube. He is credited with its foundation in AD 6, though the original fortifications have not yet been located.[72] The command of the western forces was assigned to one Sentius Saturninus.[73] The historian C. Velleius Paterculus, a participant in this campaign,[74] has Tiberius ordering Saturninus to enter Bohemia by crossing the land of the Chatti and then razing the Hercynian Forest, the forested mountain ranges including the Central Highlands, the Ore Mountains and the Sudeten Mountains, an overly ambitious task. This order implies that the western force probably would be assembled at *Mogontiacum* and by advancing due east along the river Main, enter Bohemia through the Eger Gap. However, when one considers the supply problems, such long approaches into central Bohemia, about 500 km from the Rhine and 300 km from the Danube, suggest that at least the western rallying point must have been closer to the objective, perhaps near the headwaters of the Main in the land of the friendly Hermunduri, or on the Elbe, or both. The advance upon the Marcomanni will have consisted of several columns converging on Bohemia. The strength of the Roman forces must have been great, though probably not as great as that of the twelve legions suggested by Tacitus in his *Annals*. It is unlikely that the northern provinces would have been denuded of all the troops stationed there in order to be concentrated in one adventure, especially in view of neither *Germania* nor *Pannonia* having yet been won over entirely to Roman ways. As it happened, according to Velleius Paterculus, the two advancing pincers were only a few day-marches apart[75] when *Pannonia* and *Illyricum* broke into open revolt over the recruiting of young men to bring the Roman units up to strength, so soon after the terrible massacres and deportations accompanying the pacification of these provinces by Tiberius only fifteen years earlier.[76] The conquest of Bohemia had to be aborted since not enough troops were left in *Pannonia* to suppress the uprising. In the end fifteen legions and auxiliaries were required to quell the revolt. Tiberius needed three years to impose the peace of a cemetery on the area but not without first having had to strain the resources of the Empire to the limit. Though the Germanic tribes had a reputation of untrustworthiness, Maroboduus and his Marcomanni did not make use of the opportunity to attack the Romans but abided by the truce so hastily agreed upon when news of the revolt reached Tiberius. These events also make it clear that the Bohemian campaign could not have been one of retaliation but was nothing other than an unprovoked incursion for conquest and annexation.[77] Subsequent events in *Germania* prevented a resumption of the designs on Bohemia.

Velleius Paterculus reports that Tiberius had just concluded the war in *Pannonia* and *Dalmatia* when within five days he received dispatches from *Germania* informing him of the death of Varus and the destruction of three legions, three *alae* (squadrons of cavalry) and six *cohortes* (units of infantry).[78] Velleius considers it fortunate that the Germani had not made common cause with the Pannonians against Rome. He thought the event of sufficient significance to go into detail. Discounting his personal admiration for Tiberius, his is the account of a contemporary. In Velleius' words the new commander in *Germania*, one Publius Quinctilius Varus, was a mild mannered, indolent and rapacious man who enriched himself in Syria while he impoverished the province, for whom the inhabitants of *Germania* were human beings only to the extent that they had voices and limbs, but who could be made pliable through Roman laws where Roman swords had failed. According to Velleius, Varus was misled by his own notions and wasted the time of a summer campaign by allowing himself to be delayed by the Germani in settling feigned legal disputes, their gratitude flattering Varus to believe himself to be a *praetor* in the Roman forum and not a military commander in *Germania*. Confident his approach was correct, he failed to heed the warning brought to him by Segestes, a loyal friend of Rome, that Arminius, a young, brave and intelligent noble who had been a constant companion to the Romans on their last campaign and who, in accordance with Roman law, had been raised into the estate of the *equites*, the knights, was plotting to take advantage of Varus' carelessness. To the old soldier Velleius the army of the Rhine was the best of all in discipline, bravery and experience. The incompetence of its commander, the deceit of the enemy and fate conspired to lead this army into a trap in which it was not deployed to defend itself. Surrounded by forest, swamps and ambushes the legionaries were cut down, impeded by the supply column, deserted by the cavalry, left leaderless through the cowardly suicides of Varus and many officers. The disaster was caused by an enemy whom the Roman army had always butchered like cattle, with no more than arbitrary restraint. So wrote Velleius.

The event reported by Velleius Paterculus took place in AD 8, when Arminius and the Cherusci destroyed legions XVII, XVIII and XIX and their supporting auxiliary units, a force of some 20–25,000 men, while they were returning to their winter quarters on the Rhine. Though this massacre almost coincided with the Pannonian revolt, it is doubtful that the two events were co-ordinated.[79] Roman intelligence in support of the principle *divide et impera*, divide and rule, would have intercepted any attempts to form alliances among its subject peoples.

Publius Quinctilius Varus, the son-in-law of the famous Agrippa, had succeeded Sentius Saturninus in AD 7 to the command of the army of the Rhine. History, following the tradition of the Roman historians, has probably treated Varus too kindly. *Germania* had been established as a province, the *Ara Ubiorum* dedicated to the veneration of Rome and Augustus was tended by the noblest chiefs enlisted in the emperor's cult and provided the cultural focus for a loyal and unified province[80] and the Roman armies were beginning to operate on its eastern frontier with an eye to setting up a new buffer zone to the east of Bohemia. Presumably an established boundary on the Elbe had been secured by agreements, so that it was time to pass from a phase of military supervision to civic administration. That this was an error in judgment committed by the high command, possibly by Augustus himself, is clear. Varus was a proven administrator with experience in Syria and Africa who was charged prematurely with the task of setting up a provincial administration. In the documents Varus is made to take the blame for a blunder made at the highest level of the imperial administration.[81] His death on his own sword, unsoldierly for a field commander, is not necessarily inconsistent with the behavior one has expected of administrative officials through the centuries. However, he had not been sent there to die a soldier's death but to introduce Roman legal practices and a system of taxation. It was in the execution of these duties that he may not have shown the required analytical skepticism. Dio Cassius[82] recounts that the inhabitants of *Germania* gradually were being converted to accept Roman ways, Roman order, urban settlements, markets and peaceful meetings without compromising their inherent character, their life style and freedom based on their fitness to bear arms. This imperceptible cultural alienation from their old ways did not stir them to resistance. On the other hand, Varus with his mandate threatened a clear break with their traditions. And much to the surprise of the Romans, here was a people which preferred its own ways to those of the Romans. Dio Cassius suggests that Varus' high-handed directives and impositions, which made it clear to them that they were to be reduced to servitude and subjugation, fanned the discontent among those who had lost their pre-eminence and those who preferred the traditional ways to foreign domination. To the historian Florus the Germani had merely been surpassed in battle, not subjugated and they looked skeptically at Roman ways.[83] The arbitrary arrogance of Varus irked them especially. Roman legal procedures and Roman justice they found to be more cruel than Roman arms.

It is apparent from the accounts that the opposition to Rome and the open revolt was engendered by overt romanization. Varus, the itinerant magistrate, was the

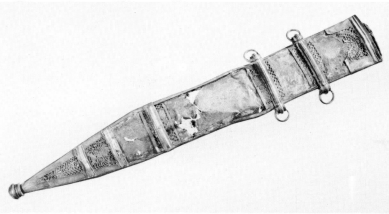

8 Helmet from Haltern. (Westfälisches Museum für Archäologie, Münster)

9 Bronze scabbard of a Roman sword, first century AD. Dredged from the river Weser near Bremen-Seehausen. (Landesmuseum, Bremen)

wrong man for the task. Rather than suppress them he tried to impress them with Roman circumstance, not realizing that these northerners had a history of institutional traditions and that the Romans were not the ones who had introduced peaceful assemblies to them. The Romans were not the last high culture to underestimate the level of cultural development in a conquered people. Hitherto, Rome's imperial expansion had been facilitated by the fact that the Roman armies conquered largely where armies of kindred cultures had conquered before them. These lands were characterized as urban civilizations, more easily subdued once the urban centers were controlled. To a degree this had even been done in Gaul. But while the early conversion of Gaul to a mediterranean culture had been extensive, to the northerners Roman ways were totally alien. In *Germania* the Romans encountered largely unfamiliar cultural conditions. Varus had gained his experience as judicial and fiscal administrator in the urban centers of Syria and northern Africa which did not serve him, the bureaucrat, in good stead when dealing with tribal structures. A bureaucratic Roman legal approach to administration was premature for a society so unlike Rome and its institutions. His experience in the Roman army taught Arminius that in a confrontation between drawn up battle lines the Romans would have little difficulty in smashing his tribal formations. For centuries to come the Germanic armies were no match for Roman equipment, discipline and battle tactics. Instead Arminius made use of intractable terrain and of extremely bad weather to attack the three Roman legions on the march in a running engagement which lasted four days as the Romans tried to extricate themselves from a hopeless situation.[84] Only a few units of cavalry escaped. It ended in a massacre which many of the officers chose not to witness to the end. The victors sacrificed the survivors to their gods. Arminius sent the head of Varus to Maroboduus, probably to incite him to join in the revolt against Rome. Maroboduus merely sent the head on to Augustus. Six years later Germanicus sought out the sites to bury the remains. Tacitus gives a detailed account in his *Annals*[85] of bleached bones showing how the Romans had fallen singly or in groups, of piles of armor and skeletons of horses, of skulls nailed to trees and of altars on which the tribunes and senior centurions had been sacrificed.[86] In spite of much interest in the subject, the site of this battle has not yet been discovered. Tacitus is the only one to speak of a *Saltus Teutoburgensis*[87] as the location of the disaster. Until the seventeenth century no region by this name was known when in 1631 Cluverius, a forgotten humanist, in his book *Germania antiqua* placed it in the forests along the Lippe.[88] Since then the mountain range has borne the name 'Teutoburger Wald.' It is not surprising therefore that over thirty sites have been proposed for the actual site of the battle.

The loss of three legions and their support units constituted a loss of three-fifths of the entire complement of the army of the Rhine.[89] Within a short time after their victory over the Romans all of the outposts were taken by the Cherusci and their allies, calling twenty years of Roman efforts into question (Fig. 8). At first the Lippe forts and a Roman relief force were able to stay the Cheruscan advance.[90] By then the two legions stationed at *Mogontiacum* had assumed defensive positions along the Lower Rhine. The coastal tribes, Frisians and Chauci, had not joined in the revolt. Their vulnerability to the Roman fleet may have bolstered their loyalty.

According to Suetonius[91] Augustus was grief stricken over the loss of his legions. In commemoration he ordered that their permanent serial numbers and distinctive titles never be used again. Suetonius recounts that during months of mourning and depression he would sometimes thump his head against doorposts, crying out 'Quinctilius Varus, give me back my legions.' Even if this and other accounts of omens and drastic measures taken in Rome itself are only partly accurate,[92] it appears that the Varus defeat was more than a lost battle to Augustus.[93] Nevertheless, he does not appear to have given up his project of securing an Elbe frontier, for neither Augustus nor his successor, Tiberius, proclaimed an official renunciation of the annexation of *Germania* between Elbe and Rhine.[94] Even in his testament[95] he continues to speak of the Atlantic and the North Sea coast to the mouth of the Elbe as the limits of the territories he had pacified and of Elbian tribes such as the Semnones. Their ambassadors had once solicited his friendship and that of the Roman people. These statements suggest that he had retained control of the coast and that the rivers continued to provide access to the interior (Fig. 9). The instruction to his legates contained in his last papers advises them to refrain from any further extension of the Empire but to keep it within its bounds. It is likely that he spoke of the Elbe and not of the Rhine.

The rest is quickly told. Following the disaster Tiberius immediately assumed personal command on the Rhine, refraining from crossing the river until AD 11 and drawing additional reinforcements from Gaul to bring his forces up to a strength of eight legions.[96] The sources are scanty, but Arminius and Maroboduus appear to have been at war with one another which allowed Tiberius to re-establish some of his lost bases beyond the Rhine. Co-ordinated operations between army and fleet may have continued. In AD 13 Germanicus, the son of Drusus, was ordered to the Rhine with explicit orders not to engage in offensives. When Augustus died in AD 14 all legions were stationed west of the Rhine,[97] perhaps because revolts were feared in Gaul. That same year mutinies broke out in the northern armies. The legions were reluctant to accept Tiberius as the appropriate successor of Augustus. Germanicus' declaration of loyalty to Tiberius persuaded the legions to remain loyal.[98] To channel their pent-up frustrations, that autumn Germanicus, much to his discredit, launched a totally unjustified campaign of extermination against the Marsi settled between the rivers Ruhr and Lippe. While there, he destroyed the sanctuary of the goddess Tanfana, perhaps a Celtic divinity. This distraction cost him dearly, for during his withdrawal the legions were badly mauled by neighboring tribes, the Rubantes and

Usipetes. It is possible that the preceding year had served organizational purposes, because between AD 14-16 Germanicus resumed the offensive. In AD 15 Germanicus designed another joint operation against the Cherusci. With four legions and 5000 auxiliaries, as well as other Germanic troops from the left bank of the Rhine, his lieutenant Caecina headed for the river Ems, while he, Germanicus, approached the Chatti with a similar force from *Mogontiacum*.[99] Though the Romans were not successful at first, later that year the Roman party among the Cherusci led by Segestes, a former priest at the *Ara Ubiorum*, solicited his assistance against Arminius and his supporters. In a pitched battle Germanicus prevailed, recovering the standard of the *legio XIX*, along with booty and many of the possessions lost by Varus. Among the prisoners was Thusnelda, daughter of Segestes and wife of Arminius. She would figure prominently in the triumph with which Germanicus entered Rome in AD 17. His return from the campaign in AD 15 was almost a double disaster, when the disembarked troops on the navy transports were caught by the tide and almost drowned while the land forces were caught once again in the northern moors. Near panic broke out along the Rhine frontier as yet another disaster became a possibility. A successful pincer campaign in AD 16 suffered a similar reversal of fortune, when the naval arm was broken by a storm and dispersed eastward and the troops, held to ransom by the natives, had to be bought free.[100] This loss of prestige had to be redressed and two more punitive raids were launched against the Chatti, Bructeri and the Marsi. From the latter another eagle standard could be recovered, although the actual recovery of the 'province' was feasible no longer. Roman methods only moved the natives to greater resistance. Germanicus had concentrated on the river Weser and though he, generally, was victorious, his victories cost dearly in prestige and the Elbe was not anywhere in sight. His annual incursions were expensive raids rather than consolidating campaigns. Whatever gains had been made during the summer vanished during the following winter months. Roman efforts in *Germania* resembled attempts at sweeping water. Probably convinced of the futility of any further efforts in the north, Tiberius cancelled all further designs in AD 17 and invited Germanicus to enjoy his triumph in Rome. The festivities were a cover for the lack of final success in the north. Rome had renounced the annexation of *Germania*. It was hoped that without Roman pressure and by means of clever diplomacy the tribes might be set to fighting one another, and thus neutralize their potential threat to Rome in hereditary dissension.[101] The policy was to prove effective, for already in AD 17 war broke out between the coalition under Arminius and Maroboduus' Marcomannic federation. Deserted by Semnones and Langobardes the war went against Maroboduus who had to ask for Roman support. Remembering that Rome was not bound to pledges made with barbarians, Tiberius rejected the possibility of Roman intervention[102] and stimulated intrigue against Maroboduus instead.[103] When the latter fled to the Romans in AD 19, he was interned in Ravenna where he died eighteen years later.[104] Civil war broke out among the Cherusci. Arminius, motivated by his military and political successes, apparently sought the kingship. Family intrigue brought about his end in AD 21.[105]

In view of the very limited economic and military value which this *Provincia Germania* represented, it is difficult to justify the military and financial cost which Augustus was prepared to invest in conquering it. The first-hand knowledge which Tiberius had of the northern problems of terrain and population pressures must have induced him to insist on a strictly defensive policy, to curtail all future projects

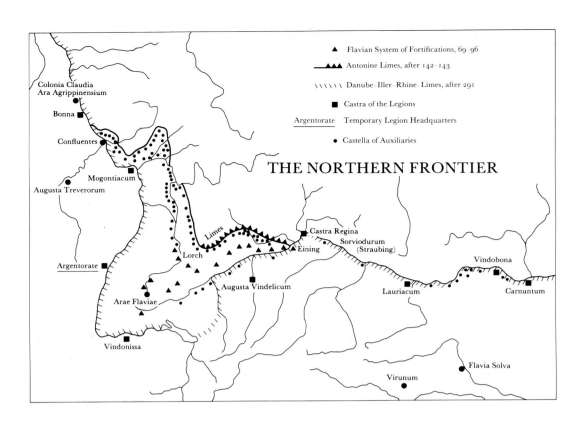

Flavian System of Fortifications, 69–96
▲▲▲ Antonine Limes, after 142–143
\\\\\\ Danube-Iller-Rhine-Limes, after 291
■ Castra of the Legions
Argentorate Temporary Legion Headquarters
• Castella of Auxiliaries

THE NORTHERN FRONTIER

Colonia Claudia
Ara Agrippinensium
Bonna
Confluentes
Mogontiacum
Augusta Treverorum
Argentorate
Limes
Lorch
Castra Regina
Sorviodurum
(Straubing)
Eining
Vindobona
Arae Flaviae
Augusta Vindelicum
Lauriacum
Carnuntum
Vindonissa
Flavia Solva
Virunum

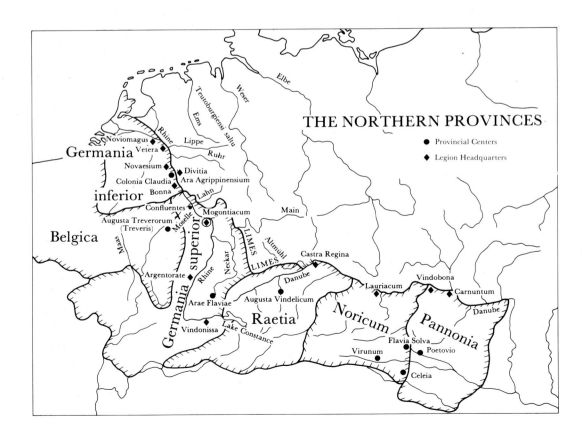

THE NORTHERN PROVINCES

● Provincial Centers
◆ Legion Headquarters

Elbe
Weser
Teutoburgiensi saltu
Ems
Lippe
Rhine
Ruhr
Noviomagus
Vetera
Germania
Novaesium
Divitia
Colonia Claudia
Ara Agrippinensium
Bonna
Lahn
inferior
Confluentes
Mogontiacum
Main
Belgica
Augusta Treverorum
(Treveris)
Moselle
Germania superior
Maas
LIMES
Altmühl
Castra Regina
Argentorate
Neckar
Rhine
LIMES
Danube
Augusta Vindelicum
Lauriacum
Vindobona
Carnuntum
Arae Flaviae
Raetia
Noricum
Danube
Pannonia
Vindonissa
Lake Constance
Flavia Solva
Poetovio
Virunum
Celeia

18

10 Hollow brick, bearing the stamp of *legio XXII Primigenia pia fidelis* (Sammlung Nassauischer Altertümer, Wiesbaden)

beyond the Rhine and Danube and to consolidate these against inevitable attacks.[106] Not until the reign of the emperor Vespasian (AD 69–79) and especially that of Domitian (AD 81–96) was the 'wet border' replaced in part by a fortified line, the *limes* between the Middle Rhine and the Upper Danube, the most docile of areas. Nevertheless Roman self-glorification led to the issuing of coins with the legend *Germania capta* during AD 85–87.[107] It was only now that the military districts were reorganized into provinces: *Germania inferior* with *Vetera* as its military base and *Germania superior* around *Mogontiacum*.[108] On the Rhine military districts organized around *Vetera* and *Mogontiacum* became areas of military concentration when 8 legions, 16 *alae* of horse and 49 cohorts of other auxiliaries were distributed along the Rhine. In all, between 40,000 and 50,000 men, one quarter of Rome's armed forces, made the Rhine the eastern border of what was left of the *Provincia Germania*.[109] The crystallizations around key installations are a reflection of the increasing rigidity of the military planners. It will have been noticed that most operations set out from the forts of the Lower Rhine. No attempts appear to have been made to incorporate the area between Danube and Main either before or after the defeat of Varus. A much smaller area, though more difficult of terrain, it might have been a more realistic objective. It seems though that very early the theaters of operation were fixed. The overall plan of the conquest appears to have lost its flexibility within only a few years, set as it was on an eastward sweep along the coast and up the Elbe, a mirror design of Caesar's conquest of Gaul. The failure of this grand design was due only partly to the defeat of Varus.[110] One reason why the three lost legions were not replaced was the growing depletion of manpower available to Rome, which was particularly acute at this time.[111] However, the conquest of Britain demonstrates that Rome was still capable of great efforts and determination when it came to executing clearly defined objectives. Internal rivalries during the first century often removed not only the focus from northern conquest but most of the northern legions as well. Rome had increasing problems elsewhere. As it was, the frontiers were already overextended. Frustrated by logistics and events, the conquest of central Europe had ceased to be a priority after the death of Augustus in AD 14. Henceforth, the Roman administration implemented the earlier policies which saw the Rhineland as a buffer zone, a catchment to absorb and channel intruders beyond the Rhine and to protect Gaul, Rome's new supplier of food for the Empire and manpower for its legions.[112] The avid nationalists of the nineteenth century on both sides of the Rhine made much of both events, the

11 Two Roman soldiers. A relief formerly part of a larger triumphal monument of the second century AD. The block of stone was later used in the wall of the *castellum*. (Historisches Museum, Basel)

Germans because their freedom loving 'ancestors' had repelled the enslaving Romans and the French because they saw themselves as the heirs of a superior Roman civilization. As regards that, the events described were of great significance for western Europe.

Behind the loosely defined northern line of demarcation, the legions could devote themselves to the non-military aspect of their presence in the land, the conversion of conquered territories into productive provinces. A legion's aim to achieve self-sufficiency in all things made it possible for the troops to perform a great variety of tasks including such vast engineering projects as the drainage of swamps, building of canals, fortifications, harbors, roads and bridges as well as aqueducts which brought water over great distances. They stabilized the cultivation of the land and increased its yield, founded new settlements, emphasized crafts and trades by developing the exploitation of natural resources, building up local industries and fostering and regulating trade and commerce.[113] Within a short time prosperity characterized the land. In their wake the military forces brought an organized society, stratified along Roman lines into which the local social structures eventually were incorporated. In due course this gradual integration behind secure borders gave rise to a provincial culture determined largely by the army stationed in depth in the frontier provinces, one which in its regional differentiations extended along the Rhine and Danube from the English Channel to *Noricum* and *Pannonia*.

The Roman preference for brick has proved a boon to historians, because the brickworks of each legion stamped each brick with the legion's number (Fig. 10).

With this information it has been possible to establish the posting of the legions along the frontier, as well as the approximate time of their transfer to other positions along the frontier, because bricks generally were made for local use. These stamps, along with other sources, indicate that approximately forty legions saw service on this frontier, either stationed permanently in their bases or transferred to trouble spots from other parts of the frontier or from other parts of the Empire, unless they happened to be marching on Rome to impose a new emperor. Already at the time of the Varus defeat the *legio XX Valeria victrix* under Tiberius had marched from *Pannonia* to the Rhine. The *legio XXI rapax* reflects something of the history of the border territories. The legion probably had been raised expressly for the conquest of the Alps and of *Raetia* by young Tiberius before 15 BC, had been with Tiberius on the Lower Rhine, had been moved back to *Vindonissa* among the Helvetii in the time of the emperor Claudius, was involved in the revolt of Antonius Saturninus in AD 89 and was transferred to the Middle Danube, only to perish there a few years later in the reign of the emperor Domitian.[114] Following that revolt Domitian bestowed upon the legions of the *exercitus Germanici inferioris*, the army of the Lower Rhine, which had remained loyal, the honorary title *pia fidelis Domitiana*. These were the *legio I Flavia Minervia*, newly raised by Domitian and stationed at *Bonna*, *legio VI victrix* at *Novaesium*, *legio X gemina* at *Noviomagus* and *legio XXII Primigenia* at *Vetera* and all of the associated units of auxiliaries. Another similar example is that of the *legio XXX Ulpia victrix pia fidelis* to be stationed at *Vetera*, raised by the emperor Trajan in *Pannonia* and bearing his name Ulpius, the number *XXX* in honor of all the existing legions in the Empire during his reign and the title *victrix*, the victorious one, after its successful activities during Trajan's wars against the Dacians on the Lower Danube. Here too the title *pia fidelis* was added later for trustworthiness and loyalty. The legions were named either after the emperors who raised them (*Flavia*) or the region of their origin (*Gallica*), with honorary titles (*martia*) and with nicknames (*alaudae*—the larks). Though their numbers remained the same, the names changed. Thus the *legio XXII Primigenia pia fidelis* was later known as *legio XXII Constantiniana victrix*.[115] *Legio XXX* had been moved to *Vetera* in AD 119 to fill the gap left in the frontier defences when the legions stationed there had been withdrawn to reinforce the army on the Lower Danube. *Legio XXX* was to remain at this base until the Romans withdrew from the Rhine almost 300 years later. Already in AD 185 the *legio VIII Augusta* gained the title *pia fidelis constans Commoda* and held it until the assassination of Commodus in AD 192. During the reign of the emperor Severus Alexander (AD 222–35), the *legio XIV gemina martia victrix* bore the honorary title *Severiana*.

The pressure along the frontier of the Middle and Lower Danube coincided with generally peaceful conditions along the Rhine and the Upper Danube. These conditions made it possible to reduce the Rhine garrisons from eight legions with 50,000 men to four legions stationed at *Castra Vetera* near modern Xanten, *Mogontiacum/* Mainz, *Argentorate/*Strasbourg and at *Vindonissa/*Brugg in Switzerland, and after AD 161 along the Danube one legion each at *Castra Regina/*Regensburg, *Lauriacum* near modern Linz in *Noricum* and at *Vindobona/*Vienna and *Carnuntum* in *Pannonia*. In times of crisis these units were reinforced. During the second and third centuries these forces proved insufficient, yet Rome could not afford to increase the number of legions.

The legions were the core of the Roman army (Fig. 11). During the Imperial Period a legion consisted of about 6000 men drawn from the Roman citizens of the Empire.[116] In AD 213 the emperor Caracalla bestowed Roman citizenship on every

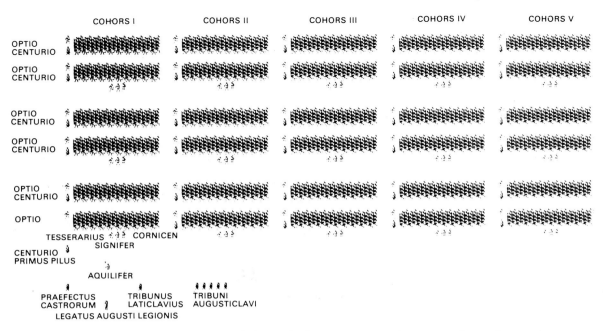

	COHORS I	COHORS II	COHORS III	COHORS IV	COHORS V

OPTIO
CENTURIO

OPTIO
CENTURIO

OPTIO
CENTURIO

OPTIO
CENTURIO

OPTIO
CENTURIO

OPTIO

TESSERARIUS   CORNICEN
SIGNIFER

CENTURIO
PRIMUS PILUS

AQUILIFER

PRAEFECTUS   TRIBUNUS   TRIBUNI
CASTRORUM   LATICLAVIUS   AUGUSTICLAVI
LEGATUS AUGUSTI LEGIONIS

12 *a and b* The Roman legion of the early first century AD: its command structure and disposition. (Westfälisches Museum für Archäologie, Münster)

free born inhabitant of the Empire, which then made it possible for the legions to fill their complements from among the inhabitants in whose territory the legion was stationed. This practice eventually would affect the ethnic composition of a legion. In principle after *c.* AD 80 a legion was subdivided into 10 *cohortes* of which *cohors I* was nearly doubled to be 800 men strong while the other 9 cohorts were 480 men strong (Fig. 12). The first cohort was subdivided into 10 centuries of 80 men each. 6 centuries made up each of the other cohorts. A detachment of cavalry about 120 strong for reconnaissance and communications completed the legion. Each of the 60 centuries was commanded by a centurion, legionaries who had risen through the ranks, the backbone of the legion. The senior centurion of the legion, the *primus pilus*, commanded the first cohort. The legion commanders, the *legati Augusti legionis*, and their seconds in command, the *tribuni militum legionis laticlavius*, were not professional soldiers but administrators of senatorial rank in their 30's and 20's respectively. The legate was supported by five junior staff officers, the *tribuni militum augusticlavi* of either senatorial rank or of the equestrian order, whose functions were not defined specifically (Fig. 13). Legion headquarters were under the command of a *praefectus castrorum*, the quartermaster of equestrian rank, whose duties included much of the administration of the legion, camp maintenance, engineering projects and supplies. Since the military forces also had to fulfill administrative functions and vouch for the security of the area entrusted to them, until the late third or early fourth century the legate was usually the civil and military governor, the *legatus Augusti pro praetore Germaniae superioris/inferioris*, for instance. Upward mobility was extremely rare.[117]

Of special interest are the auxiliary units which complemented the legions' fighting strength and effectiveness. It was Augustus who had organized the native forces assisting the legions, into regular army units, the *auxilia*, closely linked to the legions

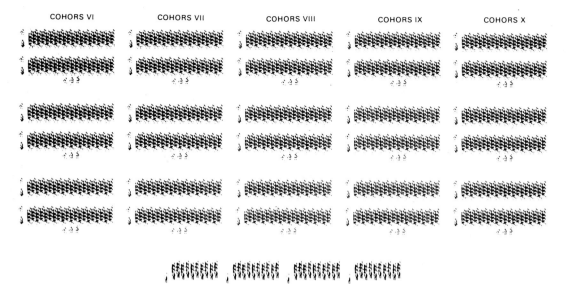

COHORS VI	COHORS VII	COHORS VIII	COHORS IX	COHORS X

120 horsemen for reconnaissance and communications

until the middle of the first century AD. They often shared the same camps. Only later when the *auxilia* assumed specific duties on the borders did the auxiliary units act under the jurisdiction of the legions.[118] Each legion was supported by auxiliary units of infantry and cavalry, usually at a ratio of 6 or 8 *cohortes* of infantry to 2 *alae* of cavalry.[119] An *ala*, a cavalry regiment, or an infantry cohort varied in size, being nominally either 500 or 1000 men strong and therefore identified either as a *quingenaria* or a *milliaria*.[120] A *cohors quingenaria* might be commanded by an equestrian with the rank of *praefectus*. Tribunes might command larger units such as a *cohors milliaria*. An *ala quingenaria* was subdivided into 16 *turmae*, an *ala milliaria* into only 24 *turmae*, each *turma* consisting of 30 or 40 horsemen respectively under the command of a decurion. The infantry cohorts were modelled after those of the legion and divided into either 10 or 6 centuries.[121] Mounted infantry units, *cohortes equitatae*, either *quingenaria* or *milliaria*, i.e. of 6–10 centuries of infantry and of 120–240 horsemen divided into 4–8 *turmae* respectively, were also known.[122] The number of men in the auxiliaries approximated the number of legionaries. After AD 100 still smaller auxiliary units of infantry, *numeri*, or cavalry, *cunei*, were organized for frontier duty.[123] In addition local levies could be mobilized in support. These auxiliary units were recruited from among the non-Roman population of the Empire and usually from the population of the land in which the units were stationed. The names of these units reflect their tribal origins (*cohors Raetorum*), the province in which they were raised (*cohors Germanica*), the officer who raised them (*ala Longiana*), an imperial name (*ala Flavia*), honorary titles (*pia fidelis*) or their armament (*cohors sagittariorum*). For instance the *Cohors I Flavia Canathenorum milliaria sagittariorum*, was a milliary unit of archers raised in the Near East in Flavian times and stationed at *Sorviodurum*/Straubing on the Danube.[124] Raising these recruits was usually the function of the local native administration.[125]

23

13 Early Roman officer's dagger with silver and brass inlay. From Oberammergau. (Prähistorische Staatssammlung, Munich)

In difficult areas, for reasons of security the young men, sometimes as young as fifteen, were enlisted in the auxiliaries and then stationed in some foreign part of the Empire.[126] In definitely loyal areas they assumed full responsibility for the border defenses in their own land. Military service increased the rate of romanization and the use and spread of Latin.[127] While service in the legions was barred to the natives, their sons could join the legions since their fathers were mustered out as Roman citizens. The army also taught trades and crafts, contributing to the rapid increase in prosperity. After AD 14 and for the next 300 years, to the time of Constantine, service with the eagles was fixed at minimum terms of twenty years in the legions and of twenty-four years in the auxiliaries.[128] However, tombstone inscriptions indicate that many troopers served a longer tour of duty, twenty-eight years in one instance, probably because a sudden rush on the 'pension fund' managed by the emperor exceeded the latter's resources. Originally, upon being mustered out the legionary received a piece of land near his garrison.[129] It became customary to pay off the veterans with a generous sum of money. Auxiliaries received Roman citizenship, the *civitas Romana*.

After the middle of the first century AD the legionaries wore metal plate armor reinforced with leather, the *lorica segmentata*—a flexible corselet and shoulder guards—

14 Fragment of bronze scale armor—a *lorica squamata*. (Gäuboden Museum, Straubing)

15 Helmet from Hofheim, *c.* AD 110. (Sammlung Nassauischer Altertümer, Wiesbaden)

allowing maximum freedom of movement,[130] while the soldiers of the *auxilia* tended to wear a close-fitting scale mail shirt, the *lorica squamata* (Fig. 14), over their tunics. Chain armor, the *lorica hamata*, was also used. The cavalry wore either plate reinforced armor or scale-armor. All wore helmets (Fig. 15), legionaries carried large square, curved, or hexagonal shields, auxiliaries carried smaller oval shields, swords (Fig. 16), daggers (Fig. 17) and spears or lances. This equipment came for the most part from Italian workshops, though factories in Gaul and *Illyricum* also supplied arms.[131] It was, of course, imperative that the routes on which these supplies were transported be kept open and in good condition at all times.

Roman defensive strategy was based on the co-operation of Roman regulars and auxiliaries raised from among the local population. For the Roman army the advantages lay in that it was able to use local knowledge of language, customs and terrain. Above all, it was able to incorporate in its own tactics native arms and the local style of fighting.[132] This was best illustrated when Rome incorporated Germanic cavalry in its ranks. In the Roman army the cavalry was the orphan service. The Romans did not make use of stirrups so that the Roman horsemen rode with their knees, making it difficult for them to deliver a shock charge, while the Germanic riders, who did use stirrups, were able to wield axe and sword with much greater force. In the east the inclusion in the army of mounted archers increased Roman effectiveness against Parthians and Sassanians. Upon his retirement from the service the auxiliary veteran received his diploma of citizenship and the right to marry, the *ius conubium*. Generally this right was not granted to a soldier of fewer than twenty-four years of service.[133] Common-law arrangements must therefore have been frequent, but off-spring from such marriages were not considered legitimate until the father received his diploma. Before AD 50 auxiliary troops had not been rewarded in this way. Native officers of auxiliaries received their diploma of citizenship upon being promoted from the file to the rank of officer. Already in Julio-Claudian times, before AD 68, officers must have risen from the ranks of their own units to become centurions and decurions of auxiliaries.[134] However, reverses such as the Batavian Revolt of AD 69/70 encouraged Rome to appoint only Italian officers to the command in order to guarantee a measure of reliability and fighting efficiency, since a degree of sympathy with their tribal relatives beyond the frontier made the auxiliaries suspect of collaboration with the enemies of Rome. During this revolt most of the Gallic and Germanic units had joined the rebels and were dissolved.[135] This Batavian Revolt led Rome to make the northern auxiliary cohorts and *alae* less regional and homogeneous by transferring troops from other areas of the Empire when bringing the units up to strength. This practice accounts for the presence of some tombstones dedicated to the memory of Thracians, Iberians, Dalmatians, Gauls, Anatolians and so forth along the Rhine for instance. The reduction of the regional character of these units was designed to reduce fraternization with the local population. Only during the third and fourth centuries were units again allowed to do their tour of duty close to home.

The emperor Septimius Severus (AD 193–211), a provincial from Africa, carried out a policy of democratizing the army.[136] The changes he instituted allowed for the upward mobility of provincials and for the recruiting of peasants from the frontier provinces, even if only superficially romanized. In spite of an efficient administration, costs had risen to a level five times higher than they had been under Augustus.[137] Yet the Empire could not meet the cost of its frontier expenses at the very time when the Empire needed to increase its forces to resist the pressures from beyond the frontiers.

16 Sword— *gladius*, from Rheingönheim. (Historisches Museum der Pfalz, Speyer)

17 Dagger—
pugio, from
Rösenbeck.
(Germanisches
Nationalmuseum,
Nuremberg)

The military reforms of Septimius Severus were intended to confront this dilemma.[138] The legions were short of potential officers. Hitherto service in the praetorian guards had qualified men for a centurion's commission, but membership in these elite units had been restricted to Italians. Septimius Severus made it possible for provincials to join the praetorian cohorts, thereby removing the last criterion by which Italians were distinguished in the legions.[139] At the same time the *ius conubium* was repealed by Severus.[140] The troops now could marry before their term of duty was completed and settle their families in the villages near the garrison. As long as the Roman army had been a mobile field army the ban on marriage was justifiable in terms of the necessity of uncompromised movement when the units had to change their garrisons frequently. With large parts of the army becoming a stationary border force,[141] the ban on marriage was no longer reasonable. The benefit to the frontier defences lay in that the border army was regenerating itself, as sons followed in their fathers' footsteps.[142] However, while frequent relocations of the auxiliaries kept military traditions effective, thereby maintaining professional military standards, discipline and a state of readyness, and while a continuous process of romanization provided the common cultural denominator, the shift to permanent duty along a designated section of the border soon reduced the professional units to the level of a border militia, the *limitaneus*, prone to discontent, developing regional characteristics, regional interests, local concerns and local sympathies.[143] The debilitating boredom experienced by the troops in some forgotten border post can only be imagined. When Septimius Severus made available hereditary leases of land to the auxiliary units he indirectly made it possible for tribal units to cross the border to help 'protect' it against like-minded tribes further inland. Opening the command structure of the army and of the civil service to non-Romans and incorporating whole client-tribes into the army quickly changed the fabric of the forces at the disposal of the central command. A sedentary army compromised the necessary flexibility. Already in the time of the soldier emperors and during the subsequent military anarchy of the third century, Rome was depending to a perilous extent on military forces to protect its borders whose loyalty to Roman traditions and institutions was superficial and whose commitment to their defense was a function of their loyalty to individuals and of their own gain.[144] It is significant, in this context, to note that among the Germanic peoples the notion of statehood was not known, so that agreements could only be made between individuals and not between political units.[145] Much to Rome's annoyance, the constant changes in the Roman command necessitated a corresponding number of renegotiations. This impermanence of agreements was interpreted by the Romans as a blatant display of duplicity and untrustworthiness.

From the middle of the third century the Germanic auxiliaries played a significant role in the northern armies because the defences of the Rhine and Danube were left largely to them. By the time of Constantine (AD 306–37) the army had to be enlarged and reorganized to meet the intrusions from across the frontiers. In AD 270 Marcomanni had broken into the valley of the Po river; in AD 233 and in AD 260 Alamanni had penetrated into *Raetia* and into the Po valley; in AD 266 Franks had raided into southern Spain,[146] while in AD 267 sea-faring Goths had emerged from the Black Sea to raid Cyprus, Crete and Greece and another Germanic force had crossed the Lower Danube and penetrated into the Balkans. Sometimes defeated in battle, more often the attackers were allowed to overextend themselves and starve, as the romanized population withdrew with its livestock behind newly fortified towns. Constantine's reform of the army continued to post garrison forces along the frontiers but supplemented them by units of *vexillationes*, highly mobile shock troops stationed at strategic points, to be brought quickly to critical points on the border or to meet the intruders at some distance inland and to cut off their retreat. Such units already existed under Septimius Severus. This strategy necessitated larger cavalry forces which, ironically, had to be recruited from among the border peoples. As a result the European army became largely an army of Germanic mercenaries as the frontier garrisons were reinforced by hired warriors from treaty tribes, a solution which led to the unwholesome situation of Germanic border troops being contracted to fight off Germanic intruders.[147]

By AD 300 the border was no longer protecting a splendid realm of universal glitter enjoyed by everyone. Already by AD 200 the internal strife and the destruction wrought by aspirants to the imperial purple had filled the provinces with corrupt officials, profiteers, homeless men, ruined peasants and merchants, deserters, marauders, brigands and refugees, producing a social stratum of victims of someone's vengeance. Social order was very much a function of power, whim and arbitrary interest. To the peoples beyond the borders engaged in eking out a sparse existence not much above the subsistence line, the relative wealth of the vulnerable provinces just out of reach beyond the frontier must have seemed attractive indeed. What had begun as a reasonable principle of defensive strategy became the inherent weakness of the defensive system.[148] Within 300 years the auxiliary support units had become the main line of defense. In the first two imperial centuries the veteran auxiliaries had taken pride in adding Roman names, especially that of the emperor under whom they had received their Roman citizenship. Thereafter, this was no longer realistic and the practice became a presumptive pretence indicating in itself, however, that whatever the Empire's faults, the veterans did want to become a part of the Empire to whose service they had devoted their best years. They were not a 'Fifth Column' intent on helping the barbarian forces in the destruction of the Roman Empire.

The means by which the Romans solidified their hold on a region revolved around a strategic constant. Ever since the earliest wars of the Roman Republic, the rules of war included the standing orders that the units on the march had to set up a camp fortified with ditch, earthwork and palisade before retiring for the night. This protective measure accounts for the doggedness of the Roman military advance.[149]

During the early phases of occupation the encampments were of ditch-earthwork construction to fortify temporary strategic positions. Strings of such fortified encampments dotted the invasion route along the river Lippe almost to the Weser, with smaller defence posts located in between at intervals of about 18 km.[150] From *Mogon-*

18 Front with main gate of the 'Saalburg', a reconstruction of a
Roman auxiliary *castellum*, near Bad Homburg/Taunus.

19 *Porta praetoria*, main gate to the Saalburg *castellum*.

20 Gate of the *via principalis*, Saalburg.

21 *Principia*, the command center of the *castellum*, Saalburg.

tiacum a string of defensive positions had been established in a north-easterly direction probably at Rödgen, possibly a large supply base—3.3 hectares (8.15 acres), which had been prepared for Drusus' campaign to the Elbe in 12/11 BC. It has been found that this particular base was not a good defensible position, which allows the conclusion that it had been set up among friendly tribes from whom supplies could be readily obtained.[151] Dating from the last decade BC, some of these sites were of such size that they may have been occupied by two legions, at Oberaden for instance.[152] Evidently winterquarters were more substantial than those which served only the summer campaigns. All of these encampments were overrun after the defeat of Varus. During the reign of Claudius (AD 41–54) the ditch-earthwork-palisade encampments were converted to fortifications of stone and wood, but only if the strategic location of bases, depots and marching camps warranted their conversion into permanent garrisons to be occupied by Roman detachments. Such *castella* (Fig. 18) were not fortresses but fortified barracks of a rather individualistic character.[153] With only minor concessions to terrain, the *castra* and *castella* generally were laid out in a rectangular design according to a standardized plan established in the standing orders. Within the limits of the guidelines the builders were sufficiently free so that no two forts are identical in all respects.

The Roman command relied on the armed strength and fighting skills of its garrison troops rather than on sophisticated defensive architecture.[154] Only in the fourth century did the *castella* assume distinctly defensive features. Access to the rectangular *castellum* was provided by four gates, one in each wall. (Fig. 19). The *via principalis* linked the two gates in the long sides (Fig. 20) and intersected the *via praetoria* at right angles. On the *via principalis*, where it intersected with the *via praetoria*, the *principia* was located, the administrative nerve center of the *castellum*. The *principia* (Fig. 21) housed the *praetorium*, i.e. the residence of the *praefectus* or of another commander in chief, the *sacellum*, i.e. the sanctuary of the standards (Fig. 22), housed the altar of the genius of the unit, the treasury, a drill hall (Fig. 23) and the *armamentaria*, i.e. the arsenal, as well as representations of the ruling emperor.[155] The fortifications occupied by the legions were called *castra*, those of units of the *auxilia* were called *castella*. Whether housing a legion or only a cohort these fortifications contained no buildings other than those needed to guarantee the self-sufficiency of the garrison, such as the storerooms and granaries (Fig. 24), hospital, workshops and stables. All other enterprises, whether cultic or commercial, had to be located outside

22 *Sacellum*, flag sanctuary and treasury, flanked by statues of the emperors Hadrian and Severus Alexander, Saalburg.

23 *Principia*, forehall, possibly used as a drill hall, Saalburg.

24 *Horrea*, (below, left) the granaries, Saalburg.

25 *Centuriae*, (below, right) barracks, looking towards the officers' quarters, with entrances to the *contuberniae*, Saalburg.

the walls. However, the front of the *principia* of the camp at Haltern on the Lippe was lined with shops or storerooms facing out onto the *via principalis*.[156] Generally the civilian settlements[157] came several years later and were set up at some distance from the military establishment, but by the second century even these settlements were laid out in military style, suggesting that military surveyors were at work and that the military policed all those elements which profited from the legionaries' worldly needs.

The social differences of Roman society were reflected in the quarters which officers and men occupied. Every century (sixty, eighty or a hundred men) was housed in a wooden building (Fig. 25). This building was subdivided into a flight of ten rooms of

equal size, a *contubernium*, normally occupied by a *contubernia*, i.e. a mess-group of eight men in each.[158] At the end of the building the centurion occupied larger quarters which he had to share, however, with his second-in-command and two other non-commissioned officers. The excavation of officers' quarters has indicated that each new officer who joined a command could have his quarters remodelled and, of course, redecorated according to his own taste.[159] From Reveille at dawn until noon those not assigned to normal duties would perform all those parades and drills characteristic of army life.[160] In the afternoons those off-duty could pursue their 'own' affairs, such as the maintenance of their equipment and the care of their animals.[161] Since each *contubernia* had to prepare its own meals and the main meal was taken in the evening, much time would be devoted to its preparation. Extensive records were kept of all activities and events. Regular mini-manoeuvers to maintain physical fitness,[162] leaves of absence and numerous holidays to honor the gods and the imperial household[163] broke the monotony of barracks routine.[164] Thus the imperial cult included the annual oath of allegiance, while such military festivals as the celebration of the birthday of the unit and the cult of the *signa*, i.e. the standards, fostered the morale of the unit.

In Germany the most celebrated *castellum* is the so-called 'Saalburg',[165] a not so accurate nineteenth-century reconstruction of a permanent encampment of a mounted auxiliary cohort, located in the Taunus Mountains and built there originally in about AD 69. This cohort had been recruited in *Raetia*. For bravery it had been awarded Roman citizenship, hence its proud name *cohors II Raetorum civium Romanorum equitata*.[166] That it bore the number *II* indicates that the cohort was about 480 men strong. It was attached to the *legio XXII Primigenia pia fidelis* stationed at *Mogontiacum*. Two factors lay behind the establishment of a fortification at this site. During the Batavian Revolt of AD 69/70 it was found that the Upper Rhine–Upper Danube frontier constituted too much of an obstacle to the quick movement of troops from their bases on the Middle Danube to the Middle and Lower Rhine.[167] Shortening this line of communication was a strategic necessity. Secondly, along the Middle Rhine the Chatti assumed a hostile attitude which prompted the emperor Domitian (AD 81–96) to move against them as a preventive measure. In the face of Roman military might the Chatti resorted to guerilla warfare. The Romans in turn kept them at a distance by cutting clearings into the forests up to 180 km deep, from which they combed the woods.[168] Domitian used five legions for the task[169] and may have had more extensive plans when Dacian attacks drew his attention to the Lower Danube, preventing him from following up his advantages and again emphasizing the awkwardness of using frontiers determined by geography. Against the Chatti the Romans occupied the heights of the Taunus Mountains with a line of fortifications (Fig. 26), at the same time depriving them of their best arable land.[170] Units of auxiliaries were thrown into these encampments. In spite of the uncertain success of this campaign, Domitian nevertheless assumed the title *Germanicus*. As part of a first phase towards establishing 'dry borders', the Flavian emperors (AD 69–96) moved away from the Rhine south of *Bonna*, fortified the Taunus heights, then came south along the Main and the Upper Neckar rivers. Already in AD 73/74 units of the *legio VIII Augusta* laid out a road from *Argentorate* through the Black Forest to the Upper Danube.[171] From there a line of forts 'secured' the heights north of the Danube in largely friendly territory. The western acquisition, designated *agri decumates*,[172] was included in the province *Germania superior* which was the official designation for the

26 Reconstruction of a signal tower along the *limes* in the Wetterau, near Pfaffenwiesbach. Palisade ditch is visible in the foreground.

27 Reconstruction of a Roman watchtower behind its palisade screen along the *limes* in *Raetia*. (Open-air Museum near Schwabsberg-Buch)

province after AD 85, an area to be reoccupied by Celtic populations from Gaul.[173] An altar dedicated to the Flavians was intended to provide the new territory with a cultic focus at *Arae Flaviae*, modern Rottweil. An uprising in this sector in AD 142/43 during the reign of the emperor Antoninus Pius (AD 138–61) appears to have prompted the relocation of this defensive line further eastward meeting the new, more northerly line of defensive installations north of the Danube.[174] Interlinked with walls this line was called the *limes*. For the next 120 years this *limes* separated and linked Roman and Germanic peoples. The history of the *limes* recorded the interactions between them.

Initially, the *limes* was a patrol path cut through the forests, punctuated by watchtowers placed in such a fashion that the lookouts on each tower could see the next towers to the left and right (Fig. 27), making the rapid transmission of signal-messages possible. During its second phase, both in *Germania superior* and in *Raetia*, a palisade and V-shaped ditch (Fig. 28) protected the watchtowers.[175] In *Germania superior* the third phase, in the reign of Antoninus Pius, saw not only the eastward relocation of a straightened line but also the construction of stone towers to replace the wooden ones. In its fourth and final phase, during the reign of Caracalla (AD 211–17), the *limes* in *Germania superior* consisted of palisade, ditch and earthwork with stone towers set back behind the line, while in *Raetia* a stone wall, 3 m high (Fig. 29), incorporated stone towers without the support of any outlying obstacles (Fig. 30). The Upper German *limes* ran from the Rhine north of *Confluentes*, modern Koblenz, to modern Lorch, east of modern day Stuttgart; the Raetian *limes* from Lorch to Eining on the Danube, south-west of the later *Castra Regina*. Four or five men inhabited each watchtower. About 900 towers appear to have existed along its 500 km.[176] These two

sections of the *limes* were guarded by auxiliary units, *alae* or *cohortes*, stationed within easy reach of the *limes*. The only *castellum* assumed to have been founded by Trajan, the 'Saalburg'[177], was the third *castellum* on the site for the auxiliaries stationed there to guard this limit of the Empire. Smaller *castella* manned by *numeri* were interspaced between the *castella* of the cohorts if they were spaced too far apart. Almost 60 *castella* supported the *limes*. Simple arithmetic indicates that 30,000 men guarded the entire line,[178] or 60 men per km, a barrier as effective as a 'No trespassing' sign. Quite evidently the *limes* was not a military obstacle in the sense of a fortress but rather an administrative demarcation, designed to impress those beyond it with some intangible message. It was a political and judicial dividing line, along which the cultural differences became ever more diffused. For Tacitus, writing in AD 98, the word *limes* meant the established limit of the Empire. Later the term included the entire system of depots, roads, control points and military establishments. Owing to the great distance which separated the *limes* from the *castra* of the legions at *Argentorate* and *Vindonissa*, even at *Mogontiacum*, and occasionally at *Augusta Vindelicum*, modern Augsburg, and

28 Eroded ditch and palisade embankments along the *limes* in *Raetia*, near Schwabsberg-Buch.

29 Reconstructed stone wall, stone tower base and wooden watchtower along the *limes* in *Raetia*, near Schwabsberg-Buch.

31 Reconstruction of the defenses of *Colonia Ulpia Traiana*, with an accurately reconstructed Roman crane. C U T was erected in the vicinity of the *castra Vetera* I and II. (Open-air Museum, Xanten)

considering the acculturation of the auxiliary units, the defences of this sector of the Roman Empire were soft indeed.

The Lower German *limes* was the Rhine. From south of *Bonna* the line of demarcation ran north, overland to the Zuider Zee and then along its western shore to the *Mare Germanicum*, the North Sea. Large *castella* were located on the west bank of the Rhine, quite visible from across the river.[179] Initially, three legion *castra* had been located along the Rhine at intervals of 120 km at *Bonna*, *Novaesium*, modern Neuss, and at *Vetera* (Fig. 31). A fourth *castrum* was located at *Noviomagus*, modern Nijmegen. *Castella* of auxiliaries were scattered between them, 12–15 km apart, less than a half day's march. The great width of the Rhine was thought to offer sufficient security. Even today, contained by dikes, the Rhine is up to 400 m wide, a considerable obstacle. Under Constantine a bridgehead was thrown over the Rhine and a *castellum* was built called *Divitia*, modern Deutz, just across from *Agrippina*, modern Cologne. *Divitia* reflected centuries of additional experience in that its square outline was protected by massive bastions protruding nearly 6 m from the wall-face, from which

30 (far left) Excavated and partly restored stone gate on the *limes* in *Raetia*, near Dalkingen.

32 (left) Remnant of a Roman four-way gate, a tetrapylon. Lonely remainder of the fortifications of the civilian settlement at *Carnuntum*, near Petronell, east of Vienna.

the defenders could sweep the walls with cross-fire. The earlier *castella* did not have this feature, for it was essentially an expression of an aggressive strategy.[180]

Towards the east, the Middle Danube was a 'wet' border which, in conjunction with mountain ranges, offered enough natural protection to require only a few *castella* some 30–40 km apart.[181] In Lower Austria Roman power extended north into the Danube Plain, far too fertile an agricultural area to be ignored. The region witnessed a period of great building activity c. AD 114, not for the construction of fortifications but with an emphasis on comfort and luxury. With its many baths it appears to have been a center for the recreation of Roman dignitaries. *Vindobona*, modern Vienna, *Lauriacum* near modern Linz and *Carnuntum* (Fig. 32) were the great *castra* on the Middle Danube.

As such the 'dry' *limes* did not provide a solution for the strategic demands of the military situation. It was only a poor defensive measure, crumbling under serious pressure. As an expression of defensive policy it prevented easy access in that it channeled the border traffic through designated and specially protected crossing points. It did not hope to offer a realistic defense against a concentrated attack. We have seen that the field commanders of Augustus and Tiberius did not conceive a defensive policy along the northern frontier based on fixed lines. Even later the *limes* was of little strategic significance for an army whose legions were still geared to movement.[182] The stationary tasks were assigned to the auxiliary units of light infantry and cavalry. In view of the way in which the *limes* was laid out, it seems that the planners were not too interested in the view ahead but rather in an unobstructed lateral view between watchtowers. It was a device of limited effectiveness as long as the status of Rome commanded respect. At the same time it must be considered that the *limes* was not endangered by those groups on whose tribal areas it touched but by those tribal groups which were crystallizing in the interior. It was their movements which were creating the turmoil beyond the *limes*, in reaction to which the border tribes requested to be settled within the Empire. In the vast imperial domains they were settled as *coloni*, eventual sources of revenue.

A dividing line is also a line along which contacts are made. Along the *limes* Roman institutions, customs, attitudes and techniques were transmitted to the Germanic hinterland (Fig. 33). As long as changes beyond the frontier were taking place gradually, the Roman influence was able to contribute to a degree of romanization (Fig. 34). Thus the Hermunduri north of the Raetian *limes* had been friends of Rome since the time of Augustus. Some 200 years of contact with Rome had romanized them considerably.[183] Many Roman tradegoods have been found in their former territory. In the end, those who had not yet crossed over the border were absorbed by the Alamanni. A natural development among the border tribes would be the emergence of pro- and anti-Roman factions within each tribe as well as of pro- and anti-Roman tribes, both developments contributing to the turmoil beyond the borders as rival groups were expelled or eliminated.[184] In such situations the Roman *divide et impera* would find its most extensive application as it favored the generally pro-Roman nobility's pursuit of the benefits of acculturation, mainly aggrandizement through wealth and power, playing into the hands of Rome which saw in romanization a means of pacification. In any event, the dissension between those who resisted Roman influence and control and those who favored it neutralized the offensive thrust of the tribes. Roman support either for such puppet 'rulers' as Italicus, the nephew of Arminius,[185] in the time of Claudius or the outright installation of outsiders equipped

34

33 Bronze casserole with the name of its former owner engraved on the back. First century AD. Dredged from the river Weser. (Landesmuseum, Bremen)

34 Imported Roman bowl, wheel thrown, with impressed twig patterns and engraved animals— stags and boars, from a gravefield at Bremen – Mahndorf, third century AD. (Landesmuseum, Bremen)

with funds and just sufficient military power to maintain themselves in position complete with intrigues, assassinations and 'palace' revolutions, a policy still pursued by Caracalla 200 years later,[186] vis-à-vis the Marcomanni, did not create any great confidence in the possibly beneficial intentions of Rome. It is apparent from archaeological evidence that distinctions between kings and subjects were not known to the northern inhabitants. Though the Celts used the suffix -rix, it was Rome that had bestowed the title rex upon Ariovistus.[187] It was to be among the Marcomanni, that tribal group in the following of Ariovistus which had withdrawn to the Central Highlands from where Maroboduus had led them into Bohemia and where Tiberius had hoped to deal them an extinguishing blow, that the most blatant application of the Roman policy of furthering internal dissension was demonstrated. Brought up in Rome, Maroboduus had remained loyal to Rome during the Illyrian Revolt and had not joined with Arminius in spite of the aborted attack aimed against him. Probably in a state of social disruption after their repeated dislocations and resettlements, the Marcomanni were susceptible to outside interference, something Rome always reserved for itself once a tribe had become a treaty tribe. As clients of Rome the Marcomanni had to accept a sequence of rulers imposed by Rome whom the tribe jettisoned at the first opportunity.[188] To avoid open conflict in that sector with this potentially powerful tribal federation, Rome had to keep the Marcomanni in a state of perpetual inner strife. It was part of Rome's policy to keep the extent of support at an ineffective level, thereby preventing their puppets from gaining any real support and power which could easily be turned against Rome. Without a popular power base and with only symbolic support from Rome these 'rulers' found themselves in a state of paralytic tension, at the mercy of both parties, suspicious of all and trusted by none. Rome reserved its prerogative to ratify a tribe's choice of its leader. It follows that only he who was prepared to welcome the counsel of Rome would be found worthy of the honor. Any change of attitude would result in the withdrawal of Rome's support which would leave the renegade in an extremely precarious position. It is known that in AD 180 the emperor Marcus Aurelius had plans to extend the Roman frontier to the Bohemian and Carpathian Mountains. A policy which actively pursued internal dissension in the area would have served to undermine any effective resistance to such an annexation. Two provinces were to be added to the Empire, *Marcomania* and *Sarmatia*, to link *Dacia* to the Upper Rhine.[189] It is understandable that Marcus Aurelius was so infuriated when one of the allies of the Marcomanni, the Quadi, elected a chief other than the Roman candidate who had been found to be too eager to do Rome's bidding and consequently had been expelled. Marcus Aurelius put a price on the head of the newly elected king. Commodus (AD 180–92), the son and successor of Marcus Aurelius, tried to limit the Marcomanni to one assembly per month at a place designated by him, under the eye of a trusted centurion.[190]

By means of techniques such as these Rome had tried to prevent the effective coalition between the tribes of the Marcomannic federation. The sequence of events in this theater, however, demonstrated the futility of Rome's preventive policies.

From AD 150 Bohemia and the neighboring area were marked by unrest. Population movements north of the Roman frontier culminated in the Marcomannic Wars between AD 167 and 180 which were in themselves early indications of the great migrations.[191] A preliminary theater of war developed in the west when uprisings unsettled northern Britain and the Chatti invaded *Germania superior* and *Raetia*. Far to the east the Parthian Wars, AD 162–66, brought serious defeats to the Romans. Without having caused extensive destruction the Chatti could be driven back. Along the Danube the pressure does not appear to have been critical yet since a cavalry unit from *Raetia* and the *legio II adiutrix* from *Pannonia inferior* were sent east as reinforcements. By the end of that eastern war the deteriorating conditions on the Danube necessitated the speedy return of the troops. They returned as carriers of an epidemic. The rapid spread of this disease decimated the forces and depopulated large areas, affecting agriculture and causing severe starvation.[192] Marcus Aurelius armed slaves and recruited gladiators to regain at least some of the military strength, but beyond the northern frontier the first large concentrations of hostile forces, Marcomanni in Bohemia, Quadi in Slovakia, their neighbors the Naristae, Yaziges in Hungary, appeared before *Vindobona* and *Carnuntum*, crossed the Danube in AD 167, devastated *Pannonia* and *Noricum*, dealt a significant defeat to a large Roman force, threatened *Raetia* and appeared before Verona. For the first time in over a century troops had to be raised in Italy, the *legio II Italica* and the *legio III Italica concors*, to confront the recurring invasions, some of which reached Greece. At the same time the Chatti renewed their attacks. To organize the protection of Italy Marcus Aurelius established a military district, the *praetentura Italiae et Alpium*, and assigned the two new Italian legions to the district. After 167/68 *castella* along the Raetian Danube were destroyed as *Raetia* and *Noricum* were affected particularly. In AD 169 Marcus Aurelius started his counteroffensive to clear Italy of hostile forces (Fig. 35). By AD 171/72 the two provinces had been cleared of invaders (Fig. 36) and the *praetentura* was replaced by a line of defence north of the Alps. In AD 172 Marcus Aurelius was able to cross the Danube and subjugate the Marcomanni (Figs. 37, 38) and some of their allies to the point that he could envisage the eventual establishment of the new provinces *Marcomania* and *Sarmatia*. From about this time, the *legio II Italica* was stationed in *Noricum* and *legio III Italica concors* in *Raetia*.[193] Destruction horizons in Raetian *castella*, possibly datable to AD 174/75, suggest renewed invasions which may have reached *Augusta Vindelicum* and points south of Lake Constance. The changed status of *Raetia* and *Noricum* in *c.* AD 175 from proconsular to praetorian provinces is significant, a change

35 Details of the column of Marcus Aurelius in Rome, commemorating his campaigns against the Marcomanni. The central strip shows a captured barbarian chief being led into the presence of the *imperator*.

36 Column of Marcus Aurelius. The central strip shows barbarians paying homage to the *imperator*.

which accompanied the permanent stationing of a legion in each province. This meant that even the civil administration was placed under the commander of the legion, a senatorial *legatus Augusti pro praetore*.[194] Although the attention of Marcus Aurelius was drawn once again to the east in AD 177, the legion camp at *Lauriacum* in *Noricum* for *legio II Italica*, completed in AD 180/81, the legion camp at *Castra Regina* in *Raetia*[195] for *legio III Italica concors*, completed in 179/80, and especially the decisive defeat of Marcomanni and Quadi eliminated the crisis and stabilized the frontier. For the first time the name of the Vandals to the north appears in the reports. Of interest is evidence of a military expedition against the Buri, a tribe hostile to Rome located to the north of the Marcomanni and the Quadi in northern Slovakia. Towards the end of the Marcomannic Wars, when units of the *legio III Italica concors* were stationed near the Raetian *limes* fort at Eining, a centurion of the legion erected

37 Column of Marcus Aurelius. Continuation of the same strips. The center shows the destruction of a village. Captives are being driven off.

38 Column of Marcus Aurelius. The central strip shows the execution of barbarian captives by barbarian auxiliaries.

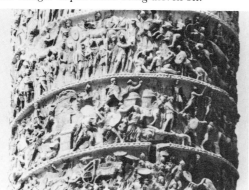

39 Stone dedicated to Jupiter Stator for the safe return of the *expeditio Burica* found at Untersaal in Bavaria. (Prähistorische Staatssammlung, Munich)

an altar dedicated to Jupiter Stator as thanks for a safe return (Fig. 39). Soon afterwards *legio III Italica concors* moved into its permanent base at *Castra Regina*. Evidently Rome did not wage only frontal wars but thrust far behind enemy lines as well. The death of Marcus Aurelius at *Vindobona* in AD 180 put an end to his grandiose plans. His son Commodus preferred to wrestle with gladiators.

A foreign policy of containment by intrigue preserved the status quo in that theater, yet was forced on Rome by insufficient military and economic reserves, disease, depopulation, decreasing self-confidence and unrest throughout the Empire. The momentum with which Marcus Aurelius had completed the defeat of the Marcomannic federation induced his generals to consider for a while the resumption of the Augustan plans of conquest in central Europe. However, the renunciation was final. In AD 193 a column was erected in Rome, 30 m high, with an ascending narrative frieze, to commemorate and illustrate the events of the Marcomannic Wars.

These wars were the prelude to the invasions of the Empire yet to come. To fight its eastern wars Rome had to strip its European frontiers of all available forces.[196] It had become customary to draw upon the experienced troops from the Rhine-Danube frontier whenever the need arose elsewhere. The troops were often replaced by levies raised among the Germanic settlers brought in to repopulate the devastated areas. The constant murders of emperors and the ensuing civil wars weakened the borders while the victimization of inhabitants and the consequent depopulation demoralized the people left on the land behind the *limes*. These factors were a standing invitation and a challenge to the tribal federations which were massing behind the romanized

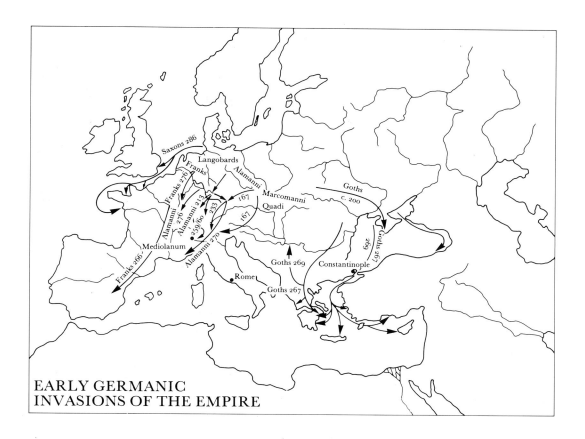

EARLY GERMANIC
INVASIONS OF THE EMPIRE

buffer-zones. The commanders tried to clear the forefield of enemies, but to do this forces had to be withdrawn from one sector to be concentrated elsewhere. This created weaknesses and invited attack. After AD 200 the Alamanni pressed from the Middle Elbe towards the south-west and crossed the *limes* in AD 213, 233 and 242.[197] Utilizing troop withdrawals to the east the Alamanni attacked. While the Upper German *limes* was held generally, in AD 233 the Raetian *limes* was destroyed extensively. Many settlements perished as the Alamanni reached the rivers Saar and Moselle in the west and Lake Constance in the south. Insufficient strength prevented the reconstruction of the *castella* after AD 233 and many *vici* were neither rebuilt nor repaired. The suddenness of the Alamannic attack of AD 233 is illustrated at the *castellum* at Pfünz, where the shield fittings were found where the shields had been leaning against the gate wall. Their bearers, the guards at the gate, had been killed before they could arm themselves. After the attack the *castellum* at Pfünz was not rebuilt.[198] Evidently the belief in the survival of the Empire was diminishing. The depopulation of extensive areas prevented a successful economic recovery. In a great military effort directed against the Alamanni in AD 235 the emperor Severus Alexander gathered an invasion force at *Mogontiacum*, including units drawn from legions stationed in Spain, Rome and *Pannonia*. Worn out by a futile campaign he retired across the Rhine to negotiate but was murdered by a dissatisfied army. Other Alamannic raids in AD 242, 253/54 against the Raetian and Upper German *limes* carried them far inland. During these early raids the destruction was great as each thrust was allowed to spend itself and the raiders died of starvation (Fig. 40). The

40 Collapsing barbarian. Fragment of ornamental horse trappings. (Kunsthistorisches Museum, Vienna)

limes had ceased to be an effective line of demarcation. The emperors of the day tried stop-gap measures, but no extensive rebuilding programs were undertaken, until AD 259/60 the largest Alamannic invasion, aimed directly at *Augusta Vindelicum*, completely destroyed the military and civil adminstration of *Raetia*. This attack was supported by parties of Goths, Quadi and Sarmatians along other parts of the border. With the exception of the *legio III Italica concors* and two cohorts, the known *limes* garrisons disappear from the records and probably ceased to exist.[199] After AD 260 the Raetian border could be secured no longer. With their settlements in ruins, trade and commerce gone, large parts of *Raetia* in Alamannic hands, the romanized population shrank to a fraction and withdrew onto small secure sites. The Empire was undergoing severe tests as in the east the city of Palmyra, under its legendary queen Zenobia, had established a separate kingdom,[200] while in the west a certain C. Latinus Postumus had established the *Imperium Galliarum* consisting of Britain, Gaul and even Spain.[201] The Alamannic incursion of AD 259/60 reached *Mediolanum*, modern Milan (Fig. 41). Other tribes, perhaps Marcomanni, closed on Rome and Ravenna. Italy was saved when co-emperor Gallienus (AD 253–68), with the help of troops withdrawn from the Rhine and from *Raetia*, fought a victorious battle against the invaders before *Mediolanum* in AD 260/61. Something of the vainglory is indicated by the fact that in the years AD 256 to 259 Gallienus was proclaimed five times *Germanicus maximus*, supreme victor over the Germani.[202] Elsewhere Rome faced disaster when another

41 Depot find of coins dating up to the time of the emperor Gallienus (AD 253–58). From a *villa rustica* at Büßlingen, near Konstanz. By then the area had been largely abandoned. Such depots of coins help to trace the general directions taken by the Alamannic invaders. (Museum für Ur- und Frühgeschichte, Freiburg)

tribal federation, the Franks, crossed the Lower Rhine into Gaul. Earlier the emperor Valerian (AD 253–60), father of Gallienus, had been captured by the Sassanians. Though Postumus cleared the Franks out of Gaul, this time the Upper German and Raetian *limes* were overrun and natural frontiers once again became the northern limits of the Empire, as the border was redrawn along the Rhine, Lake Constance, the river Iller and the Danube. In AD 267 the Goths laid siege to Thessalonica, having crossed the Danube earlier and plundered the Balkans for several years. The Heruli had even occupied Athens for a while. In the west the Alamanni attacked again in AD 267, and in 268 reached Lake Garda. A Gothic force was defeated in AD 269 by the emperor Claudius II Gothicus who, however, settled the remnants as *coloni* in the depopulated Balkans.[203] For the next 100 years the Goths were quiet. In AD 270 the Alamanni directed their attack on *Castra Regina* and on *Augusta Vindelicum*, crossed the Alps, reappeared before *Mediolanum* and defeated a Roman army near *Placentia*.[204] The crisis was such that rebuilding the walls of Rome was seriously considered. In AD 271 the emperor Aurelian (AD 270–75) defeated the raiding parties once again at Pavia, but the rebuilding of the Roman walls was begun anyway. In AD 274 he defeated the Alamanni once more in Gaul and his successes in the Empire were such that most of the old frontiers were restored. Palmyra was destroyed, its queen Zenobia graced Aurelian's triumph into Rome, and the *Imperium Galliarum* was reincorporated. However, the germanization of the Roman army was becoming more pronounced as units of Vandals, Juthungi and Alamanni were taken into its ranks. Aurelian even permitted them to fight in their traditional wedge formations. In AD 276 Alamanni and Franks invaded Gaul on a broad front and taking advantage of the disorder in Gaul, stayed long enough to capture seventy towns, a blow to the economy of Gaul. From AD 276 to 305 three successive emperors campaigned systematically to restore the former boundaries. In AD 277 the emperor Probus (AD 276–82) succeeded in pushing Alamanni and Franks back across the Rhine. He even settled Frankish prisoners on the Black Sea, but they resorted to piracy to return home, plundering Syracuse and Carthage among other cities as they went. In AD 278 Burgundians, Vandals and Goths were driven out of *Raetia* and reconstruction was begun. The seventy towns in Gaul were restored but the land beyond the Rhine, Iller and Danube was given up for lost.[205]

A new stability came with the accession of Diocletian (AD 285–305). In AD 286 he divided the Empire into an eastern and a western half, with himself as emperor of

1a The god Sol in his quadriga. Fire-gilt silver mounting from Butzbach. (Hessisches Landesmuseum, Darmstadt)

1b Dancing figure, wall painting from *Virunum*, *c.* 20 BC. (Landesmuseum für Kärnten, Klagenfurt)

1c Reconstructed mural from a wealthy house, first half of the second century AD. The mural was found under the southern spire of Cologne cathedral. (Römisch-Germanisches Museum, Cologne)

1d Grape harvest. Detail of the mural. (Römisch-Germanisches Museum, Cologne)

2a Cupids, from the Constantinian ceiling paintings at Trier. The building in which these paintings were displayed was constructed between AD 315 and AD 321. (Bischöfliches Dom- und Diözesanmuseum, Trier)

2b Lady with a jewel casket. Constantinian ceiling painting. (Bischöfliches Dom- und Diözesanmuseum, Trier)

2c Flower girl. Constantinian ceiling painting. (Bischöfliches Dom- und Diözesanmuseum, Trier)

2d Lady with a scarf. Central portrait of the Constantinian ceiling paintings. (Bischöfliches Dom- und Diözesanmuseum, Trier)

the East and Maximian (AD 286–305) as co-emperor of the West.[206] A strategic necessity, this division would remove the conflicts on an eastern and western front from the concerns of only one person. Previously the emperor's presence in any one theater brought difficulties in another, as incursions from outside and military uprisings on the inside exhausted the emperors in ineffective troop movements and frustrated most efforts to implement and supervise any of the much needed reforms. In AD 293 each half of the Empire was subdivided further in that each emperor appointed a Caesar to whom he entrusted half of his domain. Each now administered a tetrarchy. Diocletian adopted Galerius as Caesar for his northern half of the Empire, while Maximian adopted Constantius to share his power in the west. Constantius administered Britain, Gaul and Spain, Maximian governed Africa, Italy and *Raetia*, while Galerius had jurisdiction of *Illyricum* (Noricum, Pannonia, Dalmatia), *Macedonia* and *Graecia*. Diocletian ruled the rest. This division allowed greater administrative attention to be focused on each tetrarchy, concerted efforts to be devoted to each section of the frontier, but above all it allowed each tetrarch to bring the concentrated military power of his domain to bear upon critical points on his borders. A measure of cultural and social stability could return to the ravaged provinces. The attempted incursions of Burgundians, Alamanni and Heruli in AD 286/87 and of the Franks in AD 288 could be halted and driven back across the Rhine by Maximian, while Diocletian himself could repel the Alamanni from *Raetia* and even make some gains.[207] A renewed incursion in AD 291 led to the decision to refortify the Rhine–Iller–Danube *limes*.[208] Most important for the west was Galerius' victory over the Sassanians in AD 297 which gave the eastern half of the Empire a forty-year peace. The northern legions now could return to the Rhine and Danube. In AD 298 Constantius defeated the Alamanni at *Vindonissa*. None of these defeats was decisive, for in AD 302/3 another incursion of Franks and Alamanni had to be repelled across the Rhine.

With the abdication of Diocletian and Maximian in AD 305, a new situation leading to civil war was created when, with the advancement of Constantius and Galerius to the position of co-emperors, Galerius in appointing the Caesars passed over the sons of Maximian and Constantius.[209] In the end their heirs, Constantine and Maxentius, were to assert themselves, with Constantine ultimately emerging as sole emperor at the end of a war of everyone against all.[210] As sole ruler Constantine renewed the defences along Rhine and Danube and in AD 328 defeated the Alamanni decisively. In AD 332 the Goths on the Lower Danube were forced to assume the protection of the river frontier against those pushing in from further north and east. By then ever more Germanic leaders with their followings of free-lances had entered Roman military service. Eventually these leaders became officers and some rose to very high commands. During the wars of succession following the death of Constantine, Constantius, one of his successors, committed the fatal error of inviting Germanic forces to fight on his behalf.[211] This meant that Franks on the Lower Rhine and Alamanni on the Upper Rhine crossed once more into the Empire. This time (in AD 355) *Agrippina* fell after a long siege. The Alamanni were beaten once again in AD 357 and the Franks in AD 358. The importance of these wars, which incidentally coincided with wars on the Lower Danube, lay in that they reaffirmed Roman prestige among the Germanic tribes beyond the frontiers. The emperor Valentinian (AD 364–75) once again threw the Almanni back across the Rhine (AD 365), crossed the Rhine himself in AD 368 and again several times thereafter, and supervised the construction of defences along the Rhine and in the territories lost after the collapse of the *limes* in

AD 260. Valentinian's personal presence on the frontier points to his great efforts at halting the invasions and thereby saving the realm. In AD 369, by making alliances with the Burgundians living to the east of the Alamanni, he induced them to attack the latter in the rear while he attacked them from *Raetia* in AD 372.[212] Alamannic prisoners were settled in the Po valley. The stroke was not entirely successful and in the end (AD 374) the frontiers were those established under Augustus.

The death of Valentinian in AD 375 coincided with the appearance of the Huns and their client peoples from the east. This new pressure forced christianized Visi-Goths to cross the Danube into the Balkans in AD 375, to be settled by the emperor Valens in Thrace. Roman profiteering caused them to rebel and, in conjunction with Ostro-Goths, Huns and Alans who had followed them, inflict a disastrous defeat on the Romans at *Adrianople* in AD 378. A reign of devastation followed as these peoples gradually moved westward into *Pannonia*. The emperor Theodosius (AD 379-95) succeeded in settling them as *foederati* in the Balkans. The disaster at *Adrianople*, the beginning of the last phase of the Roman Empire, had been made possible by the split of the forces deployed in the West to obstruct yet another incursion of the Alamanni.

In spite of strict contravening measures, the armies were increasingly germanized.[213] For Rome there was no alternative as its eligible citizens were resorting to self-mutilation in order to avoid conscription.[214] Germanic leaders bearing the official titles *magister militum*, or *magister equitum* soon controlled the military fortunes of the Empire.[215] In fairness to them it must be said that they considered themselves Romans who espoused the cause of Rome as their own. Thus, the Frank Bauto[216] had been *magister equitum*, general of cavalry, under the emperor Gratian, had served as consul and was considered brave and incorruptible. He became the father-in-law of the emperor Arcadius (AD 395-408) when the latter married Bauto's daughter Eudoxia, a Grecified lady it would appear.[217] One Merobaudes,[218] *magister militum* under Gratian and his step-brother and western co-emperor Valentinian II (AD 375-92) and under the usurper Eugenius (AD 392-94), had served twice as consul and probably helped his fellow Franks Bauto, Richomer[219] and Arbogast into their offices.[220] Richomer and Arbogast both had served under Gratian. The emperor Theodosius promoted Richomer to the top military post. Arbogast was more of an opportunist. Expelled from his tribe he had sought refuge in Rome where he revealed himself to be a bitter enemy of the northerners. Theodosius sent him north to negotiate a peace with the Franks who had once again taken *Agrippina*. This peace did not prevent Arbogast from avenging himself on them by devastating their territory on the right bank of the Rhine. A few years later this Arbogast engineered the usurpation of Eugenius[221] in the west and as commander of the western forces he was to face Richomer, commander-in-chief of the army of Theodosius. Though Richomer died before the encounter, Theodosius was victorious and Arbogast committed suicide. In this battle Visi-Gothic troops led by Alaric fought in the army of Theodosius. Theodosius again split the Empire into western and eastern halves. Hereafter, they were not to be reunited. The sons of Theodosius were his successors, Arcadius then eighteen (AD 395-408) in the East and Honorius, only eleven (AD 395-423) in the West. But it was the prefect of praetorians, Rufinus, who ruled the East for Arcadius, while Honorius was dominated by the Vandal Flavius Stilicho (AD c. 359-408)[222] who had married Serena (Fig. 42), the niece and adopted daughter of the emperor Theodosius. Stilicho, whose father had commanded cavalry under the emperor Valens, had par-

42 Ivories of Flavius Stilicho, his wife Serena and his son. (Tesoro del Duomo, Monza)

ticipated in a mission to the court of the Sassanians in AD 384. In the war against the usurper Eugenius, Stilicho had been second-in-command of the army of Theodosius. Following the victory he was made *magister utriusque militiae*, supreme commander. In AD 398 Stilicho could persuade his ward Honorius to marry his daughter Maria and, when she died in AD 408, his second daughter Thermantia. The epic poet Claudius Claudianus, poet at the western court, from AD 395 to 404, hailed Stilicho as the leading personality of his time.[223] Not only do these few examples illustrate how undefined the divisions between 'barbarians' and Romans had become but also something of the extraordinary capabilities of these individuals. That these acculturated men rose to command the Roman armies without seizing the opportunity to claim the imperial purple for themselves, as well they might have, preferring instead to wield power from behind the throne, suggests that they must have recognized a fundamental difference between themselves and the Romans even if the concept 'Roman' was only a legal concept.[224] Stilicho was an extremely capable commander who had quelled a Moorish revolt in AD 398, had driven the Visi-Goths out of Italy in AD 396, defeated them again in AD 402/403 and had triumphed over the Ostro-Goths in AD 405. In AD 401 the Eastern and Western Empires quarreled over the possession of *Pannonia*. Alaric, *magister militum per Illyrium* stood poised to invade Italy. Stilicho withdrew the legions from Britain and the Rhine to meet the Gothic threat to Italy and hired Alaric and his Visi-Goths to fight Arcadius, thereby keeping him out of Italy. In AD 408 Honorius accused Stilicho of treason and even though Stilicho had the power to overthrow the throne he chose not to do so. By order of Honorius, Stilicho was beheaded on August 23, 408 at Ravenna,[225] the capital of the Western Empire since AD 402. The abandoned Rhine frontier was crossed easily by Alans, Vandals and Suebi (Quadi) in a thrust which took the Vandals to North Africa, the Suebi to north-western Spain and the Alans to south-western Spain. In AD 410 Alaric and his Visi-Goths took Rome.

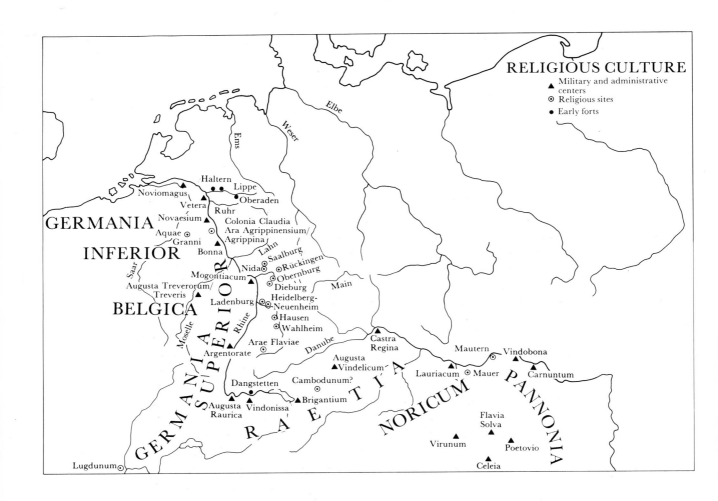

RELIGIOUS CULTURE

▲ Military and administrative centers
⊙ Religious sites
● Early forts

GERMANIA
INFERIOR

GERMANIA SUPERIOR

BELGICA

RAETIA

NORICUM

PANNONIA

Elbe
Weser
Ems
Lippe
Ruhr
Lahn
Main
Rhine
Saar
Moselle
Danube

Haltern
Noviomagus
Vetera
Oberaden
Novaesium
Colonia Claudia
Ara Agrippinensium/
Agrippina
Aquae
Granni
Bonna
Saalburg
Nida
Rückingen
Mogontiacum
Obernburg
Dieburg
Augusta Treverorum/
Treveris
Ladenburg
Heidelberg-
Neuenheim
Hausen
Wahlheim
Arae Flaviae
Argentorate
Castra
Regina
Mautern
Vindobona
Augusta
Vindelicum
Lauriacum
Mauer
Carnuntum
Dangstetten
Cambodunum?
Brigantium
Flavia
Solva
Augusta
Raurica
Vindonissa
Virunum
Poetovio
Celeia
Lugdunum

2. Roman Religious Culture along the Rhine and the Danube

The Roman military occupation paved the way for the transformation of the occupied territories. In themselves the conquests did not cause the romanization of the areas incorporated into the Empire. In central Europe the late phases of the various regional expressions of the Celtic La Tène Culture showed considerable tenacity and the necessary adaptability to provide some of the substantive substructure in the life of cultural forms. Gradually the military presence, but more importantly the administrative organization, brought about the romanization of public life. Certainly the ruthlessness with which Caesar took hold of Gaul—he bragged about the death of three million combatants and the deportation of one million prisoners[1]—or with which Tiberius pacified the areas around the eastern Alps by enslaving a significant proportion of the population both before and after the Illyrian revolt, upset the structure of the elites who were responsible for upholding their culture. Caesar's destruction of Celtic settlements, the massacres of their populations and of entire tribes, as well as his removal of the accumulated treasures of their sanctuaries bankrupted their cultural wealth and constituted a tear in the material aspects of the social fabric. In the spiritual realm a process of assimilation was to bring about a syncretism of two polytheistic religions, allowing the survival of Celtic religious forms in Roman guise. The material culture, on the other hand, survived in impoverished forms in the artistic expression of the lower social orders, while Roman forms, first as imports and then as local products, indicate the taste of the Roman population and of the romanized native 'gentry'. Here too, the works of local craftsmen, by virtue of a combination of traditional technique and an inability to match Mediterranean skills (Figs 43, 44), give evidence of the development of identifiable regional styles.

The fact that the Italian military and administrative elites were rotated through the provinces of the Empire discouraged their identification with those regions into which their tour of duty brought them, while it encouraged these officials to bring with them the latest fashions of the capital, be it in manners or in the decoration of their living quarters. The native gentry, concerned about maintaining its social role, would strive to emulate these forms at least outwardly as its own rich heritage of Hallstatt and La Tène forms was gradually eroded and replaced by the standardized forms of the general issue of the Roman military establishment. Such was the price of assimilation and Roman citizenship. Hereafter, though to varying degrees and depending on the significance which Rome attached to a given military district, the conquered territories became an integral part of the Mediterranean world. The area

43 Germanic funerary ware, early and middle Imperial Period, first to third centuries AD. Hand made. (Westfälisches Museum für Archäologie, Münster)

west of the Rhine dedicated itself especially to the imitation of its conquerors. As a result of the Roman conquest the development of its own animated originality was arrested in Gaul[2] though it was to continue in non-Roman Britain, from where it would return six centuries later to rekindle a dormant Celtic creative process.

In the meantime romanization was to be nearly completed as Roman language, life style, mode of thought and methods of production were adopted against a backdrop of almost prefabricated cities and towns, as Roman surveyors and architects laid out settlements complete with public buildings erected with almost uniform architectural features in the wake of the Roman army. 'Technocrats' derived administrative authority and even notions of human superiority from their ability to organize and systematize. To the native populations, skilled only in the use of wood for construction (Fig. 45), this authority was proclaimed by the imposing buildings of stone columns, pillars, arches and gables. The administrative palaces, the temples dedicated to the official cults, the theaters and arenas, bridges and roads impressed upon everyone the determination behind the Roman presence and the advantages for those who associated themselves with the new system. In Roman Gaul this process led to a singular history of successful colonization and such political loyalty that little more than a century was sufficient for Rome to decide to integrate Gauls into the leading elements of the Roman state, including membership in the Roman Senate. The provinces of Gaul demonstrated their allegiance a mere 120 years after the conquest, during the civil wars which followed the death of Nero in AD 38. The march of the Rhine legions on Rome would have made an attempt at separatism conceivable, yet Gaul chose to stay with the Empire.[3] Over the centuries Gallo-Roman relations were marred by few and generally only partial revolts and even the *Imperium Galliarum* (260–74) founded by Postumus, a Gaul, was not characterized by Celtic nationalism. With its residential capital towns at *Treveris*, *Agrippina* and *Mogontiacum* and supported by the

44 Germanic funerary ware of the late Imperial Period, third and fourth centuries. Wheel thrown. (Westfälisches Museum für Archäologie, Münster)

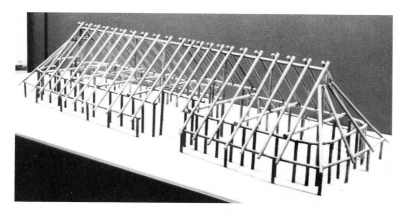

45 Germanic hall house with three naves from Albersloh, dated to the time of the birth of Christ. (Westfälisches Museum für Archäologie, Münster)

legions of the Rhine, the provinces of *Belgica*, *Germania inferior* and *superior*, the mainstay of the *Imperium Galliarum*, were in the forefront of a desperate effort to preserve this portion of the Roman Empire against attacks from across the Rhine at a time when Rome's difficulties in the East diverted all of the central authority's attention to that area. The rest of Gaul, in opposing the *Imperium Galliarum*, showed itself to be intensely loyal to the principle of legitimacy in its support of the central authority represented by the Emperors Gallienus and Aurelian.

From an historical vantage point it appears, however, that during the first century the Roman presence in the provinces to the west of the Rhine achieved only a partial romanization as the populations largely adopted only those civilizing aspects offered by Rome which suited them, while the ingrained indigenous aspects of the culture, made even more resilient by Druidic opposition to romanization, went through a lengthy process of adaptation and amalgamation without, however, surrendering their solutions to the inherent question of the deep culture. In addition to the newly found political loyalty to Roman institutions, promoted by the strategic location of the military bases which served as focal centers and from which radiated not only military power but also impulses to enrich the crafts, industries, trade and agriculture, the introduction of better implements to work the land (Fig. 46), of techniques for cultivating fields, orchards and vineyards until agricultural production rivaled that of Italy, the increasing economic importance and material prosperity gradually reawakened indigenous traditions. The urban centers were the most romanized, while, on the contrary, the countryside was characterized by a decreasing romanization. Away from the cities cultural life became ever more 'provincial', accounting for significant differences in cultural levels so that not all areas were in the same cultural phase. Wherever the native population was not affected by the influence of Rome, its attachment to familiar traditions continued to shape its interpretation of the world

46 Iron tools found in the cellar of a *villa rustica* at Mengen. (Museum für Ur- und Frühgeschichte, Freiburg)

51

47 Statuette of a native divinity. (Historisches Museum, Basel)

around it and of its place in the universe. Cut off from the movement of ideas, the rural populations clung to their ancestral pre-Roman attitudes. In their conservatism they responded less readily to Roman influences than the inhabitants of the urban centers who did not hesitate to refer to the rural populations as 'pagan', a term derived from *paganus*, meaning peasant or country-man, because they clung to the old beliefs and which would be used later by the urban Christians to describe the 'heathen'[4]. However, membership in the new order was not there for the asking. Thus a tribe as devoted to Rome as the Ubii was only slowly granted certain possibilities of social mobility. Not until the reigns of Trajan (AD 98-117) and Hadrian (AD 117-38), when by necessity the administrative weight shifted from Rome to the provinces, was a policy of deliberate romanization actively pursued[5], with the expressed aim of raising provincial standards to a parity with those of the Mediterranean areas. From now on romanization meant increased urbanization which required an increase of activity in the civic sector. Faced with a declining population, Rome had to attract the upper levels of native society to Rome's interests and blend them into a uniform political body. The process was completed in AD 212 when Caracalla bestowed citizenship on the free-born population of the Empire. Gravestone inscriptions indicate that with the second century the military predominance in society receded, accompanied by an increase of wealthy non-Roman elements in the population.[6]

The earlier program of gradual romanization under military auspices, assisted by worship of the Deified Emperor which saw altars dedicated to the emperor and tended by priests selected from among the local aristocracy, was an effective, if gradual, program of promoting familiarity with and allegiance to Rome and its institutions. Rome did not interfere with the established cults. The old gods retained their votaries, altars and sacred precincts which had been dedicated to them. During this early period the old gods retained their respective images (Fig. 47). Only with the advancing urbanization–romanization, did a new need arise for cultic centers of orientation as the population engaged in a degree of alienation from its heritage. It was only now that the external and readily apparent traits of local divinities were assimilated with the equally obvious traits of those divinities from among the Greco-Roman pantheon whose divine functions echoed those of the Celtic gods. Now the conditions had been created which favored the convergence of divine personal ties into the religious syncretism indicated by the hyphenated Celtic and Roman names of Gallo-Roman religion.[7] It was becoming an advantage for the aspiring Celtic inhabitant in pursuit of acceptance and public office to demonstrate that there was no fundamental difference between his own gods and those worshipped by the Romans, thereby removing a serious obstacle from the path towards his own acceptability. At the same time the Romans' estimation of the Celtic gods increased. No longer seen as ferocious gods of an old religion worshipped by barbarians this reassessment made it possible for Celt and Roman alike to worship at the same sanctuary, a most important prerequisite on which to base the synthesis of a new society. It is ironic, however, that while the military demands made for a certain uniformity, the civic requirements of urbanization reinforced regional cultural inclinations. This feature, as well as significant variations of standards, would ensure that the provincial culture would not attain a level of natural continuation from Italy and Rome.

It is a characteristic of the Roman attitude to religion that the cults of conquered lands were treated with tolerance, at least, once the conquered people had entered into that community of interest with Rome. It will be recalled that Germanicus in AD 14 showed little hesitation in destroying the sanctuary of the goddess Tanfana. Eventually the Romans made this open-minded attitude towards the religions of others a part of their policy of romanizing conquered peoples.[8] Taking advantage, no doubt, of a natural opportunism of those among the subject peoples who saw their fortunes to be with Rome, local gods and cults were recognized by the Romans as a legitimate component of public life alongside the official deities introduced by Rome. The provincials were permitted to worship whatever gods they wished, provided they also rendered homage to the gods of Rome, especially to the Deified Emperor. Already in the time of Augustus altars dedicated to Augustus and *Roma* had been set up at *Lugdunum*, at the *Oppidum Ubiorum* and on the Elbe. Still later the Flavians had set up the *Arae Flaviae*. Each time it had been the intention to focus the religious life of the province on these religious centers as a means of tying the new subjects closer to Rome.[9] While the natives adopted and adapted the Roman cults in their own *interpretatio gallica*, the Romans in turn recognized certain attributes of the native gods to be applicable to their own gods, the *interpretatio romana*.[10] It must be considered that the appeal of the Roman cults was waning. The gods grew paler each time they were evoked, so that the hyphenation of divine names was at the same time an enrichment, though only in the short term, since the constant assimilations led to disintegration in the end. The danger to Roman religion lay in that the enriching religious activity was taking place on the periphery of the Empire while the Roman pantheon itself grew ever more anemic, until the old Roman gods were deserted in favor of the eastern mystery religions. These added a new dynamism to the cultic life by making moral demands of their worshippers. In the former Celtic realms the humbler section of society reverted to the ritual duties of gods far older than those introduced by Rome, to nature and fertility gods whose fundamental appeal stemmed from timeless local sentiments. In the countryside the people retained Celtic and even older magical rituals[11] such as the processions in animal costume (which are still part of folklore today), probably to draw upon themselves the protection of the unknown forces. Though the gods appeared in many local variations, some common denominational relationships must have existed among the Celtic divinities and been perceived to exist between the Celtic and Roman gods as well, no doubt an echo of a related Indo-European experience which facilitated the fusion of Celtic and Greco-Roman gods. Their easy assimilation proceeded at a faster rate than that of other cultural facets, as new rites evolved in common sanctuaries.

As has been mentioned above, not all provincial areas were in the same phase of acculturation. It depended on the significance which Rome attached to the area. Thus, Trajan and Hadrian had emphasized the west in their policy of romanization, while in *Noricum* romanization was not a priority until after the time of Marcus Aurelius.[12] Before AD 180, the Flavians (AD 69–96) and Antonines (AD 138–92) had allowed the coexistence of native and Roman deities, in some instances with practically no contact between them.[13] A few joint sanctuaries have been located, but gods such as Belenus and others were not associated with southern gods in the inscriptions nor was Jupiter linked with the local weather god. These are exceptions, however, since, as was noted above, the second century witnessed the gradual syncretism of Toutates or Latobius with Mars to become Mars Latobius (see Fig. 140), or of Noreia with Isis or Fortuna or with Victoria, or at least the addition of native attributes or epithets to the name of a Roman god[14], as was done when the Celtic Wheel God was identified with Jupiter. Further east in *Pannonia* an entirely different scene prevailed as, contrary to the practices in the west, only temples dedicated to the official Roman gods were erected and hardly any names of native gods have been recorded, until the Severans began to pay attention to this province.[15] Incidentally, Septimius Severus had been proclaimed emperor in *Carnuntum* and his successor Caracalla made it a fetish to wear Germanic garb, just like his Germanic bodyguard. In fact, the Antonines stemmed from the provinces. Their policies represented a coming to terms with the new realities in the frontier provinces of an overextended Empire.

In Gaul an obstacle to romanization was to be encountered in Druidism. Apparently a late phenomenon in Celtic civilization, the absence of contrary evidence suggests that it was not a 'Pan-Celtic' institution. Evidence comes only from Gaul and Britain. Its presence in eastern Gaul, however, recommends at least a peripheral consideration in this context. Basing his comments on observations compiled by predecessors, Caesar suggests that differences between Celts and Germani also existed in their cultic attitude[16] and is correct when he identifies Celtic society as one dominated by Druids[17] while the Germanic attitude to religion, characterized by poorly developed sacrificial cults, could do without Druids.[18] The 'kingship' had developed out of an older indigenous sacerdotism in which the religious and political powers were intermingled, where the king was priest but only as priest was he also king.[19] The 'revolution' which separated the political from the religious power must have taken place after the Celtic core area had shifted into Gaul and when the sacerdotal prestige had waned sufficiently,[20] perhaps because of its inability to adjust to new socio-cultural necessities, to allow specialization in the spiritual and temporal realms. Caesar states that the Druids originated in Britain[21] and that anyone aspiring to be a Druid had to return there for his education.[22] The importance of their role in society and the political life derived from their pedagogic tasks. Aristocrats and 'clergy' alike were under their tutelage. Students of Druidism had to train their minds by memorizing great numbers of verses, so many in fact that for some it took twenty years to complete their studies.[23] They taught that all men were descended from Dis Pater,[24] the god of the underworld. As initiates into the living mysteries they were closer to the gods than their fellow men. They, must have considered that the letter deadened the spirit, hence the emphasis on an oral tradition. Caesar suspected that the maintenance of secrecy was the chief reason why their doctrines were not committed to written texts,[25] no problem in itself since the Celts did know the use of the Greek alphabet. Their religious role saw the Druids preside at all sacrifices and other religious functions. As intermediaries who knew the nature of the gods and spoke their language, they ruled over all religious questions. As the guardians of religion they conserved the cult and its traditions by interpreting the wishes of the gods and thereby regulating the cultural life in all details.[26] Highly esteemed by the people, the Druids acted as judges in all judicial matters. Their verdict was final under pain of banishment and applied equally to individuals and to entire tribes.[27] A sacerdotal corporative community, it chose a chief Druid from among its midst in a process which suggests at least that the chief Druid may, on occasion, have had to impose himself by force of arms.[28] This may have involved or deteriorated into a political process, when in Caesar's time the Aeduan Druid Diviciacus was chief of a political party ·which opposed that of his brother Dumnorix,[29] a conflict which had first brought Ariovistus and then Caesar onto the field. Versed in divination, astronomy-astrology, natural philosophy, medicine and 'science', their superior knowledge of things allowed the Druids to impose themselves on their societies, even to act as advisors to kings and as the power behind the thrones. Caesar states that the greatest emphasis was placed on teaching the imperishable nature of the soul, which after death passed into the body of another, thereby teaching warriors to shake off the fear of death.[30] In his *Natural History*, Pliny[31] indicates that the Druids knew nothing more sacred than the mistletoe, provided it grew on an oak. Oak forests contained the *nemeton*, the oak grove, the sanctuaries and no sacred acts were committed without oak leaves, prompted by the belief that the mistletoe was positive proof of the highest god's presence. The mistletoe was cut preferably on the sixth day of the moon, the day of its greatest vigor, following sacred preparations beneath the tree—a banquet and the burnt offering of two white bulls which had not yet been yoked. The mistletoe was harvested with great ceremony by white robed priests wielding golden sickles and gathered in a white cloth. The sacrifice was made to request luck and happiness.

It was mentioned above that the fusion of Celtic and Roman gods served to enrich the Roman cults. This came about through the ethical elements implied in the teachings of the immortality and the transmigration of the soul, a teaching which conceived of death as no more than the middle of a long life divided between a present life and rebirth.[32] Even metempsychosis, the passage through animal forms, is implied.[33] Already in Roman times one saw here very hastily drawn similarities with the teachings of the Pythagoreans. Orphic and Vedic teachings are related.

To the Druidic pre-eminence in the society of Gaul[34] romanization constituted a threat, as the loss of Celtic independence spelled Druidic decline. Roman urbanization selected strategic sites and communication networks which coincided only rarely with the established Celtic patterns. This dislocation, with its new urban attractions, was a threat to the traditional cultural and political focal points. Roman persistence in erecting temples on old sacred sites, the cult of the Deified Emperor tended by non-Druidic aristocrats, the presence of Roman 'advisors' and, most important, the introduction of Roman law—a direct challenge to Druidic judicial power—and of Roman education which intercepted the potential initiates to Druidism, all these deprived the Druids of their pivotal position.[35] First Tiberius and then Claudius passed decrees suppressing their activities, marred in Roman eyes by the excessive cruelty of their cults. As rare as human sacrifices may have been, they proved a convenient pretext for outlawing such a religious intertribal organization. Its end was in sight when the religious resistance to Rome proved as fruitless as the military resistance had been a century earlier and when the aristocratic oligarchies had found it opportune to join in the Greco-Roman cults. Deprived of any real political support the Druids continued 'underground' with secret meetings and surrogate practices until in the end they survived, peddling the secret wisdom of their nature religion as 'magi'' wise men and fortune-tellers.[36] With the simple people of the countryside they retained some of their influence. Centuries later the early Christian Church first combated and then absolved selectively the animistic cults centered around rocks, trees, springs, ponds, fields and forests, preserved to this day in folklore and fairy tales. Druidic resistance to Rome during the first century AD, retarded Gallo-Roman syncretism.[37] But by the second century Druidism ceased to be a cultural force.

The approach to Celtic religion must be cautious. It is first encountered in the historical works of the Greeks who, in attempting to interpret it to their contemporaries, filtered the mythical and cultic acts through their own cultural perceptions.[38]

48 Boar hunt, relief from a monument. (Steiermärkisches Landesmuseum, Joanneum, Graz)

The *interpretatio romana* in turn adjusted and assimilated all cults, leveling off the differentiating characteristics in favor of Roman practices and functions and in so doing misunderstood and misrepresented them until, in the end, evolutions and borrowings obscured the original appearance of the divinities. Even by drawing upon later Celtic traditions preserved in Ireland, the knowledge of Celtic religion remains disconnected and incoherent, creating an impression of a confusion of traditions in which religion is no more than a random assortment of cults. Almost four hundred Celtic gods are known by name but of these three-quarters appear only once. The remainder are of more than regional significance.[39] An attempt to arrange these divinities into a comprehensive hierarchy would be vain. A pantheon cannot even be contemplated since that evokes notions of anthropomorphic gods imbued with specialized functions, recognized throughout the Celtic lands.[40] Iron Age art, Hallstatt and La Tène stylistic motifs emphasized a dynamic world of organisms, of vegetation and animal life, over human forms. Only during the latter phases did human forms appear but even then not in a representational manner but as anthropomorphic stylizations. It was in this context that the scenes represented on the Gundestrup cauldron proved problematic. It is reasonable to conclude that various conceptions of natural religion attended the crystallization of the Celts. Only when they came under the Mediterranean influence were the venerated natural forces transformed into a diffuse totemistic animism without individualization, with a multitude of functions and abstract powers apparent as natural phenomena and fused into identifiable shapes so that there existed divinities with half-human and animal forms.[41] The Cernunnos representation on the Gundestrup cauldron is such an instance. As is true for most things Celtic, the characteristics of religion were also subject to regional variation.

Reference already has been made to the powerful oak, with its hold on the earth reaching upward into the sky, as the seat of the mightiest god whose presence is indicated by the growing mistletoe. Besides such an oak god, there were also gods who resided in beeches, ash trees and apple trees.[42] It is reasonable to assume that other forms of vegetation will have played a role in the mythical and religious life of the Celts, as it did among other Indo-Europeans. The transformation of zoomorphic gods into anthropomorphic forms appears to have been gradual and incomplete. In some instances, vestiges of their former animal nature were retained in the gods' attributes, such as the raven who continued to have a long career as messenger and counsellor of the gods.[43] Boars, bulls, stags, snakes and birds are frequent in the Celtic inventories, whether as independent sculptures in the round or as ornaments on

57

weapons, as embossed reliefs on vessels or as skeletal remains. Ancestral totems and tribal symbols may indeed be hiding behind these animal representations. As early as the Bronze and the Hallstatt Periods skeletal remains of pigs have figured in the funerary evidence, so that the continued emblematic and heraldic representations of the boar are not too surprising an innovation. Its fighting rage made it an exemplary adversary and a symbol of manly power. Its later association with the Celtic hammer god Sucellus, an underworld divinity perhaps of pre-Indo-European origin, seems to provide a link with its use in early funerary ritual.[44] The Celtic boar is called Moccos and will appear in its Gallo-Roman guise as Mercury-Moccos. A Roman tombstone from *Noricum* represents a boar-hunt (Fig. 48). So frequent are boar representations in Gaul that it is almost a Gallic symbol. The stag, to this day the king of the forests, has a history of religious associations, from the representations on Iron Age pottery and ritual vehicles as well as the Cernunnos representation on the Gundestrup cauldron to the St. Hubertus representations of the Middle Ages. The stag is venerated as a symbol of productivity and fertility and may have played a part in the death cult as well.[45] Bulls also have been encountered as early as the Bronze Age, on wheeled ritual vehicles associated with birds but most prominently on the Rynkeby and Gundestrup cauldrons. Bulls were a prominent feature in Druidic rituals.[46] The bull Taruos (also Tarvos) Trigaranos, a three-horned bull represented in northern Gaul especially, is a symbol of force quite unknown to the south. Such a representation has been found in the land of the Treveri.[47] The bull too is a likely vestige of earlier agricultural times, as skeletal remains and ceramic motifs in the funerary inventories would make it appear. Associated with running water it symbolized not only fertility but especially vitality and heroic feats. The smiths of the La Tène stamped both boar and bull motifs on swords during the later period.[48] Various birds, especially the raven which according to legend had shown the wandering Celts their way, but also the ram, the snake, singly or fused into the ram-headed snake and dogs as they appear on the Gundestrup cauldron, and also the bear and the horse figure among the early nature gods. Probably a manifestation of the later transition, the bear is known as the Dea Artio, the bear goddess.[49] As late as the ninth century an ivory book cover by Tuotilo from the monastery of St. Gall shows the saint extending bread to a bear in two scenes of consecutive narrative. More frequent are representations of the horse goddess Epona.[50] The Celtic word for horse 'epo' (latin *equus*), may suggest that the horse, the original object of veneration as a symbol of fertility, became an attribute of a fertility goddess as the zoomorphic conceptions gave way to anthropomorphic representations. More about this goddess will be found below. The list of sacred animals could go on. However, even these few examples indicate that the main preoccupations were with death, life, fertility and vitality.

It appears that it was the cosmic forces in these animals, which were far more powerful than man, that were venerated. Quite consistent with similar developments in other cultures, a transformation of nature gods into ethical divinities in human form took place. This accompanied an increasing socialization and urbanization, which in this instance were reinforced by deliberate romanization. To ensure that the traditional, sacred essence should not be lost, a mytho-poetic process safeguards the continuity of the old forms by means of a heritage of divine attributes.

It is fair to wonder whether the multitude of divine names need imply the existence of a similar multitude of divinities or whether these names are not diverse designations for a more limited number of spheres of cosmic activity and responsibility.[51] When

Caesar names only five Celtic gods by Roman names he may in fact have circumscribed the spheres of activity of some fundamentals in his perception of Celtic religion.[52] Caesar, and after him Tacitus, lists in order Mercury, Apollo, Mars, Jupiter and Minerva.[53] That he recognizes the pre-eminence and popularity of Mercury over that of Jupiter does suggest that he appreciated a difference in the respective divine relationship.[54] Caesar's systematization would help account for the confusing overlap of attributes and functions among the Celtic and then the Gallo-Roman divinities. The problem of course arises only for the systematizer rather than for the local practitioner of the cult who is concerned only with that image of the deity with which he is familiar in his region and that aspect of it which is of immediate concern to him in his appeal. According to Caesar the Gauls saw in Mercury the inventor of all arts, the god of travellers and merchants. To avert illness they appealed to Apollo. In Mars, they revered the god of war to whom they dedicated the spoils of war, as, incidentally, the Teutones had done after the battle of *Arausio*.[55] Jupiter was venerated as king of the gods, while Minerva taught the crafts and industries.

According to Caesar the Gauls claimed descent from Dis Pater,[56] a tradition preserved by the Druids of a subterranean god whose original Celtic name is not known. As god of the underworld he is also a god of fertility, a joint characteristic of ancient chtonic gods who are masters of life and death. For this reason the Gauls measured time not by days but by nights, hence 'fortnight', and held that the day begins at night.[57] His Roman name is an Indo-European derivation and it is likely, therefore, that an Indo-European concept provided this god's ancestry. In *Pannonia* his cult is not recorded. The possibility exists that a Roman shrine at Mautern on the Danube in *Noricum* had been dedicated to him.[58] A native stone dedicated to Dis Pater and Proserpina, hence from the Roman period, is located in the museum in Stuttgart. A specific Celtic cult to him is not indicated even in Gaul. Instead, another later manifestation of this divine principle is known in Sucellus, an underworld divinity who is god of the earth and of growth linked with the Roman god Silvanus, god of fertility and viticulture and whose hammer attribute identifies him as a chtonic deity.[59] The name Sucellus means 'he who strikes well.'[60] His dedicants, members of middle levels of society, saw in him a paternal protector who assured men the essentials of life. That he is frequently accompanied by a dog, a three-headed dog at times, recalls Pluto and Cerberus while the hammer and workman's garb link him with Vulcan, underworld deities all. Already one of the three gods represented on the deities' stone from Anderlingen, a headstone from a Bronze Age grave chamber, wielded a hammer-shaped instrument.[61] A later relationship of attribute and function can be recognized in Germanic hammer-wielding Donar—Thor. Evidently we are confronted with varying manifestations of a common tradition.

The first century Roman poet Lucan mentions three Celtic divinities to have been worshipped among the Treveri: Teutates, Taranis and Esus.[62] In accordance with the general assumption that the gods were everywhere the same and that only their names were different from region to region, the inherent characteristics of these three gods were also leveled off eventually in favor of Roman attributes so that an understanding within the framework of Roman ideas would be possible.[63] Perhaps these three deities have received an undue amount of attention in literature. Nevertheless they appear to have been the embodiments of principal ideas about divine functions among the Celts. Even the iconography on the Gundestrup cauldron lends illustrative assistance. Before attempting an individualization of their profiles, it is worth remem-

bering that each divinity had attributed to it numerous, not clearly defined characteristics and that it was the practitioner of the cult who determined in his dedication to which particular side of the god he wanted to direct his appeal.

Teutates, Taranis and Esus constituted something of a trinity imbued with poorly delineated characteristics and jurisdictions. The name Teutates is in evidence throughout the Celtic realms and as such may harbor a clue to the idea which rested behind the name. The first two syllables of the name recall the tribe of the Teutones. An etymology of 'touto-' or 'teuto-' reveals the meaning 'people' or 'folk'[64] so that Teutates may signify 'God or Father of the people' in its restricted tribal sense,[65] which each tribe then provided with its interpretive attributes and which it venerated in its own fashion. Roman interpretations saw in Teutates qualities of Mercury as well as of Mars.[66] He could be one and/or the other since he was a protective entity in war and in peace.[67] Gods assimilated into Mercury have chtonic qualities. Teutates was a guide on the roads as well as a leader on the way to the beyond. His cult was notoriously cruel and involved human sacrifice, usually of prisoners of war or of criminals.[68] Taranis is the thunder and sun god, perhaps the most sublime heavenly god, equated with Jupiter.[69] Shown holding an eight-spoked wheel, he may be a manifestation of the wheel god shown on one of the panels of the Gundestrup cauldron. With the wheel as symbol of the rolling thunder as well as the sun, he is the sky god. Gallo-Roman representations show him holding lightning rods. Holding a sword he is also the god of battles and the master of war, therefore also linked with Mars. As Jupiter-Taranis he is the god of contracts and of friendships. He reigns over the dead like Pluto or Dis Pater. A link exists with Sucellus. As sky god, holding lightning rods, he was erected on columns. In eastern Gaul and in *Germania superior* he is shown as horseman or charioteer on so-called Jupiter-Giant columns, riding or driving over an anquipede (Fig. 49), a human form whose feet terminate in writhing snakes.[70] These anquipedes may be representations of a malevolent titanic earth spirit over which Taranis-Jupiter rides in triumph.[71] Name and attributes associate Taranis with the northern Thor, another point of evidence indicating a relation of backgrounds. In Gallic guise Jupiter is also god beyond the grave. The third god, Esus, is clearly equated with Mercury but also with Mars.[72] He may have been the one of whose universal popularity Caesar spoke. The bull is associated with Esus.

These three gods demanded human sacrifice.[73] According to Lucan, ferocious Teutates could be appeased by a form of sacrifice which did not involve bloodshed, hence drowning, strangulation or suffocation were ritual features. Of Taranis, Lucan wrote that he could be placated by being venerated on altars comparable to those of the Scythian Diana, i.e. by fire. Caesar mentions huge images made of wickerwork, the limbs of which were filled with human victims, which were then set on fire.[74] Hideous Esus could only be appeased by flowing blood. The sacrifice took the form of the offering being hung from a tree and perhaps later being dismembered. One representation shows Esus striking a tree with an axe. These factors are consistent with shamanistic notions and with accounts of Odin-Wodan who, according to Tacitus, is to be equated with Mercury.[75] Altars dedicated to this divine Celtic Triad could be found in the same sanctuary.

On Caesar's list of gods Apollo ranks second. Since he does not rank very highly in the Roman pantheon, Caesar must have been struck by the importance of his cult in Gaul. Apollo came to be associated with local gods whose activities involved curative functions.[76] Thus the Celtic Borvo and Grannus were associated with hot springs venerated for their healing powers, their presence being indicated by the name of the place. It is held, for instance, that names such as Bourbon or Bourbonne are derivatives of Borvo.[77] Modern Aachen was called *Aquae Granni* in Roman times. Belenus, the god of the brilliant star,[78] an obvious Apollo association, was worshipped from Gaul to *Noricum* where his cult survived into the third century. Tertullian even states that Belenus was a Norican god. Twenty-six Celtic names of deities have been identified in *Noricum*.[79] Cernunnos, the stag god,[80] by virtue of his role in the curative realm of the sun, is also associated with Apollo. Later representations show him with money or distributing agricultural abundance.[81] This links him with Mercury. As was mentioned above, associations with Mercury link the god in question with the underworld. However, the stag itself is already associated with allusions about the underworld. As a chtonic god of plenty he is also god of the healing light. An important name is that of the god Lug.[82] Preserved on many dedications his name entered into many place names: *Lugdunum*—Lyon, or London, Leon, Leiden for instance. Even Liegnitz in Silesia has been proposed in this context. Lug was linked with Teutates, Mercury and Wodan, with whom he shared many characteristics. This cross-cultural link suggests Lug to have been of original Indo-European ancestry. Ravens are associated with him and with Wodan as well. The importance of the sanctuary dedicated to Lug at *Lugdunum* may have figured significantly in choosing it as the location for the *Ara Augusta et Roma*, established by Drusus in 12 BC. Thereafter, Lug was linked with Augustus and the cult of the Deified Emperor whose feast was celebrated on the first day of August.[83] It has been suggested that Lug's other name Find, the fair haired one, was commemorated in such place names as *Vindonissa*, modern Windisch in Switzerland and *Vindobona*, modern Vienna. His most important surname is Teutates and as Gallo-Roman Mercury-Lug he possessed all the qualities of all the gods, for whom he is the most brilliant embodiment, the only global equivalent, the 'luminous god'.[84]

It is evident that the list of gods and the ensuing array of Gallo-Roman cross-references is nearly endless, not to mention those regional deities entrusted with the protection of roads, bridges, river traffic, boating in general, and all the other areas of human activity pertaining to the workshop and the market place and all those conditions that are subject to natural phenomena. Because of their many surnames, the association with the names of the Roman pantheon is not very helpful unless one also has a clear idea of the functional capacities and the metaphysical conceptions surrounding the divinity that are hidden in his Celtic surname.[85]

Caesar mentions only one goddess, Minerva, the divinity of trade and industry, crafts and the arts.[86] Venerated by craftsmen she seems to be the goddess of lower social groups.[87] Monumental inscriptions show her to have been worshipped throughout the Celtic area. As goddess of the domestic crafts she is the protectress of the textile industry, of weaving and dyeing. In the Rhineland she was appealed to by smiths, especially during the manufacture of weapons which, by extension, also allowed her to appear as warrior goddess. In Gaul, she is most frequently represented in warrior costume. Beyond that, however, it appears that the divine principle which Caesar identified with Minerva is a summation of a nearly inexhaustible array of Celtic goddesses with many functions, diverse shapes and names characterized by common elements such as benevolence, fertility and abundance, procreation and protection. Even though purely Celtic gods such as Teutates, Taranis and Esus were not matched by feminine equivalents, the great number of female deities suggests a

50 Relief dedicated to the Celtic underworld divinities Sucellus and Nantosuelta. (Badisches Landesmuseum, Karlsruhe)

51 Relief dedicated to Mercury and Rosmerta. (Badisches Landesmuseum, Karlsruhe)

matriarchal structure not only among the gods but also in human society. During the Roman period the gods were surrounded by groups of female attendants which, however, seem to have had no individualizing identities but had merely become female personifications of the god. Only as a result of the Roman examples did the Celtic divinities begin to form pairs.[88] Thus Belisama was a likely mate for Belenus. She is brilliant and flamboyant like Minerva and like her Roman relation, she is charged with the protection of the fires, especially of the forge, of the pottery kiln and of the enameling process. Sucellus was sometimes accompanied by Nantosuelta (Fig. 50), while the fertility goddess Rosmerta or Maia accompanied Mercury (Fig. 51). Nemetona joined Mars, Sirona—a Celtic Diana—joined Apollo and Damona was represented with Borvo. These few pairs have to stand for many others.

As divinities of the forest and of the hunt, of springs, brooks and streams—hence the association with healing powers—of hills, fields and meadows, the goddesses usually appear as divine duos or trios. When they appear in this context then they are representations of Mother Earth—Terra Mater, in Gaul an intensification of a Mediterranean and Indo-European synthesis. As a source of fertility a Gallo-Roman Cult of the Mothers grew up around them[89] in which they are identified as *Matronae*, *Matrae* or *Matres*, such as the *Matres Treverae*, or the Aufanian Matrons. As objects of local cults, hence the names, their representations were venerated in monumental as well as in portable form (Fig. 52), in public sanctuaries and as part of the domestic cults. Over one hundred names are known from *Germania inferior*, fifteen names of *Matronae* alone from *Colonia Claudia Ara Agrippinensium*. It has been suggested that their origin may have been Germanic since most of the representations come from Ubian territory.[90] During Roman times especially, the tribes to the east of the Rhine worshipped mother goddesses with particular enthusiasm. Whether as stone monuments or as portable figurines, the representations follow a general pattern. The most frequent compositions show them in groups of three, usually seated, wearing large circular headdresses and ample, loosely flowing, native outer-garments fastened at the waist with a clasp. Though there is variety, it is a common feature that each one holds a bowl or basket of fruit (Fig. 53). Occasionally the middle one may be

52 The Matrons, terra cotta figurines made by Fabricius at Cologne. (Römisch-Germanisches Museum, Cologne)

swaddling an infant with the other two holding the swaddling clothes. Other attributes designating fertility may include vine leaves and grapes. They may be wearing necklaces with crescent-moon pendants, an ancient symbol of the changing seasons, cycles and rhythms of birth, life and death. They are rarely shown standing. The middle one may be smaller, perhaps conceived to be younger, and bare-headed. This difference may simply have been prompted by considerations of composition. Since the three are usually seated on a bench in an apsidal niche, a shorter, bareheaded central figure was necessary if the upper portion of the background was to be used to feature the dedicant and his family. To maintain the physical proportions, the legs of this central figure may have had to be shortened which necessitated the support of a footstool. One of the most complete of these monuments was found under the minster in Bonn, part of the wall of an early Christian sanctuary. This monument had been dedicated to the Aufanian Matrons (Fig. 54) by one Quintus Vettius Severus who had been *quaestor*, chief financial officer at *Colonia Claudia Ara Agrippinensium*, pointing to a relationship between *Agrippina*, the colony's common name, and *Bonna* which has continued right into the present. Since the dedication also lists the consuls of the year, Macrinus and Celsus, it has been possible to date the dedication to the year AD 164.[91] Venerated, protective, benevolent, vegetation deities, as *Matres domesticae* and especially as Junos, their domain also included the household and the family, the clan

63

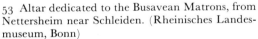

53 Altar dedicated to the Busavean Matrons, from Nettersheim near Schleiden. (Rheinisches Landesmuseum, Bonn)

54 Altar dedicated to the Aufanian Matrons, dated AD 184. It was discovered in the foundation of an early Christian sanctuary beneath the minster at Bonn. (Rheinisches Landesmuseum, Bonn)

and the tribe, which would account for their diverse names. They may even have been conceived as ancestral mothers. Sculptures and figurines have been found in graves. Especially established in the Rhineland,[92] this divine trio benefited from an ancient tradition which included the three Greek *Moirai*, the Roman *Parcae*, *tres fortunae* and *tria fata*, and the three Norns of Germanic mythology.[93] The Celto-Roman cult blossomed between AD 40 and 240 but must have remained a cultic force far into Christian times, for as late as the eleventh century Bishop Burchard of Worms[94] decreed penance for all those who believed in the three *Parcae* and in their power to foretell a person's future at birth. Mythology, folklore and fairy tales were to keep alive notions of threesomes and of their multiples, three, six or twelve Valkyries, wise women, and so forth. As late as the first third of the fifteenth century the relief of three women was mounted in the southern transept of Worms cathedral. In Cologne a group of three sisters figures in the martyrdom of St. Ursula and the eleven thousand virgins. In Christian times ideas around the three Marys would have given new focus to these pagan notions.

Their earthbound characteristics as vegetation and fertility goddesses link them with the goddess Epona, to whom reference has already been made.[95] Of Gallic origin Epona, the horse goddess, came to be venerated not only in the Roman garrisons of the north but in Italy, Spain and even North Africa. The greatest number of representations and references have been found in northern Gaul and in the Rhineland, with concentrations along the Moselle and Rhine rivers and along the *limes*.[96] Whether monumental or as portable bronzes or terracottas, the most common compositions portray Epona riding side-saddle on a horse facing 'stage left'. The horse is

55 Epona, Celto-Roman goddess of horses and the stables, shown with horses and foals, from *Brigantium*. (Vorarlberger Landesmuseum, Bregenz)

56 Epona, from Hausen an der Zaber. (Württembergisches Landesmuseum, Lapidarium, Stuttgart)

always a mare which is usually accompnaied by a foal (Fig. 55). Epona was most popular in the least romanized areas of Gaul and the two German provinces.[97] It is natural that as protectress of horses, mules and donkeys and of the stables she had a place in the cultic life of the *alae*, the cavalry wings made up of non-Roman auxiliaries of whom many were recruited from among the Celtic and Germanic populations of central Europe among whom horses were a regular part of life. Being more mobile than infantry units the *alae* could be transferred more easily to other locations which would explain the finds pertaining to Epona in unexpected parts of the Empire. Already in earlier times the horse had considerable cultic significance, playing a prominent role in the ornamental art of the Bronze Age and in the funerary ritual of the Hallstatt and La Tène Cultures. Here the emphasis is on the feminine aspects in that Epona is a goddess and the horse is a mare. The stress on fertility, reproduction and nurturing (Fig. 56), especially in those instances where a foal is present, is unmistakable. Inscriptions link Epona with the *Matronae* who are especially associated with water and since a number of Epona figures has been found in wells, springs and lakes the link with the generative and curative power of water may also be implied. To the mounted infantry of the Empire the cult dedicated to Epona may have seemed especially accessible and rewarding at a time when the mystical religions of the east, with their emphasis on the acceptance and practice of ethical principles, raised moral tensions in the conscience of the soldier. The relationship between a man and his animal allowed for companionship and a simple exchange of affection. Any service rendered to the horse, the living manifestation of the divine attribute, such as the attachment of ornaments to its harness served both as an act of cultic participation and as an expression of personal vanity.

In major cities of the Empire, the *colonia*, a temple was erected to the Capitoline Triad—Jupiter, Juno and Minerva. Though sanctuaries for the other Roman divinities existed, in the German provinces, in Britain and in north-eastern Gaul it was customary to erect columns or pillars dedicated to Jupiter as Jupiter Optimus Maximus (Fig. 58), the Best and the Greatest, and the symbol of Rome's worldly power.[98] These Jupiter columns were surmounted by various representations of Jupiter while the hierarchy of the Roman pantheon was illustrated either on the shaft of the column itself or on one or two superimposed bases (Fig. 57). Economic and easily erected, these columns, up to 8m high, provided the settlements, private villas, estates, cross-roads and cemeteries with a cultic focus by means of which individuals paid homage to the gods but by means of which the native population would also be familiarized with the gods and goddesses of the Roman state (Fig. 59). It is, of course, understood that the natives drew equations with their own divinities, thereby contributing to the Gallo-Roman, and to a certain extent to Germano-Roman, religious assimilations.[99] The form of these slender structures did not deviate from fundamental Graeco-Roman models. In *Germania inferior* these columns consisted of a square pedestal decorated with reliefs of Roman gods upon which rested column–shafts, usually decorated with a 'scale' pattern intended to be understood as leaves, and the images of three or four gods placed one above the other. On top of the capital, usually Corinthian, rested a statue of Jupiter, either standing or enthroned. The divine images shown on the shaft were usually Mercury, Mars, Juno and Minerva. By contrast Jupiter pillars represented the Roman pantheon but on three sides only, subdivided into three tiers, each showing a divinity placed in its own niche (Fig. 60). The fourth side must have been hidden from view, placed against a wall, for instance, for it remained blank.[100]

57 Base of a Jupiter-giant column from Dieburg, second century AD. (Hessisches Landesmuseum, Darmstadt)

The selection of gods reflected the local preference of the sponsors and dedicants, though the members of the Capitoline Triad always enjoyed select status. It follows from what has been observed above that the natives, whether Celts or Germanic, saw their own gods embodied in the Roman gods. The reasons for the popularity of these columns in this sector of the Empire may have had to do with related native religious ideas. Jupiter was depicted in at least five poses: enthroned, alone or as a pair with Juno; standing with a crouching giant at his side; or driving or riding over a subdued anguipede.[101] Not all five types were to be found in any one region, thus the enthroned pair and the charioteer are not evident in *Germania inferior*. In that province the enthroned Jupiter (Fig. 61) predominated over the horseman. In *Germania superior* the horseman riding over the fallen titan (Fig. 62) was the preferred representation.[102]

The interpretations of these Jupiter-giant columns are inconclusive. The first of these columns was erected in AD 66 as a salute to the Emperor Nero by the civilians at *Mogontiacum*.[103] This was in recognition of Nero's efforts on behalf of the Rhenish frontier where peace and prosperity had been established to such an extent that the *castrum* at *Argentorate* was razed and the garrison transferred while the military governor at *Mogontiacum* was replaced by a civil administrator.[104] The salute to Nero also came at a time when the Emperor had himself proclaimed as the new cosmocrator, a claim to universal dominance. The sculpture would then symbolize the victory of the supreme god over the primeval forces of the earth.[105] The fact that the capitals show four different heads, the seasons (Fig. 63), characterized by the vegetation common to those seasons introduced not only a connotation of fertility but symbolized the eternal cycle of the cosmic order established by Jupiter.[106] The Nero column was found broken into nearly two thousand pieces and buried, perhaps by zealous Christians during the fourth or fifth century. Nero's name had been erased after his death when the Roman Senate condemned his memory, the *damnatio memoriae*.

58 Capital and Jupiter-giant group from Steinsfurt, near Ludwigsburg restored, 2nd/3rd century AD. (Badisches Landesmuseum, Karlsruhe)

59 Four-divinities base with Venus and Vulcan and the quotidian gods. (Württembergisches Landesmuseum, Lapidarium, Stuttgart)

60 Divinities base with Mars. (Open-air Museum, Petronell, Austria)

Jupiter may also be represented reaching with his left hand through a wheel, a link with the Celtic sky god Taranis (Fig. 65). Such a sculpture has been recovered on the site of the *limes castellum* at Obernburg on the Main, north of Miltenberg.[107] This was an especially interesting find in that this sculpture of a Celtic god on the *limes* was probably brought there by the men of the *Cohors III Quitanorum equitata civium Romanorum*, an auxilliary unit of mounted infantry from south-western Gaul which had received Roman citizenship—Rome extended this privilege to units which had shown particular valor in the field. The sculpture also points to the pattern that horseman representations of Jupiter correspond to Celtic conceptions. The dedication and elevation of these columns was a response sensitive to the nature of polytheism. The representations of many gods preserved the balance which a worshipper believed necessary if he was to maintain that relationship between the divinities and himself which, while it proclaimed the supremacy of Jupiter, also recognized the debt owed to the other deities. Four-sided or polygonal bases and pedestals could accommodate those gods whose special protective functions the dedicant wanted to call down upon himself and on those around him (Fig. 64). From this point of view the Jupiter columns were characterized by a high degree of religious efficiency, a feature readily adopted and continued by Christianity. The inscriptions on the columns indicate that a sense of contractual fulfillment led to the elevation of these columns. At some point the worshipper had entered into a 'contract' with his god(s) that was intended to incline the divinity mercifully and benevolently towards a specific human problem in return for a pledge. The satisfactory performance of the god was followed by the worshipper's fulfillment of his pledge, such as the sponsorship of a monument dedicated to the god(s). These columns also record the ease with which the roman(ized) population was able to accommodate and incorporate religious ideologies into its

67

61 Enthroned Jupiter from a Jupiter column, early third century. (Sammlung Nassauischer Altertümer, Wiesbaden)

62 Jupiter-giant column showing Jupiter riding down an anguipede, dedicated on 28.2.221. (Sammlung Nassauischer Altertümer, Wiesbaden)

63 The Seasons: Summer and Autumn. Capital of the Jupiter-giant column from Hausen an der Zaber. (Württembergisches Landesmuseum, Lapidarium, Stuttgart)

inventory of religious cults. Barely had the Gallo-Roman synthesis begun, when the legions which had fought in the east returned to central Europe accompanied by units of auxiliaries who carried in their inventories such oriental cults as that of a bearded man with a Phrygian cap, double axe and a bundle of lightning bolts shown standing on a bull, the 'Syrian' thunder and war god Baal of Doliche. By the time of the collapse of the *limes* frontier, oriental cults dedicated to Cybele and Attis, to Isis and Serapis, to Bacchus, Dionysus, Orpheus, Sabazios (Fig. 66), to Dolichenus, to Mithras and to Christianity were practiced in the northern municipalities of the Empire alongside the gods of the Roman pantheon and those which had made the transition from Celtic times. The *limes castellum* of Nida at Heddernheim, a northern suburb of Frankfurt, yielded such an aggregate of divinities that the site might well serve as a religious microcosm of the Roman Empire.[108] In all 150 religious representations have been found, 28 pertaining to Mithras, 20 to Jupiter-Juno, 17 to Mercury, 8 each to Minerva, Fortuna and Jupiter Dolichenus, 7 to Genii, 4 each to Epona and Vulcan, 3 to Hercules and one each to Apollo, the Matrons, Venus and Bacchus, Cybele, Neptune and many for such quotidian gods as Sol, Luna, Mars, (Mercury, Jupiter), Venus and Saturn.

As was mentioned above, the ready assimilation of the gods of other lands eventually led to a debasing of the ancient religious substance until ever more Romans turned away in disenchantment. The ancient religion had been objective, one in which personal involvement had become a series of contracts. As the Roman world became ever more complex, the impotence of the gods became more apparent. Urbanization, dispersion, dislocation, impoverishment, compulsion were alienating the citizen from his state and its purposes and from himself. The myths, with which the ancients had tried to grasp the order of the world and the cosmic forces active in it, and the cults, in which the contents of the myth had gained shape in that the cultic ritual tried to make clear the happenings of the myth, had compromised their potency. The ancient gods had tired and the cults had grown ever more simplistic. Even their shadows grew paler each time they were brought into the open. In their place the Oriental Mystery Religions began to assert themselves. Hellenistic syntheses, they offered subjective involvement, demanded commitment, but most of all they held out a teleological meaning to a world reduced to the meaningless repetition of empty formulae devoid of any long-term purpose. However, as tempting as it might be to see these cults as a response to a religious crisis, it must be remembered that they were being practised quite early.

Already the Zoroastrianism of Ancient Persia had dealt with the cosmic struggle between the dualistic forces of Darkness (Ahriman) and Light (Ahuramazda) until a final resolution would be won when the new world came about and when only the followers of God would share in a second, more blissful existence. The influences of Zoroastrianism on Hellenism, Judaism and Christianity are peripheral to our concerns. Through Hellenism, however, this old Persian religion was to contribute significantly to the coalescence of the Oriental Mystery Religions in which eastern and Greek doctrines and usages were to bring into being the Mithras mysteries destined to spread over all of the Roman Empire. Much of their fascination stemmed from their knowledge of final things, escatology, the promise of a final victory of Good over Evil, from the hope of the soul's immortality with which they smoothed the way for Christianity.[109] The Mystery Religions offered the hope of salvation and redemption in place of procedural relationships. Without official support or direction they rose and fell as movements of a search on the part of some for spiritual certainty at a time which offered only material uncertainty. Yet the Empire was not overcome by a universal crisis of conscience.[110]

Of great interest among the Hellenized gods of the Ancient Near East is the local deity from the little town of Doliche in Commagene. This Baal of Doliche was linked with iron forges. He was of Hittite or Hurrian origin[111] and remained god of a people

64 Four-divinities base showing Mercury and the quotidian gods above, from a Jupiter-giant column, Walheim near Heilbronn. (Württembergisches Landesmuseum, Lapidarium, Stuttgart)

65 Jupiter-Taranis from a Jupiter column found at Obernburg. (Römerhaus, Obernburg/Main)

66 Hand raised as in an oath, possibly amulet to ward off evil eye, from Dangstetten, c. 15–9 BC. This type has also been associated with the cult of Zabazios, originally a synthesis of Zeus-Zebaoth derived in Hellenistic Palestine. (Museum für Ur- und Frühgeschichte, Freiburg)

of iron smiths and traders.[112] Following Pompey's conquest of Syria in 64 BC[113] and especially after Vespasian's annexation of the kingdom of Commagene in AD 72 and his decision to move auxilliary units from their native districts to distant frontiers to prevent the repetition of a revolt such as that of the Batavians, this iron god with his hammer, in which some see the Hittite double axe,[114] together with the god of light, Mithras, came to be the most successful oriental god in the Roman legions with the syncretic epithets Jupiter Optimus Maximus Dolichenus. The theological content of the cult is lost. Over 250 monuments erected to him as supreme sky god have been found throughout the Empire bearing personal dedications by senators, governors, traders and soldiers.[115] From the time of Pompey, Dolichenus appeared allied to the *imperator*[116] which no doubt furthered his cult in the Roman army. The earliest datable inscription, however, is found in Africa in a dedication of the year AD 125/126.[117] While the monuments show that the cult of Dolichenus in the army was largely supported by orientals, no doubt the cult was also gaining non-oriental adherents in the interim for entire military units came to make dedications to him. The cult's popularity reached its peak during the reign of the Severans (AD 192–235),[118] a dynasty of Syrian and African origins, in whose time the cult may have enjoyed particular Imperial toleration. Long held to be the god of battles and the protector of soldiers, and quite erroneously even the titulary god of the armies, it has been found that fewer than 40 per cent of the dedications mention soldiers, officers, veterans or military units[119] and although the cult was very popular in the *castella* along the Danube, the Rhine, the *limes* and in Britain, dedications from the non-military regions of the Empire show strong civilian support for the cult. Dolichenus is often described wearing an officer's uniform, a circumstance used to designate him a soldiers' god but one which ignored monuments from such military camps as *Carnuntum* on which he was dressed in the loosely-fitted civilian garb of the east (Fig. 67) while civilian dedications show him wearing body armor. It has been pointed out that the closely fitting, contoured cuirass of the Greeks had been adopted in the Hellenistic Near East as the official costume of gods and rulers[120] and had become a standard feature of Greek art when representing oriental Gods. By the time the cults had reached the west, the costumes had become convention without functional implications. The anatomical cuirass had been the reserve of officers, emperors and gods. Soldiers wore mail and/or flexible linked metal plates. It is the image of the emperor which is reflected in the god.[121]

67 Dolichenus in non-military garb, from *Carnuntum*. (Museum Carnuntinum, Bad Deutsch-Altenburg, Austria)

The cult of Jupiter Dolichenus incorporated other gods and goddesses, thereby providing the cult with that same type of syncretic infra-structure which had integrated the Celtic divinities into the divine personalities of Rome. Evidence from Rome dated to *c*. AD 150 shows that Apollo and Diana had come to play a part in the Dolichenus cult.[122] From the *castellum* at Mauer an der Url in *Noricum* come bronze figurines, the inventory of a Dolichenum, two of which show Dolichenus in contoured cuirass, free-flowing cloak and Phrygian cap, standing on a bull (Fig. 68). One of these is part of a group which also shows a goddess standing on a deer. Variously named, Juno Regina, Juno Dolichena, the goddess is a derivative of Diana. Other similar representations have raised questions about the identity of this pair. As Juno Dolichena she stands on a hind, holding the sistrum of Isis, that jingling instrument used by the Egyptians in their religious rituals, and wearing the characteristic head-gear of Isis (Fig. 69). From the municipality of *Virunum*, the most important center of the cult in *Noricum*,[123] a funerary monument shows Jupiter Dolichenus

68 Bronze figurine of Jupiter Dolichenus, from the sanctuary at Mauer an der Url. (Kunsthistorisches Museum, Vienna)

69 Dolichenus with a female divinity identified as Juno Regina standing on a hind. Her attributes would link her with Isis. (Kunsthistorisches Museum, Vienna)

standing on a bull with Juno Dolichena on a hind on his left (Fig. 70). Between them is a wreath, perhaps meant to be held up in her right hand. The group is shown in a temple setting flanked by two pilasters with an eagle occupying the gable above their heads. The radiant head of Apollo in the top corner stage right and that of Diana crowned with a crescent moon in the top corner stage left, representing sun and moon, combine with the eagle or other elements shown on the relief to form a cosmic relationship.[124] Apollo may be represented here as Sol Invictus, the Invincible Sun and Diana as Luna. Quite evidently the male principle of Sol, Dolichenus and the bull form as iconographic a group as do Luna, Juno Dolichena and the hind. It is just as evident that for military and civilian worshippers,[125] the iconography points to a theological relationship as well. Elsewhere representations of Castor and Pollux are present on cult objects. The unending course of Sun and Moon, as measure of infinity, represents eternity, while Castor and Pollux represent the two hemispheres.[126] The interlink between this cult and others is even more extensive in that the Dolichean sun god Sol Invictus (Fig. 71), inferior to Dolichenus, frequently represents Mithras, who was worshipped in Dolichenus temples in Rome, on the Danube and in the east.[127] As Juno Dolichena is revered as Isis, so Dolichenus is linked with the Egyptian Serapis, a further syncretism between Egyptian and Dolichean gods.[128] The rich complexity of the religious confluence may even account for the appeal. The wreath mentioned above may symbolize Victoria, not necessarily in any military sense but as the all-pervading cosmic victoriousness of Jupiter Dolichenus.[129] The

70 Monument dedicated to Dolichenus and Juno Regina, from the Lamprechtskogel near *Virunum*. (Landesmuseum für Kärnten, Klagenfurt)

dedications to Dolichenus also contain the wording *pro salute et victoria dominorum nostrorum*.[130] We have seen already that the Jupiter column at *Mogontiacum* had been erected as a salute to Nero. Hence, the *pro salute et victoria* to 'our lord' the emperor can be symbolized by the victory wreath since the link between Dolichenus and the emperor has already been commonly accepted.

As was indicated briefly above, the oriental gods never came to be accepted as official gods of the Empire or of any of its institutions. In spite of their popularity among all levels of society the cults were rejected officially and did not find a place on the religious calendar.[131] For all of his popularity with the military, Dolichenus was not introduced into the official sanctuaries. Like the other cults, that of Dolichenus enjoyed official toleration and respect but that was all. By the time the emperor Aurelian proclaimed the cult of Sol Invictus as the supreme god of the Empire and his own protective divinity in AD 274, a cult in which he hoped to reconcile the various religious trends in the Empire, the 25th of December was the

71 Bronze votive offering to Jupiter Dolichenus from Frankfurt-Heddernheim. Dolichenus, holding axe and lightning bolts, is shown standing on a bull. Above him are Sol and Victoria. On the base below can be seen Juno Dolichena standing on a hind, flanked by figures bearing representations of the moon (*l.*) and the sun (*rt.*). (Sammlung Nassauischer Altertümer, Wiesbaden)

date of Sol's annual festival,[132] the cult of Dolichenus was no longer a vital force. Its rather sudden decline appears to be linked to the accession of Maximinius Thrax (AD 235–38). During his reign all the Dolichenus sanctuaries were pillaged and destroyed,[133] not so much for religious reasons but rather as the effect of a fund-raising drive by the new emperor who was desperately in need of money.[134] The wealthy temples of small communities of rich, perhaps disliked Orientals fell easy prey to the hazards of the anarchic early decades of the third century. That a soldier-emperor would risk estranging his troops by violating the sanctuaries of a presumed soldier-cult suggests that the influence and pre-eminence of the Dolichenus cult may have been exaggerated. Archaeological evidence indicates that the sanctuaries were not rebuilt and the buried religious treasures were not recovered, circumstances which hint that the religious communities were either deported or completely wiped out. Much weakened, the cult of Jupiter Dolichenus continued in a few communities. The last known inscriptions named the emperor Gallienus (AD 253–68).[135] Even in its area of origin the cult disappeared when the Sassanian king Shapur I destroyed the town of Doliche. Prior to this obvious demonstration of his impotence, Jupiter Dolichenus had been revered among soldiers and civilians for the power and vitality he exuded as preserver of heaven, sustainer of men, invincible god of light and master of the cosmos.[136]

The mystical content of the Dolichenus cult reveals itself only by association with other pronounced mystical cults dedicated to deities incorporated into the Dolichean pantheon. Reference has been made to Isis and Serapis; others were Cybele and Attis

72 The goddess Cybele, from Gauting, south-west of Munich. (Prähistorische Staats-sammlung, Munich)

and of course Mithras. The Hellenistic mystery religions are of interest for they offer a glimpse of the intellectual and spiritual climate of the Mediterranean world in which Christianity arose and spread. In brief, the Phrygian cult dedicated to Cybele and Attis, a cult to a mother goddess, was widely practiced along the Rhine. The high-point of the mystery was the baptism of the initiate with the sacrificial blood of a bull and the mystical union of the believer through the symbolic death and rebirth in Attis or Adonis.[137] Cybele was not only an urban goddess but also a goddess of vegetation and salvation (Fig. 72). Venerated as *Magna Mater*, her cult contained orgiastic and ecstatic rituals. It centered around the shepherd and divine youth Attis-Adonis. Of Greek origin, the myth around him had Zeus sentence him to spend two-thirds of the year with Aphrodite in the realm of light and one-third with Persephone in the underworld. An ardent hunter, he was mortally wounded by a boar and died under a pine tree. While searching for him in the woods Aphrodite was ripped by thorns. The drops of her blood made roses grow; the blood of Adonis brought forth anemones. In Greece and Rome his festival was celebrated with great splendor.[138] He became a symbol of the birth and death of nature. His spring festival was characterized by the cutting of a pine and its decoration in the sanctuary and by Cybele-Aphrodite driving through the country side in search of Attis, who is finally found.[139] Attis was associated with darkness and with light and figured on funerary monuments as well as in statements of life.

The significance of the mystery cults lay in that they raised the initiate above the forces of fate as represented by the stars; even though these might affect the body, the soul would rise beyond their reach into the divine realm and so be saved. By seeking a personal mystical union with the god who had himself died and risen again, the initiate became as the god himself. The euphoric knowledge of 'knowing' the god, of salvation, was an emotional rebirth.[140] From Egypt came the cult of Isis, Serapis and Anubis, the god who led the souls to the realm of immortal life. The Isis cult stressed that the goddess offered immortality and triumph over Fate. Serapis, a Hellenistic synthesis, became the universal ruler. His sanctuary in Alexandria was destroyed in AD 391 by the bishop Theophilus.[141] Serapis was much overshadowed by his divine consort Isis, the greatest of the Hellenistic deities. As Isis Myrionymos, Isis of the Myriad Names, she was identified with almost every goddess. To her followers she was Lady of All, omniscient, omnipotent, queen of the inhabited world, lawgiver, savior, grace, beauty, fortune, abundance, truth, wisdom and love.[142] All civilization was her gift and in her care. Depicted as a young woman in modest dress sometimes associated with the crescent moon, she occasionally carried in her arms the infant Horus. Her festival in November represented the passion and death of Osiris-Serapis, her search for his body and his resurrection. Fasting and lament accompanied the passion and death of Serapis, rapture and joy accompanied the finding. Isis' spring festival witnessed the ceremonial launching of her ship to celebrate the opening of the shipping season. The novice wishing to enter her cult had to await her call, sometimes for years. To enter her shrine uncalled meant certain death. Once called, his entrance was symbolic death and rebirth to a new life of salvation, free from the oppression of fate and death. A goddess of all women in need and suffering, especially of mothers and wives, a Mater dolorosa, she survived into Christianity as her adherents shifted to the worship of the Virgin Mary.[143] In Cologne the churches of St. Gereon and of St. Ursula are most probably located over or in the immediate vicinity of the Isis sanctuaries.[144] An altar dedicated to Isis Myrionymos was found under

73 Mithraic
relief from
Virunum
illustrating
aspects of the
cultic belief.
(Landesmuseum
für Kärnten,
Klagenfurt)

St. Gereon, the ashes of the last sacrifice still on it as well as a coin of the emperor Constans, son of Constantine, showing that as late as *c.* AD 345 the cult of Isis was still practiced. A stone dedicated to the Invincible Isis had been carved into a Romanesque capital and built into a wall of St. Ursula.[145] It need not have come from that site though. The cognition of the divinity, the associated ethical laws aiming to promote the purest existence and a bodily life in the eternity of the beyond in constant blissful contemplation of the deity offered a new purpose to life. By means of a fixed daily ritual of devotion, of acts of purification and consecration, life was a continuous preparation.

Many variations of these themes animated the cults which the Roman Empire had inherited. Only passing reference has so far been made of the cult dedicated to Mithras (Fig. 73), the most significant manifestation of antique paganism.[146] The cult of Mithras, god of light, entered the Roman realm of awareness with Pompey's victory over the Cilician pirates in 67 BC. With the annexation of *Cilicia*, just west of Commagene, the cult of Mithras began to make its way west. However, it is first documented in a monumental inscription in Lower *Moesia*, dated reliably as from the third decade of the second century. The cult may have reached *Pannonia* as early as AD 71 in the reign of Vespasian when the *legio XV Apollinaris* returned to *Carnuntum* from the east but before AD 114 when Hadrian finally transferred the legion to *Cappadocia*.[147] The evidence is an altar dedicated at *Carnuntum*. A Mithraeum dated between AD 71 and 162 appears to have been erected by customs officials at *Poetovio*.[148] AD 148 is the earliest date in the west when an altar was dedicated to Mithras at Böckingen on the Neckar.[149] Just as with Dolichenus, the soldiers from the east, the administrative personnel and the slaves were among the first followers of the cult of Mithras. Inscriptions and excavated sanctuaries suggest that this cult was spread by missionaries, especially successful after the Marcomannic wars when eastern military units were brought to the Danube.[150] The missionaries of Mithras found an atmosphere ready for new religious stimuli since under the Severans the romanization of the region was being pushed with greater determination, thus causing greater estrangement from their native gods and religious traditions. Already in *Pannonia*, at *Carnuntum* for instance, sanctuaries dedicated to Dolichenus and to Mithras are often found in adjoining buildings, occasionally they even share the same sanctuary.[151] In *Noricum* the cult spread more widely than that of Dolichenus.[152] Apart from soldiers and easterners, slaves found the message of the cult particularly rewarding. The sanctuaries were not located very close to the frontiers but mainly in the south-eastern parts of the province. The same holds true for *Raetia* where Mithraea were located only in the south of the province and for the two Germanies where, to be sure, Mithraea were located not only along the *limes* but in the interior of the provinces as well. So many sanctuaries have been located that it would be quite futile to name them all. Some municipalities had several.[153]

The fortunes of the Mithras cult were rather different from those of the cult of Dolichenus. Its sanctuaries were more numerous, its support base in the population was founded more widely[154] as all social strata from the most highly educated to the lowliest slave could share in the mysteries[155] and it did not become the object of attack until early Christian times when, in their religious zeal, the Christians sought out and destroyed whatever Mithraea they could. During the last decades of the third century and the very early fourth century the cult of Mithras enjoyed its most significant peak when in AD 303 the emperor Diocletian reorganized the Empire from

74 Detail of the Mithraic relief from *Virunum* showing Mithras stepping onto the chariot of Sol. (Landesmuseum für Kärnten, Klagenfurt)

75 Mithras altar with revolving central panel, from the Mithraeum at Heddernheim. (Sammlung Nassauischer Altertümer, Wiesbaden)

Carnuntum and dedicated the offering of thanks to Mithras rather than to Jupiter.[156] Shortly after, in AD 312 Constantine converted to Christianity. His Edict of Milan of AD 313 granted the Christians full religious freedom without, however, instituting a religious policy that exceeded general toleration, for Christianity was far from being accepted as the universal religion.[157] Only after Julian the Apostate's (AD 361–63) attempt at reviving and restoring the religions of antiquity did Christianity assert itself. That he ordained the restitution of pagan temple property confiscated by the Christians suggests that the Christians, as a privileged religious denomination, had begun their persecuting activities in deeds as well as in their writings. The last known Mithraeum dates from AD 325, at Gimmeldingen in the Palatinate.[158]

Superior in moral and ethical content to the other oriental religions, the Mithras cult was the arch-enemy of early Christianity which persecuted it with vehemence. The reasons for this antagonism lay in that the Mithras cult knew the mysteries of baptism, the sacred meal, ascension, judgment day and the resurrection of the dead. The god Mithras was conceived as the completion of the antique genealogy of the divinities. Because the Mithraea were generally placed in caves or in cave simulations and because the Mithraic communities had sufficient warning to bring their temple treasures to safety, something the Dolichenus sanctuaries were not able to do,[159] the very large number of finds has made it possible to reconstruct something of the lost Mithraic doctrine.

A derivation of Persian religious dualistic thought, the Mithras cult has been interpreted as spiritualizing the need for constant struggle in a conflict which saw Mithras as the God of Light and the Spirit of Good triumph daily over Darkness and Evil, thereby extending a constant challenge to falsehood in the world.[160] The

3a Orpheus Mosaic from the baths at *Arae Fla-viae*, (detail) early third century AD. (Stadtmu-seum, Rottweil)

3b Bacchus Mosaic. (Rheinisches Landesmu-seum, Trier)

3c Mosaic of the Muses, second century. (Rheinisches Landesmuseum, Trier)

4a Dionysus Mosaic, illustrating the pleasure theme. (Römisch-Germanisches Museum, Cologne)

4b Terra sigillata bowl with acanthus leaf pattern. (Römisch-Germanisches Museum, Cologne)

4c Cups with hunting scenes, from Weil am Rhein. First century AD. (Museum für Ur-und Frühgeschichte, Freiburg)

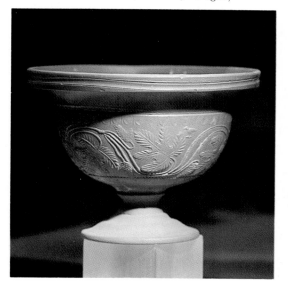

76 (left) Cautopates relief from the Mithraeum at Heddernheim. (Sammlung Nassauischer Altertümer, Wiesbaden)

77 Mithraic relief from Heidelberg-Neuenheim. (Badisches Landesmuseum, Karlsruhe)

universe is seen as a stage on which the world is both scene and prize in the eternal battle between Good and Evil, gods and demons. The believer could draw the moral that life is a relentless combat with the hellish forces of darkness over which he had to be victorious. Mithraism taught the ideal of struggle and the virtue of endurance.[161]

Having only very little in common with ancient Zoroastrianism, the central motifs of the cult revolve around the myth of the creation of Mithras by Ahuramazda out of the rock and Mithras slaughtering the bull, the first of living creatures created and symbol of earthly power, whose blood bestows fertility to the earth. Having protected the first humans against misfortune, Mithras joined the sun god Sol in a sacred banquet and ascended into heaven in the chariot of the sun (Fig. 74). If the bull is the primordial being, then as a creation myth this one fits into the category of the dismemberment myths since the bull's carcass becomes the universe. However, eastern Mithraism does not know the significance of the bull.[162] The mythical sequence of events is not entirely clear since the sources of information are mainly the narrative friezes of the religious monuments on which the narrative scenes were carved without necessarily giving a sequential account. Nor do they all depict the same scenes. It is also difficult to reconcile the pictorial evidence with Mithraic 'philosophy' as expounded at great length in the literature dealing with Mithras. The consistent motif in the western sanctuaries shows Mithras, always represented in oriental garb with a cloak flowing behind him plunging his dagger into the bull's throat, its blood fertilizing the earth, the realm of creation where the snake, the scorpion, the dog and the lion long for the blood's invigorating powers (Fig. 75). The dog and the snake are frequently shown lapping the bull's blood from its throat.[163] Flanking this sacrificial group are two youthful figures, each bearing a torch. To the left stands Cautopates with the torch lowered to signify dusk, the setting sun, the night and autumn (Fig. 76) while to the right Cautes raises the torch to signify dawn, the rising sun, the day and spring. They also personify Occidens, the west and death and Oriens, the east and life. Neither derives from Iranian mythology.[164] The bull sacrifice, the tauroctony, which brings life to the earth, symbolizes expiation and salvation. With Cautes

80

and Cautopates the group forms a Mithraic Trinity of which it is accepted that the two are hypostases of Mithras himself.[165] As with the Dolichenus cult, the divinities of light, Sol and Luna, are represented in the upper corners, a persistent motif still found in the religious art of the Middle Ages. Sol and Luna symbolize the extent of Mithras' cosmic realm ruled by the youthful cosmocrator and victorious sun god, a realm which he saved from darkness and loss and to which he brought light and salvation.

The narrative frieze of the Heidelberg-Neuenheim Mithras relief is taken here to represent many other similar friezes (Fig. 77). The left vertical panel, from top to bottom, shows Mithras' birth from the rock holding high a disc or globe, then two figures identified as Saturn handing Jupiter a thunderbolt over a blazing altar,[166] a male figure identified as Saturn–Chronos,[167] the *Deus Mundi* as *Genitor invictus*, the Invincible Creator,[168] holding a sword or a bundle of lightning rods, reclining on a rock and finally Atlas-like, a youth wearing Phrygian cap and billowing cape carrying the globe or world disc on his shoulders.[169] The right panel depicts the grazing bull, then Mithras carrying the bull slung around his shoulders to the cave, to be sacrificed presumably, Mithras having tackled the escaping bull by clinging to its neck, and finally Mithras dragging the recaptured bull to the sacrifice. This narrative sequence is almost exclusive to the regions of the Danube and the Rhine.[170] The horizontal panel at the top, moving inward from the corners, shows a wind god in each corner, Mithras cutting branches on the left, and hiding in the crown of a tree on the right, then two pictures show Mithras shooting arrows into the clouds. Of the two central panels the right one shows the descent of the Moon goddess in her biga, a chariot drawn by two horses, while the left panel shows Mithras ascending a mountain with Sol guiding his quadriga, a chariot drawn by four horses, while Mithras himself crowns the charioteer.[171] By virtue of the birth of Mithras out of the rock, his epiphany, the god breaks through the darkness. To cover his nakedness he cuts branches from a tree, hence they are sacred to him. During his stay on earth he helps many by freeing water from the clouds in times of drought. The birth of Mithras was celebrated on the 25th of December. Born in a cave, which was regarded as a symbol of the celestial vault and of the cosmos, shepherds, perhaps Cautes and Cautopates,[172] were present at his birth and were the first to see the glowing light. These two elements account for the significance of light in the cult and for the location of the Mithraea in caves, especially if these could be associated with sources of water. On other friezes the meal between Mithras and Sol is also represented.

The Mithraic cult was a mystery cult accessible only to those initiated into its rituals following a baptism with sacrificial blood. The initiate had to pass through a hierarchy of seven grades. Over a ladder of seven rungs through seven gates his purified soul would be led by Mithras into heaven. Descent into the sanctuary was over seven steps and the life-giving water was caught in seven basins.[173] The Mithraic eucharist, consisting of bread and wine,[174] not only made the participants brothers but also made possible the mystical union between man and his god.

By means of mystical consecrations the initiate passed through an ascending gradation of degrees—Raven 'corax', Bride 'nymphus', Soldier 'miles', Lion 'leo', Persian 'Perses', Courier of the Sun 'heliodromus', and Father 'pater'—as recorded in a letter of St. Jerome.[175] The three lowest grades were 'attendants', the higher ones were 'participants', expected to share in the sacred meal.[176] During the initiation, wearing the identifying masks of his respective levels, the initiate submitted to a series of trials

81

78 Mithraic ritual
vessel from Cologne.
(Römisch-
Germanisches
Museum, Cologne)

and tribulations designed to test his endurance and to confirm his virtues.[177] In his last stage as Father, the initiated became the god's deputy on earth. His final reward was the ascent and salvation of his soul.

The association between Mithras and Sol, the sun god, led to an identification of the two to be known as Sol Invictus Mithras. As Sol Invictus (Plate 1a), the unconquerable sun was proclaimed as the supreme god of the Empire by the emperor Aurelian, who hoped to unify the various religions in this cult.[178] Sol Invictus was Constantine's favorite god,[179] the Mithraic sword and crown symbol being emblazoned on the shields of his western legions. His legendary adoption of the cross as the sign under which he would triumph was a Christian reinterpretation of the adapted sun-symbol.[180] Constantine never ceased to be a vainglorious pagan who also aimed at the unified evolution of a synthesis of cultic forms. Of interest is a vessel (Fig. 78) showing Mithras flanked by his two companions and by eight-armed crosses representing the sun ✳ a symbol of the god's might and victory and one which Christianity had no difficulty imbuing with its own meaning, adapted to ⚹ a combination of the Greek letters Chi=χ and Ro=ρ, the first two letters of the name Christos, it became the symbol of Christ, the horizontal cross-bar being replaced by the letters alpha A and omega ω placed to the left and right of ρ. It was a very persistent motif in Christian art.

From its earliest times a certain 'military' ethic was attached to the Mithraic dogma of unflinching persistence and final victory. This characteristic accounts at least in part for the cult's popularity in the Roman legions. Soldiers who had undergone the Mithraic initiations not only proved to be the bravest and best-disciplined in the Roman army[181] but, with their conviction to be the soldiers of Mithras fighting on behalf of Light and Good, they brought to their activities a higher degree of self-worth. As Mithraic soldiers the normal soldierly impulses to fight were enobled by a heightening of values, as worldly causes were transformed into 'just' causes on behalf of the cosmic balance of power. In the struggle to combat evil every individual had to be totally and constantly engaged.[182] The notion of setting out on a military pilgrimage, of engaging in good and holy warfare was not a Christian innovation.

The military ethic also accounts in part for Mithraism's failure in that, in the west at least, it did not include women at a time when women were assuming a more active role in religious matters. That Aurelian's mother had been a priestess in the temple of Mithras in Iran suggests that there, at least, the cult did not reject women.[183] The Mithraic brotherhood, however, as appropriate as it may have been for the military life was not readily transferable to western society at large. The more egalitarian nature of Christianity made it more acceptable to all segments of society, although even today the role of women in the Christian Church is by no means clarified.

At Dieburg, 15km east of Darmstadt, a Mithras relief has been found, interesting for its difference, for its central motif shows Mithras hunting on horseback, cloak flying, armed with bow and arrow, accompanied by three dogs.[184] At the feet of Cautopates is a hare, perhaps the object of the chase and by association perhaps a force of darkness. Ferocious hares will recur on Romanesque friezes. Two other representations of Mithras riding have been found; a small low-relief at Neuenheim (Heidelberg)[185] showing Mithras (Fig. 79), cosmic orb in hand, riding a horse past seven trees and accompanied by a snake and a lion,[186] and another one found at Rückingen, some 8km east of Hanau.[187] Here on the reverse of the bull sacrifice riding

79 Mounted Mithras from Heidelberg-Neuenheim, *c.* AD 200. (Kurpfälzisches Museum, Heidelberg)

83

Mithras is ready to throw a lasso. In an attempt to see Germanic influences in these hunting scenes, one inferred from the proximity of these sites to the Odenwald, which is an area rich in Germanic lore, an indebtedness to early notions about the god Wodan, the 'Wild Huntsman'.[188] However, Mithraic hunting scenes are documented in the east. It has been observed above that mounted gods are a Celtic characteristic. A link may exist here with the Jupiter-giant representations rather than an example of a Germanic influence on Mithraism. The Mithras–Jupiter connection is the more compelling as Jupiter–Saturn scenes, not of Iranian origin, do appear on the narrative panels flanking the tauroctony, as do scenes in which Jupiter having received dominion from Saturn then destroys anguipede giants.[189] However, in view of the absence of any written accounts the relationship between Mithras and Jupiter is not at all clear.[190]

Reference was made above to the adaptability of the Jupiter columns. One Jupiter-giant column of great interest in this connection probably once formed part of a Mithraeum at Wahlheim (Fig. 80), north-west of Ludwigsburg.[191] The shaft of this column shows the conventional 'scale' pattern on the lower half while the upper half is decorated with vines, grapes, snakes, eros-figures, gatherers of grapes, birds (especially a raven), nudes, men in Phrygian caps, a man wearing a lion's mask, details which point to the Dionysian and Mithraic mysteries.[192] The Dionysian grape symbolism will reappear in Christian catacomb art. The lion, snakes and raven have Mithraic connotations; the snake as earth symbol, the raven as messenger sent by Sol to Mithras, the lion and raven representing grades of Mithraic initiation. The nudes represent the individual initiated into the mysteries, his soul stripped of all earthly pretense, a feature that will still appear in the mystical terminology of the Middle Ages.

This syncretism of cultic motifs points to the common features found in the religious trends of the Roman Empire. Just as the other cults, Mithraism was not an exclusive religion. Mithras was identified with Serapis-Osiris and hence with Isis.[193] Venus, Luna, Hecate and Diana were venerated as part of the Mithras cult. Cybele and Adonis were readily associated with Mithras Invictus and Isis Invicta. In fact a statue of Isis has been found in the Mithraeum at San Stefano Rotondo in Rome.[194] The members of the cults evidently participated in the other cults as well. Mithraic missionary activity did not emphasize exclusive membership making for an apparent tendency of religious drift, were it not that for the Mithraist the human community was linked with the structure of the universe.[195] All the cults witnessed a god-man or woman assume human form of his or her own will in order to lead men towards salvation. Christianity differed in its militant insistence on exclusive adherence. Able to make and keep converts, it assimilated from the other cults what was psychologically and spiritually potent. Christianity's insistence on exclusivity encountered a large degree of willingness to abandon an empty polytheism in favor of fewer gods or even of only one omnipotent god who could save man from his earthly anxieties. Such savior religions as those of Mithras and Isis are of interest and significance in the history of religious belief, not only in themselves but for their contribution to the acceptability of Christianity during the fourth century.[196] Not to be overlooked is the organizational ability of Christianity which understood the necessity of providing not only a religious but also a socio-political order to rival that of the state, an order which survived the collapse of the Empire as it rescued Roman administrative concepts and organizational units in their religious end stage.

80 Shaft of the Jupiter-giant column from Walheim. (Württembergisches Landesmuseum, Lapidarium, Stuttgart)

3. Arts and Crafts

In central Europe Roman civilization was a function of Rome's military presence. Just as the army was an amalgam reflecting the ethnic composition of the Empire so the army and its multinational infrastructure is reflected in its cultural contribution to life in Rome's central European provinces. This has been demonstrated with religion. It also holds true for the arts and crafts. Uniformity of taste need not be expected as members of the diverse regions of the Empire carried their portable objects and personal ornaments with them wherever their duty, administrative assignments or mercantile interests took them. Despite being of interest as an indication of the far-flung relations which existed in the Empire, objects of African or Syrian origin cannot concern our discussion. Rather, the question concerns the continuity of artistic intent in this area of central Europe and the changes to which artistic efforts were subjected.

Eastern Gaul and the Rhenish provinces responded differently to the romanization of their respective cultures (Fig. 81). The late La Tène ceramic culture of the Hunsrück-Eifel mountains showed little marked difference from Roman Provincial culture which was establishing itself. However, in the land of the Treveri the archaeological funerary evidence underscored a clear break with the late La Tène as early as the time of Augustus in that no cemetery demonstrated continuity of burial into Roman Provincial times.[1] With the advent of the Flavians, however, evidence of romanization is available (Fig. 82), there being some variation between the more accessible river valleys and the less accessible hill country. The adoption and imitation of things Roman were accompanied by changes in mental and spiritual attitude as well as in taste. Richly decorated jewellery gave way to richly decorated, high quality pottery (Fig. 83) and sophisticated glassware (Fig. 84), inscribed grave stones and stone architecture until the indigenous Celtic features were no longer readily apparent. By contrast, in the British Isles the displacement of things indigenous was never so complete.

Elsewhere, in our discussion of Celtic artistic motifs it was demonstrated that Celtic style was characterized by an absence of figural representations of man or animal. The artists opted instead for ornamental dismemberment rather than for the depiction of whole shapes.[2] It is not surprising that after the dislocation of social and urban patterns caused by the Roman conquest, different forms of artistic expression should emerge as Mediterranean craftsmen, following in the wake of the Roman forces, executed the commissions entrusted to them by civilians and the military alike. Just

81 Pottery for everyday use from Dangstetten. It shows continuity of indigenous Celtic characteristics. (Museum für Ur-und Frühgeschichte, Freiburg)

82 Urns from a Roman gravefield at Hüfingen. A coin issued under Vespasian helps to date the gravefield to the first century AD. Also included are mirrors and a tile bearing the stamp of *legio XI*. (Museum für Ur-und Frühgeschichte, Freiburg)

as ever more commissions came from the non-Roman population, whether in the towns or in the military encampments, so ever more natives will have served their apprenticeship with master craftsmen accompanying the Roman armies, until native workmanship became identifiable by the peculiarities of its execution even though the craftsmen had adopted the Mediterranean content of the works commissioned. The very fact that sculpture in relief or in the round was so very much in demand demonstrates that a new beginning had to be made by the native craftsmen who now entered this new medium. Though the Celts did know work in stone, what was to be demanded of the sculptors now bore little relation to their earlier activities.

As was pointed out above, the Roman presence effected a rupture in the cultural, especially the stylistic, development of central Europe by replacing earlier indirect cultural influences with direct cultural domination. The new cultural climate allowed very little room in which indigenous cultural elements could develop. Some skills and practices native to the provinces, such as the firing of pottery, the working of iron, enameling and certain cottage industries, were assimilated with Roman ones. At the same time new ones, such as the making of glass or of *terra sigillata* pottery (Fig. 85), rose to great heights, owing to the ample presence of certain natural resources in some areas. However, eventually the importation of new products from the Mediterranean world and the introduction of new techniques overshadowed local traditions (Fig. 86). The craftsmen were not necessarily Romans. Though all the nations of the Roman Empire were represented with their special skills, the predominant group would have been composed of freed-men and slaves, largely of Greek origin. That the natives could learn their lessons well is demonstrated by the Jupiter column erected in Mainz, dedicated to Nero and executed in the Greco-Roman style by Samus and Severus, sons of Venicarus, who were probably natives from Southern Gaul.[3]

In view of the general absence of signatures, the question of native participation in Roman provincial art can only be addressed with caution. To attribute the poorer works to native craftsmen exclusively would be too facile, but it is unlikely that the apparent lack of high artistic quality evident in provincial sculpture, for instance, is an expression and continuation of deliberate native stylistic traditions, reflecting the initial efforts made by native craftsmen in creating a native style. It is a curious fact that such a style in Roman provincial art did not survive the collapse of the Roman Empire. As such, the effect of the Roman presence on the history of style in central Europe is a severing of that link between man and the mythical view of his world and its symbolic interpretation by the intrusion of forms characteristic of Mediterranean civilization to which he could not relate easily.[4] It is, therefore, not surprising that the art forms north of the Alps were long considered as stepchildren.

We saw that while the romanization of Gaul and *Noricum* was well under way by the early first century AD, the same process along the Rhine and Danube required at least another two generations. During the first phase of colonization the effects of native elements can be detected only barely if at all. In the course of a continuing romanization the Celto-Germanic elements could assert their presence in the foreign art forms introduced by the Romans, yet only with the beginning of the second century AD is there any sense in seeking out native elements.[5] From then on, however, the tendencies of development were quite different from those in Italy. It is an every-day world which is reflected in the artistic endeavors of the northern Roman provinces, most evident in the realm of sculpture in the round and in relief. Commissioned at first by the military and soon after by the wealthy administrators, landowners, merchants, traders and manufacturers, the themes translated into visual form reflect a certain 'middle class realism', documenting the daily activities of this group both in their private and public lives (Fig. 87). In time the romanized provincial high society strove to display its education and cultural sophistication.[6] Its inventory of themes reveals their very deliberate intention not to appear to be lagging

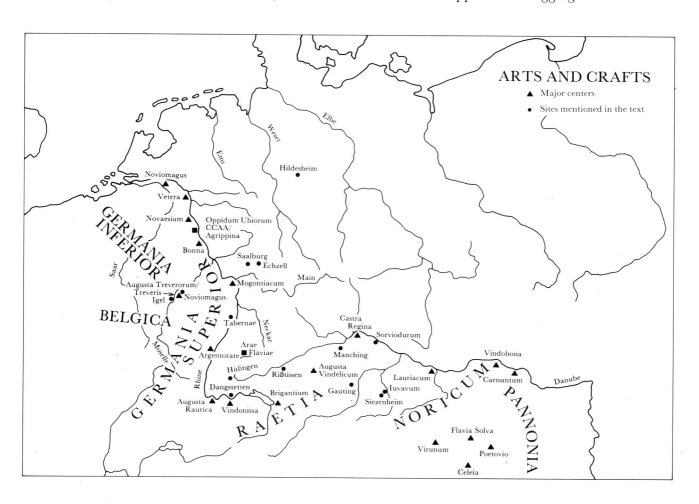

83 Jug and beakers from Hüfingen, terra sigillata plates from Schallstadt. (Museum für Ur-und Frühgeschichte, Freiburg)

84 Bluish-green glass jug with chain-like handle, third century AD. (Mittelrheinisches Landesmuseum, Mainz)

85 Terra sigillata from Dangstetten. The potter's seal is clearly visible at the center of the plate. (Museum für Ur-und Frühgeschichte, Freiburg)

86 Cup with appliques from a cremation grave. (Römermuseum, Augst)

87 A cloth-merchant displays his merchandise to a customer. Relief from a funerary monument at *Noviomagus*, modern Neumagen. (Rheinisches Landesmuseum, Trier)

behind the Greco-Roman cultural centers of the Empire (Fig. 88). In this they were impressively successful, when by AD 300 the administrative and economic centers of the northern provinces also became focal points of great cultural significance and independence. Post-World War II archaeology has brought to light convincing evidence of very demanding expectations with which they were to enhance the quality of their life. This is reflected in the elegance of their surroundings, the stylistic refinement and the astonishing quality of their fine pottery and glassware as well as those articles fashioned of precious and other metals (Fig. 89). This cultural awareness was echoed in their interest in literature, philosophy and the fine arts. In this manner people of means displayed their education, their intellectual attitudes and an enthusiasm for their cultural heritage. However, even though the formative arts offer an indication by which to assess the spiritual and intellectual life of that society, the details of this rich and refined lifestyle in which certain social levels indulged cannot be assessed easily nor entirely. It is apparent though that favorable conditions for a future synthesis of style did exist. While at some workshops native traditions were relentlessly continuing and others were content to duplicate the official styles of the court and the cities,[7] the work emanating from cities such as *Augusta Treverorum* or the *Colonia Claudia Ara Agrippinensium* revealed great vitality of stylistic independence, skill and originality of themes.

No attempt will be made here to come to terms with the great wealth of material found at the various sites. Even a brief summary of Roman provincial art in the northern provinces of *Germania inferior*, *Belgica*, *Germania superior*, *Raetia* and *Noricum* has to include reference to sculpture, wall painting and floor mosaics, pottery and

88 Mythological scene from a grave monument. Daphne is being transformed into a laurel to avoid Apollo's pursuit. Daphne's hands show the early stage of transformation. Apollo approaches from the right. The stone was built into a church at Rißtissen, near Ehingen, south-west of Ulm.

89 Venus statuette of bronze. (Römermuseum, Augst)

work in metals and glass. In general it can be said that while the area sheltered behind the 'dry' *limes* of *Germania superior*, mainly an agricultural area settled by veterans, does not develop any artistic standards beyond those of the taste of the common soldier,[8] the areas behind the 'wet' *limes*, the Lower Rhine and the Middle Danube, allowed the flowering of Roman provincial culture. In the north, monumental artistic representations in stone were the exception rather than the rule, and even then such pieces as there were had to be attributed to Mediterranean influences.[9] The arrival of the Romans in the north introduced a very marked change in that from now on monumental representations in stone are very much in evidence. Even without additional evidence the relatively abrupt appearance of monumental art in central Europe would point conclusively to the establishment of a new culture. There is no demonstrable continuity from Celtic to Roman treatments of stone.

During the first hundred years following Caesar's arrival on the Rhine and prior to the arrival of civilian institutions, the legions were the dominant cultural force in the conquered territories.[10] Busts and heads of Augustus and his immediate family, as well as those of later emperors and their families, belonged in the domain of so-called propaganda art which was produced in Italy and distributed throughout the Empire.[11] Since military commanders and high officials, retired legionaries, even natives and especially women, recognizable by their particular headdress,[12] were also represented among the sculptures, one must assume that itinerant sculptors plied their trade in the new territories. Reference has already been made to the great number of monuments dedicated to the various divinities representing the official cults as well as those appealed to on special occasions.

In the first century AD most of the commissions for monuments, mainly gravestones, were placed by relatives on behalf of soldiers who had died in Rome's service.[13] Most frequently one encounters stones commemorating auxiliaries. It appears that the workshops prepared a number of typical stones from which the client made his selection.[14] Two basic designs stand out: a cavalry man rides down an enemy barbarian; the deceased is shown reclining on his couch enjoying his funerary meal, a motif which gained in popularity after *c.* AD 50, and a sub-type which combines the funerary meal on the upper portion of the stone while on a lower panel a servant leads the warhorse of the deceased if he had served with the cavalry. The workmanship of these monuments is generally unsophisticated so that it seems safe to seek

TRADELINKS
IN CENTRAL EUROPE

LIMES
Tradelinks
Bordertrade
Important Roman cities and roads

90 Funerary monument of Romanius, typical of the first century AD, (AD 50–70), showing horseman riding down a barbarian. The deceased had served with a Norican *ala* for 19 years. (Mittelrheinisches Landesmuseum, Mainz)

91 Funerary monument of Titus Flavius Bassus from the second half of the first century AD. (Römisch-Germanisches Museum, Cologne)

92 Funerary monument of Dolanus, after serving 24 years in the fourth Thracian cohort. (Sammlung Nassauischer Altertümer, Wiesbaden)

the craftsmen among the better stonemasons attached to the military units.[15] The inscriptions often are amateurish and not without errors. The unifying stylistic characteristics identify the sculptures as belonging to the limited types of popular and provincial art found in Italy and from Spain to the Rhine.[16]

The motif of the horseman riding down the enemy[17] was known since about 400 BC and was especially popular during Hellenistic times.[18] It reached the Rhine from northern Greece and Thrace during the first century AD.[19] This motif also appeared on such portable objects as jewellery and it is so popular in the funerary art of the auxiliaries that it can be termed the characteristic fashion of the first century (Fig. 90). If one considers that prices for monuments ranged from 1,200 to 100,000 sesterces and that a soldier's annual wage during the first century AD was only 1,500 sesterces,[20] then these monuments represent a very determined attempt, it seems, to demonstrate the integration of these provincials into the Roman social order. By joining a burial club a legionary could pay for his monument by annual subscription. The excessive costs account for the great number of abbreviations and the repetition of formulas in the commemorative inscriptions. The chiseled inscriptions were retraced in paint, thereby allowing the correction of errors in spelling.

To preserve the deceased's fame for posterity he is represented in a victorious pose overwhelming his enemy (Fig. 91), usually recognizable as 'barbarian from the north' by his knotted hair-do, nudity or trousers, shape of shield, savage and dishevelled appearance and coarse facial features, whether either Celtic or Germanic.[21] In this, no real attempt is made to indicate authentic ethnicity. Instead one is content to cast general types so that it is clear to the beholder that the enemy is from beyond the *limes*, beyond the limits of civilization. Here the Romans are the heirs of earlier Greek attitudes which conceived of the barbarian as wild and uncouth. The scene is placed in a niche, usually without any consideration given to the relative proportions of men and animals. The action appears to be of paramount importance. Great attention is paid to such details as armor, weapons and horse trappings, mane and tail.[22] Partly obscured by the horse it is usual to represent an arms bearer, his inferior station indicated by his smaller size, carrying one or two additional spears. The horseman appears poised to thrust his spear as the horse bounds over the fallen foe. To accommodate the spears in the niche it is not unusual to extend them into the frame. Whether arched or rectangular, the frame tends to be embellished with vegetative patterns, laurels perhaps, to express the hope of immortality. That some of the soldiers bear the names *Titus Flavius* followed by their own name in accordance with the Roman legal requirements concerning the *tria nomina* indicates that they had been granted Roman citizenship in the reign of the emperors Titus (Flavius Vespasianus) or (Titus Flavius) Domitianus of the Flavian dynasty. The names would date their funerary monuments into the period AD 79–96. The monument of one Dolanus (Fig. 92), son of Esbeni, of the Fourth Thracian Cohort is interesting on two counts: to accommodate the extra spears the armsbearer has to reach out of the composition, thereby breaking the confining limits of the frame, in itself not too significant a solution to a compositional problem, were it not for assertions that such a reluctance to submit to the confines of formal composition demonstrate native, especially Celtic, attitudes to form; the arch of the niche is flanked by two crouching lions. Lions sculpted either in relief or in the round (Fig. 94) are found frequently on monuments and on graves as protectors against evil spirits. Lions and sphinxes (Fig. 95) were also credited with the ability to frighten off grave robbers; the sphinxes crouched as though ready to swoop down on anyone daring to violate the grave.[23]

The second type of funerary monument represents the funerary meal (Fig. 93). This type develops during the first century.[24] It generally shows the deceased reclining on a couch, drinking from a cup, attended by a servant, whose lower status is indicated by his smaller size. If the deceased was a horseman, then a lower panel shows his horse held in readiness (Fig. 96).[25] While considerable care is taken with the detailed representation of the furniture, the treatment of the figures and their garments tends to be beyond the stone carvers' skill as they avoid poses natural in such a position. Apparently unable to depict a half-turned body in perspective, the deceased faces the viewer in a stiff and unnatural frontal view. To see in these products examples of a deliberate 'expressionism' would be too apologetic.

Not only auxiliaries but legionaries also had funerary monuments erected on their behalf. The stone dedicated to one Caius Valerius Crispus, a Roman citizen serving in the *legio VIII Augusta*, shows him facing us in full military gear (Fig. 97). His equipment is itemized carefully to show his curved wooden shield reinforced with

93 Funerary monument of Titus Flavius Celsus, from the second half of the first century AD. (Sammlung Nassauischer Altertümer, Wiesbaden)

94 Lion—guardian of the tomb and symbol of invincible death, from a monument at *Castra Regina*, after AD 180. (Städtisches Museum, Regensburg)

95 Sphinx, from a funerary monument. (Römisch-Germanisches Museum, Cologne)

metal edges and a rectangular metal boss in the center, his spear in his right hand, the short sword hanging at his right side, his lower abdomen protected by metal-reinforced leather straps hanging from his waist. A Macedonian of stocky build, he died at the age of forty after twenty-one years of service. He probably died at *Mattiacum*, a casualty during the Chattian wars of the emperor Domitian, AD 83–86, when the *legio VIII Augusta* was moved north from *Argentorate*, its base since AD 71.[26] A more accomplished relief, it portrays the man in a more natural pose, resting his weight on his right leg, his left leg slightly angled and just a bit forward. Though the composition is sober it hints at greater freedom, as the articulate treatment of the lines suggests a new naturalism.[27]

While the hostilities along the Rhine frontier during the first century appear to be reflected in the military themes of the funerary monuments, the monuments erected by the military forces stationed along the middle Danube, an area rather becalmed during the first century, reflect other themes. At the risk of overgeneralizing on the basis of scanty evidence, the themes represented in *Noricum* and *Pannonia* reflect the civilian interests of a stable population. Military themes are rare even on the tombstones commemorating officers and men of the legions.[28] The agricultural scene depicted at the top of the momument set up for one Caius Attius Exoratus (Fig. 98) of the *legio XV Apollinaris* and dated to the end of the first century AD may serve to illustrate the difference in tone prevalent along the middle Danube during the first 150 years following the arrival of the Romans in *Noricum*.[29] The monument shows a

96 Funerary monument of Longinus. (Römisch-Germanisches Museum, Cologne)

97 Funerary monument of C. Valerius Crispus, of *legio VIII Augusta*, who received his stipend after 21 years of service. (Sammlung Nassauischer Altertümer, Wiesbaden)

four-wheeled cart drawn by a team of oxen. Facing the oxen but on a somewhat lower base line stands a man, a whip in his right hand. Another man, whip in hand, stands on the cart. A small dog following the cart provides a touch of comic relief. No other details fill the scene. Executed in low relief, the composition is framed by flanking fluted pilasters with simulated 'Corinthian' capitals. An arc closes it off at the top. Quite unnecessarily in view of the vacant scene, the man facing the oxen reaches into the frame to wield his whip. Poor planning rather than deliberate adherence to the demands of a local style may be held responsible for this feature. One must assume that the scene expresses the wishful thinking of this legionary for whom a cart and a team of oxen would fulfill his fondest hope in the beyond, just as the funerary meal is an expression of the wish to spend the life after death indulging in luxury, pleasure and leisure.

Of interest is a very crudely worked and awkwardly inscribed tombstone from *Carnuntum*, dated to the first half of the first century. A rough head surmounts a hunting scene in which a mounted hunter and a dog pursue a boar. The commemoration is very surprising, being of one Atpomar, son of Ilonis, aged twenty-five, to whom Brogimar, his brother, erected this monument. The names are evidently Germanic. What may their function have been at *Carnuntum*?

Since civilian camp followers were not accommodated within the fortifications, small settlements quickly sprang up in the vicinity of the *castella*. When needed, the populations of these communities would place orders for tombstones, if not with the

98 Gravestone of Caius Attius Exoratus, soldier of *legio XV Apollinaris*, stationed at *Carnuntum*, dated to the first century AD. (Museum Carnuntinum, Bad Deutsch-Altenburg, Austria)

99 Gravestone for Aurelius Patruinus, of *legio III Italica concors* stationed at *Castra Regina*, from the end of the second century AD. (Städtisches Museum, Regensburg)

95

military stonemasons on active duty, then certainly with such craftsmen who, like themselves perhaps, took their retirement from active service in the *vicus* or small town adjoining the *castellum*, probably joining their families and thereby legalizing their common-law marriages. It is evident that the civilians requested different motifs for their gravestones, usually family groupings. A convenient example demonstrating the coming together of the military and civilian traditions is an unassuming stone from *Castra Regina* (Fig. 99), evidently of local workmanship, commissioned by an armorer to commemorate the death of his beloved son, *filio carissimo*, Aurelius Patruinus, aged twenty, of the *legio III Italica*. Since Marcus Aurelius raised this legion for the express purpose of preparing for war with the Marcomanni—Aurelius Patruinus may first have gained his citizenship on enlistment, hence the name[30]—and since this legion built *Castra Regina* between AD 174 and 179, the funerary monument can be dated to this general period. The change in taste which had taken place by then is reflected on this stone by a shift in emphasis. While the earlier monuments depicted the deceased in an heroic posture, the relatives often remaining anonymous, here the dead soldier is represented by a modest bust in a gabled setting while the main pictorial area is occupied by a group of civilians, most probably the soldier's family, two men and a woman.

Such groupings reflect the middle-class tastes of the inhabitants of the cities who also favored the representation of hunting scenes, mythology and fantastic creatures. In south-eastern *Noricum* the cultural centers of *Virunum*, *Flavia Solva* and *Celeia* especially hosted skilled stonemasons and flourishing workshops, particularly during the Flavian and Antonine period from AD 69 to 192. Besides mass-produced tombstones without representational scenes, these studios also produced very complex monuments ranging from relief portraits to ostentatious architecture.[31] In the time of Hadrian (AD 117–38) a master sculptor, probably of Italian origin, aided by native assistants,

100 Family monument intended to secure lasting personal prestige for the deceased. Third century AD. (Museum Carnuntinum, Bad Deutsch-Altenburg, Austria)

101 Horseman, one of the Dioscuri, altar stone from Lienz. (Tiroler Landesmuseum, Ferdinandeum, Innsbruck)

102 Horseman, one of the Dioscuri, altar stone. (Steiermärkisches Landesmuseum, Joanneum, Graz)

furnished *Virunum*, the Norican capital just north of modern Klagenfurt, with exemplary religious statuary. The inventory of scenes draws heavily on classical mythology, an obvious indebtedness to southern influences.[32] A local theme is the representation of people in native dress (Fig. 100). These are characterized by a lack of pretension, typical of Roman provincial sculpture in portraiture. The figures are naively conceived, simply articulated, unemotional, stiff and linear; several are crowded into too confining an area. To accommodate the group the figures generally overlap, hiding the left arms. Even as inhabitants of cities they exude a rustic air. Few portraits reveal a personal individuality. Considerable care is taken to indicate the folds of garments without, however, succeeding in dematerializing the stone or in lending balance and harmony to the composition as a whole. A vivid illustration of the difference in articulate skills between an Italianate (Fig. 101) and a local work (Fig. 102) is only too evident in the execution of the horseman motif—one of the Dioscuri—shown.

Noricum also produced a type of ornate funerary monument termed mausoleum.[33] The one shown here is a partly restored fragment of the type (Fig. 103). In the south-east of the province the portico rests on a huge block of stone richly decorated with naturalistically carved mythological scenes or with ornamental friezes of lush vegetation, vine leaves, grapes, tendrils, populated by birds, symbolic of a hoped for idyllic and bucolic life of Dionysian pleasures in the beyond. Sheltered by the portico the back wall displayed busts, torsos worked in relief or seated figures sculpted in the round. The modest mausoleum shown here may have been such an upper portion. Monumental architecture of such proportions testifies to the great prosperity enjoyed by the provincial upper social groups.

At Cologne there is preserved a funerary monument (Fig. 104) of truly extravagant proportions.[34] Formerly located 1 km outside of the Roman city on the road to *Bonna*,

103 Canopy of a mausoleum typical for south-eastern *Noricum* (Steiermärkisches Landesmuseum, Joanneum, Graz)

104 Funerary monument of Lucius Poblicius of *legio V Alaudae*. First century AD. (Römisch-Germanisches Museum, Cologne)

105 Funerary monument at Igel, east of Trier. The only one of its kind to have survived north of the Alps, it was erected in AD 240 by the Secundini, a family of wealthy cloth-merchants. Originally multicolor, the narrative friezes show them engaged in their social and business activities. Mythological scenes represent the victory over death. Height: 24 m.

106 Monument at Igel. Detail, showing the transport of large bales.

107 Wineship from a funerary monument at *Noviomagus*, modern Neumagen on the river Mosel. Second century AD. (Rheinisches Landesmuseum, Trier)

it had been erected by one Lucius Poblicius, originally from the region north of Naples and veteran of the *legio V Alaudae* which had been stationed on the lower Rhine between AD 9 and 70. Upon his retirement he had received a cash settlement of 12,000 sesterces to invest in some commercial enterprise.[35] Evidently quite successful, he had erected for himself a mausoleum 14.5 m high. The economic boom which had followed the conquest of the area had put this commoner Lucius Poblicius in a position where he could afford to compete in pretension if not in good taste with anyone. Here too the ornamental details which have been preserved on the monument show intertwining vines and blossoms, inhabited by birds, while enraptured Maenads and Pans in a state of sexual arousal signal Dionysian orgiastic frenzy. These are cultic references to the natural rhythms of life and death. These representations are the stock motifs of the Mediterranean south as executed by the artists of the Empire during the middle decades of the first century of our era. No distortions, stiff poses, lifeless bodies or expressionless faces here, rather a wealth of playful ornamental detail, rich in vegetative, anthromorphic and zoomorphic forms.

The location of *Augusta Treverorum* on the crossroads between the Rhineland and *Belgica* and Gaul, favored its citizens to enjoy great prosperity.[36] The range of their mercantile activities found its way into the themes of the stone cutters (Fig. 105), attracted by the generous economic support which the citizens could offer them. In the commissions placed with them the craftsmen working there placed provincial art on a parallel course with Italy and Rome.[37] With their work narrative techniques of representation dominated the approach to sculpture and to work in relief. The artists recorded on the funerary monuments the activities of their patrons, the provincial nobility in and around *Augusta Treverorum*, its administrators, its wealthy merchants dealing in textiles (see Fig. 87), wine, transporting their goods (Fig. 106), travelling by boat (Fig. 107) or by carriage, paying taxes, collecting money (Fig. 108), a lady at her morning toilette assisted by her personal attendants (Fig. 109), a teacher and his pupils (Fig. 110), and field hands harvesting with a reaping 'machine' (Fig. 111).

108 Collecting the tax. Scene from *Noviomagus*. (Rheinisches Landesmuseum, Trier)

109 Lady with her attendants. Scene from *Noviomagus*. (Rheinisches Landesmuseum, Trier)

110 School scene from *Noviomagus*. (Rheinisches Landesmuseum, Trier)

111 Gallo-Roman harvesting machine in use. Scene from *Noviomagus*, reconstructed from fragments and with reference to other better preserved examples. (Rheinisches Landesmuseum, Trier)

These monuments have preserved the image of a society which obtained its wealth from the manufacture and exchange of goods, facilitated by the strong support of agriculture.

Through the use of roundness, perspective and depth the artist created shadows through which he achieved a softening of outlines, an emphasis on bodies and on differences of texture, the creation of moods. The panels project an invitation for a society to see itself. As such, the sculptures provide a record of life in a romanized provincial city at the turn of the second century. The choice of topics invites the term 'Middle Class Realism' to be applied to these reliefs from *Noviomagus*. The term is apt in that the craftsmen did not strive to project a glossy idealism[38] but rather, to hold up a mirror. The reliefs are self-contained scenes characterized by the objective and accurate observation of detail. The people depicted are aware of their respective positions as members of a well-situated social group. This awareness is apparent in their poise, their faces, in which one can read their moods and sentiments. It is apparent in the individualized treatment with which they are represented, as the personalities present in each scene are shown in relation to one another, assuming individual attitudes, executing complicated turns of their bodies as though deliberately excluding the viewer, and interested only in one another and the task facing them, as if life went on as usual.

In the present discussion nothing has been said about the southern regions of *Germania superior*, partly because this province does not differ significantly from the other provinces along the Rhine and the Danube (Fig. 112) with regard to funerary monuments.[39] As has been shown in the discussion of religion, however, it was the

112 Funerary monument of the family of T. Flavius Primanus of *legio III Italica concors*. The legion was stationed in *Raetia* from AD 171/72 onward. From *Augusta Vindelicum*. The form of this monument is representative for many such monuments which lined the approaches to the cities. (Römisches Museum, Augsburg)

113 Reliefs showing hunters returning from the chase: man with a net slung over his spear (*l.*); two men carrying an animal (*rt.*). The stone probably formed part of a funerary monument and is now a corner stone of the village church at Rißtissen, near Ehingen, south-west of Ulm. An inscription found in the wall of the church can be dated to AD 201.

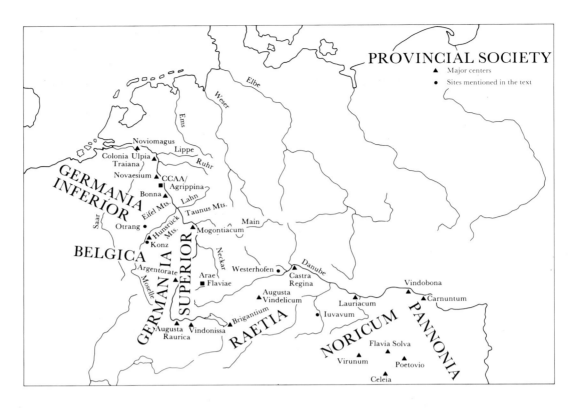

province of *Germania superior* in which a notable number of the religious sculptures were discovered. These sculptures were detailed in our discussion of the Roman cults. In all of the northern provinces monuments of a distinctly Italian character have been found which have not been drawn into the discussion (Fig. 113).

The discovery of Roman living quarters in the *castra* and *castella* and in the cities of palaces, villas and more modest homes shows that the Romans took delight in embellishing their immediate surroundings with colorfully decorated walls. Without hesitation they brought with them some of the ornamental themes of the Mediterranean and applied them to the walls of their homes. Indifferent to any motifs which might have been available in the northern environment, Roman taste for decoration was satisfied by southern plasterers, painters and decorators who, in their pattern books of stock motifs, could offer a wide selection of mythological events, creatures and allegorical figures, of architecture and of brilliant colors. Of course, compared to the wealth of decorative themes available at the core of the Empire, the selection was much more limited in the north and not entirely representative of the Roman decorative arts.

The introduction of this desire for beautification depended on the presence of certain skills. Since plaster is the common base for wall paintings, its ingredients had to be easily accessible. For instance, it is documented that from the first to the end of the third centuries the calcium deposits (Dolomite) of the Eifel Mountains at Iversheim were worked by special units of the legions stationed along the lower Rhine, the *legio I Minervia* from *Bonna*, later (after AD 98) the *legio XXX Ulpia victrix* from *Vetera* and still later (*c.* AD 260–70) a special unit of the *legio III Cyrenaica* originally stationed in Arabia.[40] Their function was to burn the lime to meet the demand for the vast quantities of mortar and plaster needed by the building trades. The quality of the plaster would vary with the expectations it was to satisfy since different degrees of quality affect durability and stability.[41] The quality of the plaster wall depended on the quality of the wall painting for which it was to serve as a base, the poorer the painting the coarser the base finish. To receive high quality painting the surface would be subjected to vigorous polishing until it assumed the smoothness of marble. Utilizing a fresco technique the artists applied the background color(s) while the plaster surface was still fresh and damp. This produced very durable surfaces.[42]

The colors were obtained from mineral, vegetable and animal sources.[43] While earth colors derived from ochres were quite common, colors derived from such rare minerals as heavy metals or from minerals used to make indigo, for instance, were rather expensive and available mainly by trade. Chemical or other substitutes had to meet this demand. Reds, browns and yellows were generally derived from ochres, ferric oxides or leads; blues and some greens from copper carbonates, silica and calcium; white from lime and black from such carbons as lamp black. Ochres containing ferric oxide produced a purple color when heated. The Roman artists evidently had an extensive range of colors at their disposal.

The background colors applied to the wet plaster frequently sectioned the wall into alternating fields of red and black, framed by separating borders of the other color. These borders could simulate such architectural features as pilasters—flat half-columns, capitals, cornices and ledges. Guidelines for the basic designs were scratched into the plaster. More complicated details were painted on more fully. To complete the painting two techniques were available to the artist: he could use a fresco technique and so work quickly and do detailed work while his colored surface was still damp or, using tempera techniques, the pigment mixed with such binding media as the white or yolk of eggs, honey, glue, size or gum, work more deliberately on the dry colored plaster surfaces.[44] The finished paintings could be repolished, thereby eliminating brush strokes and diffusing detail and clear lines. Vitruvius, who along with Pliny[45] laid down the definitive work on the building trades, suggests that black be used in winter apartments subject to smoke stains while red be used in enclosed rooms to avoid bleaching by the intrusion of bright light. Red walls should even be waxed or oiled for greater durability.

Among the earliest examples of wall painting in the provinces of our concern are the large fresco fragments from the Magdalensberg, near *Virunum* in *Noricum* (Plate 1b). Dated to *c.* 20 BC the reassembled fragments constitute a cycle of delicately painted figures, less than life size, set against a vermillion background, sectioned off by pilasters.[46] Two larger mythological and bucolic scenes had been placed in between the red surfaces. Stylistically they have been related to Pompeian wall painting. These figures of a dancer and other frescoes once decorated the rooms of wealthy Roman merchants who commissioned painters from the south to bring the walls to life.[47]

Though only a few fragments have been found, there is evidence from Cologne that already the earliest Roman buildings at the *Oppidum Ubiorum* had painted walls.[48] Much more spectacular are the frescoes from a room, 8 × 4 m in size, found under the precinct of Cologne cathedral. Reconstructed, the walls prove to have been divided into alternating pictorial areas of red and black surfaces. On only one of the red fields could a scene be reassembled. It shows a parodistic representation of a Cupid-Bellerophon mounted on Pegasus fighting the chimera. The walls are very striking in their overall effect. The black 'frames' of the upper panel depict urns, garlands, sphynxes, gryphons and swans on the black friezes across the top. The vertical panels are characterized by two tiered stands rising out of large, two-handled amphorae and populated with legendary creatures: sirens, leopards, satyrs, a pan, vegetation, wine leaves and grapes. A Dionysus surmounts one of these 'candelabra' (Plate 1c), the goddess of fruit, Pomona, stands on another. The presence of Dionysus, the leopards, a grape harvest (Plate 1d), fauns and cupids, figures commonly counted among the entourage of the god, suggest a Dionysian program for the room, were it not for the depiction of sea-monsters not at all related to Dionysus. It is rather likely that the scenes were selected at random from the pattern-books of the craftsmen, masters of their craft in this case. The candelabra-motif is also known from *Bonna*, *Vetera* and *Augusta Treverorum*, probably the work of a workshop based on the Lower Rhine.

It was mentioned before that high officers posted to the legionary units stationed in the *castella* along the *limes* could have their quarters decorated to their taste upon their arrival. An example of such taste dated to *c.* AD 50 comes from the *limes castellum* of Echzell, one of the fortifications securing the Wetterau frontier. It is a mural dominated by a large central scene showing Fortuna, the goddess of success and fate, and Hercules (Fig. 114), a preferred divinity in the army owing to his association with chtonic powers and physical prowess, a logical scene to be commissioned by the military establishment. The scene is framed by simulated pilasters. This large picture is flanked by other scenes of legendary daring (Fig. 115). To the left, set in a design of 'Minoan double axes', a smaller picture shows Theseus poised to slay the Minotaur while in an identical setting to the right Daedalus makes some final adjustments to the wings of Icarus. Since one of the 'Labors of Hercules' was the capture of the Cretan Bull, the three scenes are associated with Crete. To refer to the non-narrative, semi-circular designs of the mural as 'Minoan double axes' is therefore not too far-fetched. Additional polishing has given the whole surface the smooth appearance of stucco marble. The 'axes', which will reappear in mosaics, are outlined in reddish brown and white, the 'blades' being colored in yellow ochre, set against a dark olive background. The dramatic scenes are placed against a turquoise background. These scenes are good in that the artist who conceived them, whether for the pattern book or exclusively for these pictures, captured the moment of greatest apprehension, just before Theseus strikes the Minotaur, just before Icarus takes flight, just as Fortuna hands Hercules the cornucopia, perhaps before Hercules sets out on his tasks. But while the figures aspire to subtlety of treatment, the poses are essentially awkward and static, the dynamism of the action being left with the viewer whose imagination may help him to animate the scene. The stationary character of the figures is re-inforced by the symmetrical groupings of the static decorative designs. The arrangement of the ornamental designs forces the viewer to focus his attention on the narrative representations.

Extraordinary examples of decorative painting come from the ceiling of the Constantinian palace at *Treveris*, as the city was then already called. During two periods of excavation in 1945–46 and 1965–68, great quantities of plaster, generally blue on one side, were found under Trier cathedral.[49] Subsequent reconstruction, facilitated by the impressed wood grain of the supporting lathing, showed this plaster to have been the suspended ceiling of one of the rooms in the imperial residence. A coin of Constantine, bearing the inscription SOL INVICTO on the reverse and struck in *Treveris* in AD 315, helped to date the room as having been in use between AD 316 and AD 326. The paintings may possibly refer to events of the year AD 321, including the marriage of Constantine's oldest son Flavius Julius Crispus to Helena, as well as the seventieth

114 Hercules accepting a cornucopia from Fortuna, part of the wallpainting from the auxiliary *castellum* at Echzell. (Saalburg Museum, Bad Homburg/Taunus)

115 Reconstructed wallpainting from the *castellum* at Echzell, Theseus slays the Minotaur (*l.*), Hercules accepts a cornucopia from Fortuna (*c.*), Daedalus makes final adjustments to the wings of Icarus (*rt.*). (Saalburg Museum, Bad Homburg/Taunus)

birthday of the emperor's mother Flavia Helena. In AD 326 Constantine had his wife Fausta and his son Crispus tried and executed, allegedly for adultery. It is conceivable that Constantine feared a plot against him.[50] The plaster debris contained a coin minted in AD 325/26, suggesting that the room was destroyed at that time, perhaps in direct relation to the execution of Crispus and Fausta and the condemnation of their memory. Constantine did not maintain his residence in *Treveris*. In AD 330 he consecrated Constantinople as the new capital of the Empire. Hereafter *Treveris* was destined to decline.

The significance of the ceiling paintings is based on the following considerations: they are an excellent illustration of the level attained by Roman craftsmanship during the early fourth century and must be among the best, as the art of the imperial court, that were produced at that time; they may show actual likenesses of the imperial family;[51] they may record practices associated with official festivities. Moreover, in general ceiling painting is very rare and for this period these frescoes are almost unique.

The room, 6.86 × 9.46m in area, also had painted walls, perhaps decorated with simulated architecture, (although the plaster fragments have not yet been assembled.) There are no reliable indications that the room had a mosaic floor.[52] The ceiling was divided into fifteen sections separated by ornamental frames of green, white and red, marked off by a golden twisted rope pattern. The sections were arranged in three rows of five pictures. The reconstruction of the pictures has shown that subsequent construction on the site has destroyed the pictorial content of one and most of another picture. Eight of these sections show pairs of cupids carrying horns of plenty, a silver globe, flaming bowls and purple strips of cloth (Plate 2a). One pair has been identified as Eros and Psyche. It has been suggested that these cupids are a part of the thematic inventory of Roman marriage scenes, inspired by antique representations of Venus surrounded by cupids and applied here to the realm of human relations.[53] The cupid scenes, contained in their own ornamented frames, were arranged symmetrically, three each in the outer rows and two in the central row. The other seven scenes show portraits of four women and two men. A third portrait could not be reconstructed. It is assumed to have been that of a man. Of these portraits four depict the radiant heads of high personages, probably ladies from the immediate imperial family.[54] One young lady is wearing a wreath of flowers in her hair and may be playing a musical instrument, possibly a lyre (Plate 2c). Unfortunately that part of the picture could not be completed. None of these female portraits has been interpreted with unanimity.[55] Most interest centers on two of the female portraits, whose heads are encircled by a nimbus. One, located in the center of the ceiling and facing the entrance to the room, is set against a deep blue background and faces the viewer frontally. An attractive, majestic woman, her eyes are directed over the viewer's right shoulder into an undefined distance (Plate 2d). In her left hand she holds a golden vessel, a 'cantharos'. With her right hand she delicately lifts a reddish scarf fastened in her hair, contrasting brightly with the off-white color of her tightly folded gown. Around her throat she wears a sapphire necklace.[56] As she only wears a chain of large pearls in her hair and a tiara studded with only three sapphires, and when compared to the wealth displayed by the detailed portrait of another woman (also set against a deep blue background[57]), this woman appears to be of inferior status. It was possible to restore this other portrait completely (Plate 2b). Silhouetted against her nimbus, her dark wavy hair is held in place by a golden band studded with pearls. A gilt laurel wreath and a tiara holding five reddish gems complete her headdress. By Constantinian times court etiquette determined a relationship between rank and the display of wealth. Turned slightly to the left, this lady wears a necklace of sapphires in settings of gold. Pear-shaped pendants hang from her ears. She too has a scarf fastened in her hair. In her left hand she carries a jewel case from which she carefully draws a chain of pearls, holding the chain with poised refinement between index finger and thumb.[58] Compared to the summary workmanship of the picture of the 'flower girl',[59] the greater attention paid to detailing the fine facial features of these two women of rank suggests that these two pictures may be actual portraits.

A fourth portrait, essentially completely restored, shows a lady holding up a mirror while she adjusts a cloak which partly covers the back of her head. Set against a blue background her head is surrounded by a nimbus. On her head she wears a golden tiara and a thin string of pearls. Around her neck she too wears a necklace of sapphires. A golden laurel wreath, pearl earrings and a golden bracelet on each arm make it clear that she is a lady of high station. That only she and the lady with the casket are crowned with golden laurels might serve to identify them as wives of Constantine and Crispus.

The completely restored portrait of the lady with the casket demonstrates the structural principles of the composition employed by the artist. These principles are deemed valid for representational portraiture until modern times. Her right shoulder turned ever so slightly forward, the figure forms a triangle, the base of which is the base of the picture. By means of converging lines the viewer's eyes are led to the apex of the composition, the lady's head, whose eyes are the focal center of the composition. Unlike the eyes of the lady with the veil whose expectant look loses itself somewhere behind the viewer, the penetrating steady gaze of the lady with the casket demands eye-to-eye contact and the viewer's full attention. Through the use of gentle lighting, soft yet luminous colors and with all details contained within the triangular composition, the portrait exudes an air of stability, composure and harmony. An erratic visual to-and-fro is counteracted by the demand for focal concentration inherent in the composition as even the viewer's eyes are led steadily into the center of the picture. The gentle shadows falling onto the folds of her garment and over the fine features of her face, the refined poise of her hand, the mere suggestion of a veil falling about her shoulders and the subtle radiance of the nimbus which surrounds her head indicate this portrait, and the others by association, to have been executed by a true master of his time who was thoroughly imbued with the principles of classical art.

It appears that following the destruction of this part of the palace, the site was given to the Church as though in expiation.[60]

Though this summary of wall paintings is far too brief, it does point to a preoccupation with man and his activities, to an emphasis on architectural forms and an interest in narrative content. Similar to the work in stone, wall painting is also characterized by a deliberate striving for closed form, attained by containing the work in a form. By contrast the northern native arts of pre-Roman times are marked by ornamental open-work techniques. Celtic work is perforated, antithetical, centrifugal, unconfined, entirely non-narrative and full of unresolved tensions. It indulges in perforation so that the antithetical play between patterns and designs silhouetted against contrasting backgrounds allows a perceptual game with positive and negative spatial patterns. It is centrifugal in that it flees any point that might be the center. It is unconfined in that it rejects any external and artificial framework, impeded only by the limitations of its own dynamics. It is an art form in which the artist has no intention other than the display of the virtuosity of his imagination. On the other hand the work of the Roman craftsmen, especially in the northern provinces, is concerned with narrative representations dominated by human forms. Ornamental patterning, geometric, vegetative and zoomorphic, is restricted to the frame. There may of course be so much geometric patterning, especially in mosaics, that the ornamental designs threaten to overpower the representational elements of the composition, but there is never any doubt in the eyes of the viewer that the ornamental

116 Theseus Mosaic from a luxury villa near Salzburg, second century AD. (Kunsthistorisches Museum, Vienna)

107

patterns have a subsidiary function to the narrative or anthropomorphic representations, for the designs converge on the center and usually the focus is on man. The Roman craftsmen give to their works a closed form, organized and orderly, in which the tensions are resolved harmoniously within the composition. The lady with the jewel casket from the ceiling at Trier is such a harmonious composition.

The Romans excelled in the art of floor mosaic. Mosaic is an art form in which pebbles, but mainly small cubes of stone, marble, glass or tile are assembled into designs and pictures for the purpose of decorating such surfaces as floors, walls and ceilings.[61] Wall and ceiling mosaics have not survived in those Roman provinces with which we are concerned though they will have existed in the villas of the rich, in the administrative centers, the religious buildings and the imperial residences. From the other parts of the Roman Empire elaborate scenic mosaics are known showing large areas of human interaction, such as the Battle of Issus mosaic at Pompeii or the violent struggles of beasts in nature settings with only the suggestion of a frame. Such displays of vigor are not (yet) in evidence north of the Alps nor have large pictorial scenes been uncovered. That these also may have existed is perhaps indicated by a rather large mosaic fragment from *Arae Flaviae*, modern Rottweil in the Black Forest. Four very simple narrow bands of mosaic constitute its frame. The subject is Orpheus playing his lyre and enchanting the birds (Plate 3a). This Orpheus Mosaic may be an exception. Wide borders are typical for most of the recovered mosaics, at least on one side, composed of multicolored bands of such varying motifs as twisted rope patterns, meanders, rectilinears and curvilinears, arcades, braid patterns, checkerboards, highly ornamented slingbands and cresting wave patterns, and so forth, skillfully joined together to form independent designs or to form varying geometric shapes which in turn function as frames for floral and geometric designs, exotic fish and birds, for legendary creatures of the sea, for muses, philosophers, gods and demi-gods, hunters, gladiators and champions, as well as diverse sordid events of the arena. In one instance at least, the Theseus Mosaic from the luxury villa at Siezenheim near Salzburg (Fig. 116), the colors of the frame fuse with the picture as the frame-become-labyrinth meanders in rectilinear fashion into the center of the picture. An invitation to bored guests, the mosaic is at least a conversation piece. At the center of this mosaic stands Theseus about to strike the Minotaur with the fatal blow. The mosaic has been dated to the second century.[62]

The fragmentary evidence makes it difficult to demonstrate a continuity in the stylistic development of floor mosaics. Two mosaics from the *Oppidum Ubiorum*, i.e. from the first half of the first century,[63] decorated a wealthy house. On one the central square consists entirely of triangularly cut black marble and greenish slate contained in a black and white frame, surrounded by an obliquely laid out pattern of alternating black and white stone. A very orderly arrangement, this band is framed by four alternating white and black bands. The other mosaic shows double circles set in double square frames. While the triangular areas of the square formed by the inset circle are each filled with a curvilinear vase from which leaves and tendrils reach out, the interior of the circle contains rectangles arranged in Y-shapes, with spaces between them filled by triangles arranged in groups of three to form pyramids. The order of this arrangement is destroyed by the insertion of a rhombus which in turn contains a red circle set with black shields. The preference for black and white motifs was to remain popular. From the end of the third century[64] comes a mosaic consisting entirely of regularly intersecting black circles on white, forming four-petaled 'flowers'.

Each space between the petals contains a little swastika, a good luck sign. In spite of the erratic effect produced by the insertion of the rhombus, the compositions demonstrate a sense of organization and geometric order, principles of form which will constitute a continuing characteristic of the mosaicist's art. It also may reflect the Romans' predilection for order.

From Trier comes one of the most famous mosaics, the Mosaic of the Muses (Plate 3c), dated into the second century.[65] This mosaic demonstrates very well the desire to display one's cultural awareness, education and interests in the arts and sciences, especially in literature. Badly damaged, enough of the muses have lost their attributes to leave absolute identification in doubt. However, the examination of each frame reveals that the five muses placed diagonally are situated in identical frames. The inner line of the central frame is outlined in red, thereby singling it out, while the remaining four again are placed in identical frames, but significantly different from the group of five muses. In all, three muses are unidentified: the one at center, at lower middle and at lower right. In the group of five the following have been named: top left Thalia, Muse of Comedy; top right Clio, Muse of History; bottom left Urania, Muse of Astronomy. Since epic poetry is of central importance in Latin literature, it is reasonable to propose that Calliope, the Muse of Epic Poetry, occupies the central frame. In view of the negligible place of tragedy in Latin literature it is reasonable to propose that Melpomene, the Muse of Tragedy, occupies the square at bottom right, diametrically opposite to Thalia, the Muse of Comedy. Of the group of four Terpsichore, the Muse of Dance, is placed at top center; Euterpe, the Muse of Lyric Poetry, is placed at left center and Erato, the Muse of Love Poetry, is placed at right center, leaving Polymnia, the Muse of Sacred Poetry, to assume the remaining square at bottom center. These four muses would even be related thematically. It is likely that the plan evident in the ornamental detail also expressed a thematic program. The ornamental details conform to the decorative conventions one finds in these frames. A twisted rope pattern properly 'spliced' at the intersections runs between the 'portraits'. At top and bottom we encounter bands of confronting ∫-curves, i.e. lyres. A band of meander and another of stars surrounds the entire composition. Once again the emphasis on diagonals as well as the thematic arrangement of the composition invite the eye to travel from the decorative frames into the center.

Into the same category falls a mosaic from Cologne, which is composed mainly of hexagons, triangles, squares and trapezoids and is fitted into a frame of antithetical and complementary 'double axe' designs.[66] Six hexagons are grouped around a central hexagon. Each hexagon contains the bust of a philosopher; the one at the center frames the bust of Diogenes, the cynic. The actual 'portraits' are anachronisms, as hairdos and garments point to the third century.[67]

Commanding a great deal of every Roman's attention, the public games staged in the arena also found an echo in the residential decor. In Cologne a fragment was found showing enough to identify the rim of a circus scene. Combatants are not only represented, they are also named, indicating that the patron commissioned the commemoration of a specific set of events in the arena.[68] Off to one side a group of men is shown, perhaps trainers and coaches, but also one with a meat hook under his cape, the one whose task it was to drag out the dead. At Trier a floor mosaic has been unearthed,[69] which celebrates one Polydus, *Compressore*, a victorious charioteer standing in his *quadriga*, a palm branch in his left hand, holding high the wreath of victory (Fig. 117). Framed in an octogon, a cresting wave pattern surrounds this

inner hexagon. The hexagonal pattern makes up a large portion of the floor mosaic. As a space-filling device the hexagon is particularly helpful since it allows natural progressions by means of which the mosaicist can group arrangements of triangles, lozenges and cross-over rope patterns around an expanding center. Allusions to vegetation fill the corners. Twisted rope patterns and bands of braid square off the composition. A checkerboard pattern, meanders and upended squares complete the mosaic.

Religious themes also were used for purposes of decoration, a Dionysian theme, for

117 (far left) Charioteer Mosaic, completed by space filling pattern, found beneath the Constantinian Baths at Trier. (Rheinisches Landesmuseum, Trier)

118 Dionysus Mosaic from a *collegium* of Dionysus worshippers at *Virunum*. (Landesmuseum für Kärnten, Klagenfurt)

instance, showing the God of revelry following a pair of tigers led by a bacchante, one of his attendants (Plate 3b). The theme, from its festive side, is most fully developed in the famous Dionysus Mosaic found in Cologne (Plate 4a) and dated to the second half of the third century, *c*. AD 270, a period of great political turmoil when the frontier was also harried by invaders from beyond the Rhine.[70] The wealth represented by this mosaic must have been truly great. By means of lozenges, triangles, cross-over rope patterns this mosaicist created similarly laid out parcels of decorative designs as they appeared on the Charioteer Mosaic. While the latter presented only one picture, the Dionysus Mosaic of Cologne groups thirty pictures of various levels of relative importance to the theme around the central picture. Six scenes could not be restored. At the center the philosopher Epicurus is shown unable to sustain a precarious list were it not for a satyr, one of the helpful companions of Dionysus. Originally Epicurus had taught that excessive indulgence in pleasure was detrimental to one's equilibrium and would bring pain. Misinterpreted, his philosophy was taken as a directive to pursue pleasure with abandon. It is this misinterpretation which motivates this mosaic, as is evident from the Bacchic details itemized in the composition. The companions of Dionysus are everywhere: satyrs pursue meanads, a Silenus rides backward on a donkey, a Pan leads a goat, a satyr amuses himself with his own music, others ride a lion. A leopard hints at the presence of the god himself. The carnival atmosphere of frenetic music, ecstatic movements, exotic foods, explicit eroticism and precarious intoxication point to the voluptuous abandon that was at least conceivable in the northern provinces. The skill of the mosaicist was extraordinary; they overcame the material obstacles encountered when working with

119 Dionysus Mosaic, corner detail of a Medusa, from *Virunum*. (Landesmuseum für Kärnten, Klagenfurt)

120 Floor mosaic from the ante-room of the *frigidarium* of a villa near Bad Vilbel. The name of the master mosaicist, Pervincus, is visible at the center. (Hessisches Landesmuseum, Darmstadt)

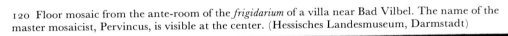

stone chips with the artistry of a painter. The forms are entirely natural in their suppleness, enhanced by the subtle effects of color, shadow and light, all the more persuasive when seen against the linear rigidity of the space-filling geometrics.

Interesting for the contrast it provides with the Dionysus Mosaic from Cologne is the Dionysus Mosaic (Fig. 118) from a *collegium* of Dionysus worshippers at *Virunum* in *Noricum*.[71] Dated to the same period, *c.* AD 290,[72] this mosaic suggests pleasure but not orgiastic abandon. Not entirely accurate, it too follows a hexagonal plan as the central rectangle framing the god forms two sides of a hexagon whose sides are formed by two cross-over triangles, Star of David motif, which are contained in turn by a still larger hexagon which finally is contained in a square. Any triangle formed by the skillfully 'spliced' twisted rope lines of demarcation is filled with birds. Each of the lozenges is occupied by satyrs and meanads. The first outside frame is formed by an intricate meander. At each corner the meander meets a square containing the head of a Medusa (Fig. 119). The final frame is made up of the same broad band of 'double axes' that surrounded the Philosophers Mosaic in Cologne. The work of an accomplished artist, this beautiful mosaic radiates control, balance, poise and the resolution of tensions. Even the furies have lost some of their frightfulness.

Mosaics were laid over hypocaust systems on a layer of mortar or on a specially prepared floor of stamped layers of stone debris and mortar (Fig. 121). Guidelines for the basic patterns were then marked on the surface before the colored stone chips, the *tesserae*, were bedded into a small thin layer of mortar just large enough to allow the mosaicist to follow his outline and the mortar not to dry prematurely. Three methods were available to the mosaicist: a direct, an indirect and a reverse method.[73] As the term 'direct' implies, the *tesserae* were set directly into the mortar bed. This meant that the mosaicist and his helpers had to work quickly in a limited area with a larger margin of error. The cost would be great. The indirect and reverse methods offered the advantage that such decorative motifs as twisted rope, meanders and so forth could be fabricated during lull periods.[74] Considering the complexities of the design layouts, mass production of patterns will have eluded them, however. With

121 Illustration of a hypocaust and mosaic floor. (Museum Carnuntinum, Bad Deutsch-Altenburg, Austria)

5a Terra nigra with barbotines, first and second centuries AD. (Gäuboden Museum, Straubing)

5b Glazed vase with decorative reliefs depicting hunting scenes. (Römisch-Germanisches Museum, Cologne)

5c Jug with heads of the Medusa. (Museum für Ur-und Frühgeschichte, Freiburg)

5d Bronze jug from a depot of eight large pieces of bronze at a *villa rustica* near Waldkirch. (Museum für Ur-und Frühgeschichte, Freiburg)

6a (above) Athena emblem and bowl, silver, part of the Hildesheim treasure. It consists of pieces dating from the last century BC to the middle of the first century AD. (Antikenmuseum, Staatliche Museen Preußischer Kulturbesitz, Berlin)

6b Silver vessel from the Hildesheim treasure, possibly part of an amphora, showing Gallic workmanship. (Antikenmuseum, Staatliche Museen Preußischer Kulturbesitz, Berlin)

6c Selection from the late Roman silver treasure found at *Augusta Raurica*. (Römermuseum, August)

122 Terra sigillata bowl from Gauting,
Bavaria. (Prähistorische Staatssammlung,
Munich)

123 Terra sigillata mold. (Historisches
Museum der Pfalz, Speyer)

124 Terra sigillata produced at
Haltern, i.e. before AD 9.
Reconstruction. (Westfälisches Museum
für Archäologie, Münster)

the indirect method the colored stone fragments were set firmly in a bed of sand. Upon assembly, paper or fabric was glued over them and, once firmly attached, lifted into the desired place in the mosaic. The backing was then soaked off with hot water. The reverse method resembled the indirect method except that each *tessera* was glued down on a colored cartoon. The same procedure was followed. The result differed in that the pattern came to lie in reverse of the original floor plan. As anyone who has hung wallpaper or laid carpet knows only too well, lines often do not meet. Once laid in place fine mortar was poured into the cracks and when hardened, the entire surface was polished with abrasives until it reached a high gloss.

As was the case for wall painting, here too the recurrence of certain motifs, especially of the decorative ones, suggests the existence of pattern books which enjoyed wide distribution as indicated by the contemporary appearance of the 'double axe' motif in *Germania inferior* and in *Noricum*, or the popularity enjoyed by certain workshops whose skill was in demand throughout a given area. No doubt both situations applied. The main pictorial themes, however, seem not to recur among the evidence and probably were custom work and executed by the master mosaicist himself (Fig. 120).

In Roman pottery something of the synthesis which forms and techniques underwent in the Roman Empire is reflected (Fig. 122). From the Greek world had come ceramic forms, decorations and the colors black and red, though by the Roman period the color preference was red.[75] Embossed Hellenistic silverware provided the models for relief ornamentation and for figures (Fig. 123). At *Arretium*, modern Arezzo in Italy, red gloss techniques were developed which Italian entrepreneurs took into

125 Gladiator relief on a terra sigillata jug from Rheinzabern. (Historisches Museum der Pfalz, Speyer)

126 Terra sigillata plate. (Historisches Museum der Pfalz, Speyer)

Gaul during the first century of our era. There Italian and Celtic ceramic skills and motifs united to produce an industry which created a very characteristic style of red gloss pottery, the *terra sigillata*. While the Arretine ware appears to have been the work of Greek craftsmen, the pottery produced in the factories of southern Gaul was made by local potters whose skill in producing highly ornamented ceramics was great, but who did not succeed in the representation of figures.[76] On the other hand, Arretine ware stands out for the skill of its figural representations.

It is a well-known archaeological fact that pottery tends to be used locally, that it is not generally traded, thereby making it possible to draw the demarcation lines which identified the various regional ceramic cultures. In Roman times this was still partly true in that some pottery forms from *Belgica* reflect a style quite distinct from Raetian or Norican ware, as everywhere traces of earlier native regional traditions are still in evidence, especially in the manufacture of wares destined for domestic use, though here too Mediterranean influences or direct imports played a role. However, *terra sigillata*, the best dinner ware of its time, was not confined regionally but traded from identifiable manufacturing centers throughout the Empire. In its rise and decline the rise and fall of the Roman Empire is mirrored. From *Arretium* it was traded into *Noricum* during the early Empire.[77] Since the army was the main customer, the relocation and stabilization of the northern frontiers drew the Gallo-Roman *terra sigillata* factories out of southern and eastern Gaul,[78] so that by the end of the first century the centers had shifted north to *Augusta Treverorum*,[79] by AD 120 into *Germania inferior* (Fig. 124) and *superior* where by mid-century the workshop at *Tabernae*, modern Rheinzabern (Fig. 125, 126), came to be the dominant center on the Rhine,[80] and into *Raetia* and *Noricum. Noricum* and *Pannonia* were supplied by shops at modern Pfaffenhofen and Westerndorff on the river Inn.[81] Where *terra sigillata* appeared it asserted itself as the dominant ceramic type. Contrary to the large manufacturing centers in southern Gaul, in the frontier provinces the industry was in the hands of family units.[82] As is to be expected, this dispersion was accompanied by a regression of quality.

The Roman name for this ware is not known; perhaps the technique of its manufacture was expressed with the term *ars cretaria*.[83] The modern term derives from the stamped seal, *sigillum*, of the potter who made the pottery and which identifies much of this ware (Fig. 127). In addition the decorative patterns were created by means of carved stamps. Here too the stylistic variations in these stamped designs, a reflection

127 Terra sigillata plate with clay drinking cups from Dangstetten. The plate bears the potter's seal—L. Tetti Samia, *c.* 15-9 BC. (Museum für Ur-und Frühgeschichte, Freiburg)

128 Mold for terra sigillata ware with the potter's seal—Abbofe. From Riegel near Freiburg. (Museum für Ur-und Frühgeschichte, Freiburg)

129 Terra sigillata plate and vessels with ground-in patterns. (Historisches Museum der Pfalz, Speyer)

of the taste of the day, are an aid in establishing chronologies. Dinner sets of un-decorated plates, cups and beakers are identified by the particulars of the rims. Each setting was completed by richly ornamented vessels (Plate 4b).

The mass production of this pottery was facilitated by the use of molds into which the desired ornamentation had been pressed with precarved stamps (Fig. 128). The clay was then worked into the molds, particular care being taken that the ornamental details were properly filled.[84] The inner cavity of the desired vessel was then finished and smoothed. The drying process would cause the clay to shrink, thereby releasing the new clay form from its mold. Premature removal would scar the ornamental relief. A barbotine technique saw ornamentation raised on the surface. Decorations were cut or rolled into the wet surface as well, either by a high-speed rotating wheel being feathered against the rotating vessel, already fairly dry (Fig. 129), or by means of a wheel with cut-in decorative detail being rolled over the surface. Most of this ware also bore the maker's or the factory's stamp in its base, making it possible to fix the location of its manufacture. Only now was the red gloss applied. This was a solution of clay particles containing iron oxides.[85] Once this solution had thickened to a creamy consistency by evaporation the vessels were dipped into it, judging by the fingermarks on some of the bases. The gloss may also have been poured over the finished pot. Stacked upside down on central supports, the pottery was fired in updraft kilns at temperatures ranging from 1050-1200°C.[86]

As may be expected, the decorative reliefs consisted of vegetative and figural motifs which may reflect a blend of Celtic and Mediterranean attitudes to design (Plate 4c). However, the vegetative motifs consist largely of acanthus leaf patterns and other southern vegetation while any animal motifs are not of the type familiar from earlier Celtic approaches. On the *terra sigillata* the tail of a Mediterranean fish-motif may terminate in an ivy leaf (Fig. 130). That the repetitive decorations strive for symmetry may be the result of using stamps. Closed compositions on the other hand are rare. Instead the potters frequently used the stamps at random, as though horrified by empty space, until the surfaces were covered with unrelated motifs. Closed compositions are seen to have been dependent on models provided by repoussé silver work. The overall impression is one of generally classical forms and motifs (Fig. 131).[87]

While the simple firing of pottery with the ready access of oxygen, as practiced around the Mediterranean, resulted in the pottery being mostly white, yellow, buff

119

or red the northern techniques generally were more complex.[88] In the north, pottery was fired preferably in a reducing atmosphere, i.e. without oxygen. For this purpose the kiln had to be sealed off carefully, the inflow of oxygen restricted, to maintain temperatures varying between 900–1000°C. This technique resulted in pottery shades ranging from light greys to deepest blacks. In the Rhenish provinces such black ware enjoyed particular popularity, especially black gloss beakers decorated with floral motifs bearing inspiring inscriptions normally associated with the pleasures of wine. During the first century AD so-called *terra* nigra, smoke blackened and polished ware was a prominent feature. Probably the expression of an indigenous Celtic manufacturing tradition, it was displaced by the decorated black gloss ware.[89] From *Raetia* came an effective type of black gloss pottery (Plate 5a). Here the black gloss had been applied to the outside of red ware decorated with linear barbotines or geometric incisions. While the black gloss may have worn off the raised designs, it appears more likely to have been wiped off those areas marked by incisions, thereby creating a pleasing effect. The province *Belgica* made a humorous contribution to the inventory of Roman provincial ceramic forms, face urns with grotesque physiognomies on the urns.[90] It formed part of the funerary inventory (Fig. 132).

During the first century of our era glazing techniques were discovered in the Near East: lead silicate gloss to which such coloring agents as cupric oxide for green and ferric oxide for brown had been added.[91] It was fired at *c.* 700°C. Generally the outside surface finish varied from a pale to a rich lime green (Plate 5b) while the inside was of a honey-brown. With glazed pottery too, molds were used to form the decorative reliefs. The sticky glaze made it necessary to place the vessel upside down on pointed prongs for firing.

Fine white pipeclay, readily available near Cologne, was ideally suited for the manufacture of terracottas and also was used for fine ceramic ware and such curios as cultic or theatrical masks. The pottery is wheel-thrown (Plate 5c). The terracottas are molded miniatures of known sculptures, mainly of divinities of Roman or local

120

130 Terra sigillata jug. (Mittelrheinisches Landesmuseum, Mainz)

131 Terra sigillata drinking cup with leaf pattern and inscription. (Westfälisches Museum für Archäologie, Münster)

132 Grotesque face urn, part of a funerary inventory. (Mittelrheinisches Landesmuseum, Mainz)

origin such as the Matrons (see Fig. 52). For the family-owned pottery workshops the trade in terracottas (Fig. 133) must have constituted a lucrative side line. Simple forms were molded in the whole. More complex figurines were molded in parts and then assembled.[92] Before firing at no more than 950°C. a white clay slip was applied. After firing, the polychrome detail would then be painted on. With such binding mediums as gum and honey the use of natural colors proved only partly satisfactory since they were not wear or moisture resistant.[93] Glosses or vitreous glazes were more durable. Some truly precious figurines may have been covered in gold leaf. The availability of portable divinities and votive offerings would have been greatly appreciated by a culture so oriented on religion. In the sphere of cultic games and, by extension, in the theatrical context as well, masks were a requisite (Fig. 134). These too were painted with brilliant 'make-up'.

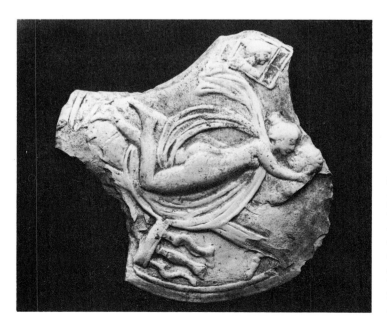

133 *Oscillum* of pipeclay. In Italy and the western provinces of the Empire one used to hang up carved marble discs in breezeways, in honor of Bacchus, the god of wine. Discs of pipeclay were manufactured in central Gaul. Pressed into molds, only one side was raised in relief. The themes dealt with legends, religion and love. (Römermuseum Augst)

121

134 An actor's mask, terracotta, early second century AD. (Sammlung Nassauischer Altertümer, Wiesbaden)

135 Oil lamps with gladiator scenes from the legion camp at Haltern. (Westfälisches Museum für Archäologie, Münster)

136 Oil lamp with facial features. (Gäuboden Museum, Straubing)

The standard method of lighting saw candles and tapers fixed on wooden candlestick holders for common use and on bronze candelabra in more ceremonious situations.[94] Wax was cheaper than olive oil which had to be imported. Nevertheless, the numerous oil lamps in Europe's museums indicate that lamps of clay and bronze were popular among those who could afford the imported oil. A simple device, consisting of oil chamber, nozzle and linen wick, oil lamps were another line in the potter's merchandise. It can be imagined that one lamp could not possibly give off enough light. In attempting to increase the amount of illumination, lamps with as many as five nozzles were made.[95] However, economic considerations will have placed a limit on the number of oil lamps used at any one time. Whether as hanging or as portable lamps they will not have created more than a 'romantic' atmosphere. Ranging from plain and merely functional to very ornate creations (Fig. 135), perhaps in competition with the highly ornate designs made by the casters of bronze lamps, the potters also tried to follow the dictates of taste. Usually made of gypsum plaster, the lamps were formed in clay molds,[96] such molds usually bearing the maker's stamp in their base. The top surface of the circular oil chamber was either plain or decorated with a molded relief or modeled into animals or into stylized human heads (Fig. 136). To add luster and to make the lamp less permeable to the oil at the same time, the finished lamp was dipped into a slip of the same clay, usually without total success.[97] Since the designs were not protected by law it was not unusual that imported lamps were used to make new molds. Not only did the name of the original manufacturer

137 Bronze lamp with human face. (Gäuboden Museum, Straubing)

138 Bronze lamp from a grave at Wehringen, Bavaria. (Prähistorische Staatssammlung, Munich)

139 Mercury
statuette, bronze.
(Römermuseum,
Augst)

get transferred to the pirated copies, but the ornamentations deteriorated while the lamps underwent a reduction in size.

Alongside the flourishing business in olive oil and ceramic wares, metals and metal objects of all types (Fig. 137, 138) were part of the lively trade among the provinces of the Empire. Of special interest are portable bronzes for cultic and ceremonial use.[98] The presence of clay molds indicates that such bronze objects as vessels and lamps for instance, or handles and decorative attachments on vessels and garments were made in the workshops of the northern provinces. These provinces, of course, had long–established traditions in the mining and working of metals, but generally for the northern artisans such work in the round as the Urnfield ducks and Hallstatt horses or the Plastic Style of the Celts had been something of an exception. With the advent of the Romans not only was the industry reorganized but the traditional inventory of Celtic motifs was displaced by the artistic execution of human and zoomorphic forms

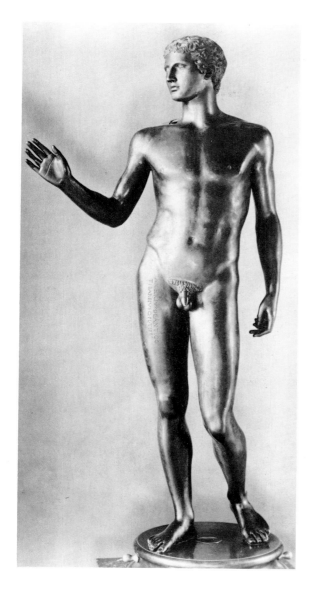

140 Cult statue of Mars, perhaps of Mars-Latobius, bronze from the Magdalensberg near *Virunum*. (Kunsthistorisches Museum, Vienna)

demanded by the official and cultic representations of the Greco-Roman world (Fig. 139). The Plastic Style of the Celtic fibulae, for instance, came to a rather abrupt end shortly after the arrival of the Romans in the Celtic territories. As was observed in the other art forms, human representations in relief and in the round assumed a central position in the inventory of forms. At first bronze vessels, statues and statuettes reached the north as objects of trade.[99] But at the same time the existing workshops soon found themselves joined by new studios as southern craftsmen expanded their activities into the new territories, especially into the new urban centers, in order to supply the growing citizenry, a mixture of natives and other peoples of the Empire, with the forms and motifs current in the Empire (Plate 5d).

That this southern influence was exerting itself in a northerly direction already before the transformation of the independent *Regnum Noricum* into the Roman province *Noricum* in 15 BC is indicated by the significant find of a life-size bronze statue

141 Model of a charioteer with movable arms, funerary gift, third century AD, from Mainz. (Mittelrheinisches Landesmuseum, Mainz)

142 *Lares*, part of the Straubing treasure. (Gäuboden Museum, Straubing)

143 Face mask of the Hellenistic type, from Straß-Moos, Bavaria. (Prähistorische Staatssammlung, Munich)

from the Magdalensberg (Fig. 140), near *Virunum*/Klagenfurt in Austria. As was noted before, the oppidum on the Magdalensberg had been the jumping–off point for merchants from Aquileia trading into the eastern Alps. This bronze statue of a naked youth, reflecting the school of Praxiteles[100] from the mid-fourth century BC in the youthful softness of its molded form, was dedicated to Mars. Originally it had been the cult-statue in a temple on the Magdalensberg. An inscription on the right thigh and another on the shield, now lost, identified the figure to be Mars, probably Mars-Latobius, an example of early syncretism. The inscriptions identified the dedicators to have been a Norican slave, three other freed-men from the south and a Celt, probably the native trading partner.[101] Statues of this type generally have not survived in the north although fragments indicate that many large ones did once exist.

More frequent are the small portable bronzes, carefully articulate in their detail, such as the Dolichenus and Isis group (see Fig. 68, 69) found in the Dolichenus sanctuary near the *castellum* at Mauer an der Url in northern *Noricum*. There are no clues to the origin of these portable bronzes.[102] If made locally then the molds probably were imported from Italy or even the Near East. It has been suggested that for such complex statuettes as the Dolichenus, the body parts were cast separately and then assembled.[103] A good example of this technique is the charioteer (Fig. 141), a unique votive gift of the third century found at Mainz. It is apparent that the hands and especially the arms were joined to the body in a secondary process.

Superb examples of the bronze caster's art came to light as part of the Straubing treasure.[104] In all, a group of seven *lares*, the Roman household gods, has been found

144 Face mask of the Oriental type, part of the Straubing treasure. (Gäuboden Museum, Straubing)

(Fig. 142). They have been dated to *c.* AD 200. Most impressive is a gracefully dancing god, 'baroque' in execution, holding a rhyton—a drinking horn—in his right hand and a sacrificial plate in his left, his graceful movements belying convincingly the metallic rigidity of the swirling flow of the garments; a genius carrying a double cornucopia in his left hand and a votive plate in his right and clad only in a draped cloak; a Fortuna carrying a double cornucopia; a Mercury. A curious member of the group is a 'cute' running figurine of a helmeted boyish god wearing the molded body cuirass normally associated with Dolichenus, discussed earlier, holding out the seed capsule of a poppy.[105] While Dolichenus usually wears a Phrygian cap, the helmet of this figurine is surmounted by a sphinx which suggests something of the shape of the traditional Phrygian cap. Contrary to the usual heroic motifs which decorate the conventional cuirass, here the body armor as well as the greaves are decorated with flowers. Its beardless face framed with curls, the suggestion of frivolity is rather strong, calling to mind the regal body armor of seventeenth-century French court theater rather than the sobriety of life along the *limes* frontier.

One of the units stationed at the castellum of *Sorviodurum*, modern Straubing, was the *cohors I Flavia Canathenorum milliaria sagittariorum*, a Syrian auxiliary cohort of 1000 archers. About AD 140, the unit took over garrison duty on this section of the middle Danube, east of *Castra Regina*. It is believed that this cohort counted cavalry in its complement. Associated with its presence on the Danube is the unique ceremonial cavalry armor found during construction in 1950. Found near the site of a Roman *villa rustica* it is assumed that a scavenger had plundered the *lararium* of the villa, added the *lares* to his loot of bronze face masks, greaves, knee guards and the protective head covering for horses and buried it all in a large copper kettle. Nearby was found a great number of iron tools and weapons. Perhaps the unknown plunderer was merely a dealer of scrap metals who had buried his hoard hoping to retrieve it at a less critical time. This particular crisis is commonly held to have been the Alamannic incursion of AD 233 when the *castellum* and the neighboring village at *Sorviodurum* were overrun and destroyed.

The copper kettle also contained seven face masks,[106] four of an Hellenistic type and three of an Oriental type, as well as an odd plate for the back of an Hellenistic mask, five greaves, six knee guards and five head pieces of hinged sheet bronze armor for horses. The Hellenistic face masks (Fig. 143) are known from several sites.[107] They appear to have been cast around molds. They are characterized by a double curl rising above the forehead in the fashion generally similar to the Head of Alexander by Lysippus, court sculptor to Alexander the Great.[108] On the masks meticulous attention was paid to the wavy hair, the detailed sweep of the eyebrows and the neatly trimmed sideburns. The determined mien is striking with the contrast between the furrowed muscular forehead and the gently contoured beardless face. The Hellenistic masks were silvered. The Oriental masks (Fig. 144) differ in that they were gilt, the face framed in a peaked headdress, most of it covered with tightly wound curls. No hair is visible though the cap itself may have been intended to simulate some curly animal skin. Traces of luting suggest that these masks also were decorated with colorful stones.[109] The setting of the eyes and the simulation of the iris give to these Oriental masks a somewhat empty stare. Of the body armor only five greaves and six kneeplates exist. Two of the greaves could make a matched pair. All of them are decorated with embossed representations either of gods, Hercules and Mars, or of heads, including one with Phrygian caps, of fish, eagles or of such fabulous beings as fishtailed leopards. The knee guards show either profiled busts of Minerva, the god-

145 Horse armor with Gorgon-headed eye guards, Mars perhaps, anguipede and crested heads. (Gäuboden Museum, Straubing)

146 Horse armor with Mars, anguipede and Dioscuri. (Gäuboden Museum, Straubing)

dess of war, or full views of faces executed in a style to be encountered again during the period of sixteenth-century Mannerism. Of special interest are the hinged head plates of the horse armor. Using a bold embossing technique the artist drove a high relief out of the sheet bronze. Adjustable so as to fit the shape of a horse's head, basket-like protrusions of network or Gorgon heads protected the eyes. The plate covering the forehead bore a divinity, usually Mars, holding an oval shield in his left hand and resting on a spear in his right. It is noteworthy that on two of these plates Mars, or perhaps it is Jupiter, is held up by an anguipede, a snake-legged giant (Fig. 145). On one plate the snake heads terminate in radiant crests. On this plate the crest motif appears frequently, by itself and as 'helmet' crests on two busts. The 'Mars' of the central panel also wears a stylized and crested headdress. The presence of Phrygian-capped heads of the Dolichenus or Mithras type is surprising. The work-man of this headplate went to great lengths to cover every surface with asymmetrical space-filling ornaments, including legion standards, geometrics, an eagle and fabled fish-sphynxes with wings. Winged Victories soar into the center extending wreaths. More orderly and less busy in the arrangement of its figures is another headplate showing a naked 'Mars' wearing a crested Corinthian helmet pushed back on his head, leaning on a spear, holding an oval shield in his left hand (Fig. 146). This 'Mars' is surmounted by an eagle, normally associated with Jupiter, a wreath in its beak. The god too stands on an anguipede, the snake heads writhing upward. The Dioscuri, the divine twins Castor and Pollux patron gods of the Roman cavalry, are shown on the cheek-pieces. Slithering snakes move around the perforated eye guards and across these panels linking the Dioscuri with winged Victories. The unworked surfaces are finished with a pattern of closely interlinked rings.

This richly ornamented parade armor, too thin for actual combat, was used on ceremonial occasions when the cavalry units performed tournament-like rides de-signed to demonstrate their effectiveness while at the same time entertaining the troops. The historian Flavius Arrianus in his treatise on the war of AD 136 has left a record of these colorful spectacles.[110] Those horsemen singled out by rank or merit were allowed to attract attention with their gilt helmets decorated with flowing manes of blond hair. Equipped with light and very colorful shields, the emphasis was on speed and elegance of movement. Instead of body armor the horsemen wore scarlet, purple or colorful garments and tightly fitting breeches. The horses wore only head-plates to protect the eyes. No other horse armor was needed since the lances did not have metal points. These ceremonial tournaments are the context for the Hellenistic and Oriental masks, for it was on these occasions that the two parties re-enacted the 'Trojan War', the *Troiae Lusus*, a ceremonial ride of complicated figures which prob-ably was accompanied by the martial music of horns and kettle drums.[111]

The origin of this ceremonial horse armor is not known. It is conceivable that these pieces are the work of one or more itinerant bronzesmiths. The differences in taste evident in the abundance of accumulated random detail on one headplate and the sober elegance achieved on the other, not to mention the stark tectonic simplicity of a third piece, suggests that the craftsman decorated one basic design of the armor according to the wishes of his clients. Beside the hinged rectangular three-piece design described above, there was one that covered less of the horse's head with an elongated, decorated octagon with the perforated eye covers set into hinged wing-shaped side pieces.

The most spectacular closed find of Roman silverware was found in 1868 near Hildesheim, far from the Roman frontier. The nationalistic enthusiasm of the time was quick to identify the seventy pieces of silverware as the dinner setting of none other than the unfortunate Varus who was overtaken by disaster in AD 9 somewhere to the west of Hildesheim.[112] Stylistic analysis has since dated the manufacture of the various pieces to range from the last century before our era to the reign of the emperor Nero, 54–68 AD.[113] That not all pieces of this dinner service were buried on this site can be deduced from missing pieces of some matched sets. The fact that the total weight of a given setting was engraved on the underside of the plates and other articles helped to determine how many pieces were not buried here. Three large silver mixing vessels, a situla, a crater and a cantharus, held all the smaller pieces. Together they present a cross-section of the inventory of different forms animated by such ornamental motifs as vines and garlands of fruit, flowers and ivy leaves, masks of Dionysus, satyrs, maenads, Sileni, Pan and theatrical masks, drinking horns, musical instruments as well as animals and such marine creatures as sea-snails, shells, mussels and crayfish. Most of this ornamental detail is worked in relief.

The pieces can de divided into three basic groups: display pieces, drinking, pouring and mixing vessels, and eating and serving dishes. Of the display pieces, designed to demonstrate the wealth which the host had at his disposal, the most spectacular is the principal piece of the find, a bowl containing a large relief emblem of the goddess Athena (Plate 6a). Seated on an outcrop of rock, she leans on her shield. The silver parts of the relief, the arms, neck and face of Athena, as well as the background contrast with the gilt of the garment, the helmet, the shield and the rock. The ornament inside the bowl, a luxurious growth of leaves and palmettes also plays with those two colors. The casting of the complex Athena emblem speaks even more highly of early Roman skills in the craft than did such bronze figurines as the 'Dancing Lar' discussed before. For gilding, the artist had command of two methods: he could cut gold foil to shape and glue it to the silver surfaces with some suitable adhesive, or he could combine gold and mercury into a mixture, paint it onto the silver and by heating the object cause the mercury to evaporate leaving the gilt surface. To achieve an effective contrast, gilding was seldom used to cover the entire surface. Details of figure or ornament were highlighted by the incision of deep lines which were then filled with *niello*, a powder compound of silver sulphide which hardens upon heating and which can then be polished to a shiny black finish.[114] Several of the drinking vessels of this hoard had been embellished in this manner.

Some pieces are held to be examples of work done in the workshops of Gaul. What singles out these pieces is a technique which created the outline of figures and of ornaments by means of punches. Three such pieces are flat rectangular plates bearing punched representations of floating ducks. The largest Gallic piece is a tall silver vessel (Plate 6b), probably the remains of a jug to be completed with shoulder and pouring spout into the form of an amphora. In addition to lush vegetation, the 'vase' is circled by a relief showing the combat between a lion and a bull.

These examples, though they are not at all typical of the other pieces, must suffice to represent other and later evidence of the art of the silversmith. Roman silverware was characterized by a remarkable similarity throughout the extent and duration of the Empire. Hardly any of the early ornamental styles fade in popularity.[115] Of the Hildesheim treasure all pieces show traces of wear, many show alterations and repair. Of the four emblem pieces, three had two or three previous uses before ending up in their final settings. Of three elongated plates, one appears to be a replacement made in the provinces. On other pieces holes have been repaired, dents beaten out and all

show evidence of frequent polishing. Style and quality suggest most of these pieces to be the products of the finest studios in Rome and in the Campagna.[116] Some seven pieces came from Gaul. Dinner sets of four reflect Greco-Roman eating practices, sets of three or multiples of three, those of Gaul. Repairs and modifications point to the possibility of itinerant silversmiths moving about freely. The copper and bronze hoards of earlier periods are often accepted to have been the inventory of traders plying their wares among the natives.[117] The same explanation may apply here. Having carefully stored away his possessions, the owner was later prevented from retrieving them. Needless to say, this aspect of the silversmith's art with its classical motifs and mythological allusions came north as imports and exerted only the faintest of influences on the native metal workers beyond the *limes*. The entire complex of Mediterranean forms was too alien to the northern sense of form (Fig. 147). Only where the metalworker made available such portable objects as ornamentation for belts, weapons and especially fibulae for garments did the Roman and Germanic realms demonstrate a ready continuity. From the Romans they will learn fire gilding, the luting of granulation and of filigree onto surfaces, the encrustation of gems and the embellishment of metallic surfaces with colorful glass enamel. That is not to say that Roman silverware could not be appreciated by the tribal chiefs of the interior. The instability of the population may account for the fact that no other similar treasures of this period or even numerous pieces of any consequence have been located in the Germanic interior of central Europe. To the west and south of the *limes* finds of Roman silverware are not unusual (Plate 6c).[118]

Glass is the last major industry to be dealt with here. While pottery was sufficient to meet the daily needs of most segments of the population, glass was in demand to

147 Silver treasure found in the earthwall of the former Celtic oppidum at Manching, probably from the middle of the third century AD. It may have been the temple silver of a nearby sanctuary hidden during a raid. (Prähistorische Staatssammlung, Munich)

148 Roman glass of the first three centuries AD. (Sammlung Nassauischer Altertümer, Wiesbaden)

satisfy the needs of luxury. Initially glass was ground from a block, or cast in closed molds, applied to a pre-formed breakable core or by arranging glass rods around such a core.[119] This method was inefficient and uneconomic so that the invention of the glassblower's pipe in Syria at the beginning of our era must have been a welcome event. Only now, as the glass industry was completely revolutionized could glass become more readily available for the average household. Glass now had economic significance. Not only did glassblowing allow for an increase in quantity and variation but it soon displaced the other methods of making glass.[120] In the north before AD 150 glass generally was imported from Italy and southern Gaul; thereafter, production centers sprang up wherever the necessary raw materials were available. Though it varied with the characteristics of the raw materials, the glass was generally 'dirty' (Fig. 148). A bluish-green glass was usual for domestic use.

In the north the *Colonia Claudia Ara Agripponensium* was destined to become a unique center of manufacture, especially of luxury glass (Fig. 149). While other centers could only produce plain glassware, just west of *Agrippina* great quantities of such pure diluvial quarzite sands were available[121] that the Romans were already making use of the site before AD 50 and factories arose there much earlier than in other northern provinces.[122] Another factor affecting the location of glassworks was the supply of fuels, of wood at first and then of coal. In the second century it was discovered that through the use of manganese the blue-green glass could be decolored, making possible a clear crystal. Very up-to-date with the newest techniques, the Rhineland and especially Cologne began to make this colorless glass.[123] It was to continue to do so until the middle of the fourth century. At first the glassworks imitated the most common Italian forms such as ribbed bowls, oil flasks, embalming and bath oil bottles

133

149 Bluish-green glass with
chainlike handle, third
century AD.
(Mittelrheinisches
Landesmuseum, Mainz)

and perfume vials, some with bronze chains for hanging on one's arm or to fasten
stoppers or corks. Among the earliest local products were funnels, siphons, ink-wells
and other toilet articles, mainly of that bluish-green glass.[124] It was the iron content
present in all sand and the absence of other minerals which produced the bluish-
green glass (Plate 7a). If such mineral coloring agents as metal oxides were added
then the glassmakers had a remarkable range of colors at their disposal. The addition
of copper made for dark blue (Plate 7b) and dark green, but also for ruby or opaque
red glass, depending on furnace conditions. Manganese helped make yellowish or
purple glass, cobalt a rich deep blue, antimony an opaque yellow, while iron produced a pale blue or bottle green glass, but also amber or black glass.[125] The de-
coloring processes made glass available for lenses, window panes and mirrors 1mm
thick, with a quicksilver backing.

Within a hundred years Rhenish glassware challenged Mediterranean work as new
and independent forms were developed and exported as far as Egypt.[126] Decorative
forms such as square or folded vessels were produced from molds. Shoulders, necks,
rims and handles would be hand-made, sometimes flattened or from drawn glass
arranged in wavy line designs, more decorative than functional.

Glass production at *Agrippina* represents the peak of the art in the Empire during
the early fourth century. One particular ornamental detail which enjoyed special

popularity among the glassmakers and their clients in Cologne is the so-called 'Schlangenfaden', snake trail (Plate 7c).[127] A development by second century Syrian craftsmen, the technique probably was brought to Cologne by eastern glassmakers.[128] The resultant snake trailed glass had either white or colored glass flux applied to glass vessels in a cursive, 'signature' fashion. With great skill drawn trails of opaque glass, usually white or blue but also reddish-brown and yellow, were bent to the desired shape over a flame or laid out into the desired shape on a heated sheet[129] of metal and then applied to the heated glass. Vessels, especially flasks, of great splendor were produced at Cologne in order to astonish the guests and to impress them with the wealth of their host (Plate 7d). A unique example of the glassmaker's art is a pair of oil flasks, part of a funerary inventory, worked in the form of glass slippers (Plate 8a). Hollow, of almost clear, colorless glass decorated with white and blue serpentines, these 'shoes' could be slipped on. Of course, the glass is too fragile. Two questions arise: how were these slippers made and, aside from their obvious role as flasks containing some precious liquid, what symbolic significance did these slippers have in the funerary inventory?

Other types of decoration took the form of marvering, an old Egyptian technique whereby glass trails of contrasting colors, laid out in intricate designs, were rolled flush with the surface of the heated vessel.[130] One technique saw drops of colored glass dripped onto a soft glass surface to produce fanciful combinations of extraordinary effect. Another technique fused sections of variously colored glass mosaic in the millefiori or thousand flowers design (Plate 8b).

The most spectacular demonstrations of the glassmaker's art are the so-called 'cage cups' (Plate 8c), luxury articles of the first order. Of these *diatreta* glasses only about eighteen have been found.[131] The word *diatarii* derives from the Greek meaning pierced ware.[132] This term refers to the ornamentation of a blown blank cup by means of a technique which represents the ultimate development of Roman glass cutting techniques. With water-driven grinding wheels the *diatretarius* carved, ground, and undercut a lace-like screen of interlocking designs into the mold to appear apart from the cup as though suggesting the dematerialization of the glass. Above the glass screen the cups usually bear a Greek inscription, reminding the owner of the pleasures of drink. Usually made from colorless, almost perfectly clear glass, very expensive in itself, the blown form was under high tension so that while grinding out the fragile screen, losses through breakage were frequent. Made on commission, the manufacturers were protected legally against any damage of their work in progress unless such damage resulted from their own carelessness.[133] These cage cups were considered to be such great treasures that the *diatretarii* of the late Empire were exempt from taxation. The finished object itself suggests that these were not for daily use but commissioned for special occasions, perhaps intended to become part of the grave inventory of a wealthy Roman.

With infinite patience and amazing skill a *diatretarius* of Cologne produced an extraordinary varicolored cage cup. Working with a blown glass which had been dipped into green, yellow and red liquid glass, the *diatretarius* had ground out and undercut the glass screen and the stems which attached the perforated glass cage to the cup, the yellow collar and the red inscription. In Greek, it invites its owner to drink, that he might always live well.[134] The delicate workmanship of this expensive piece will have prevented its frequent use. It was found in a coffin. Whether it was intended primarily for funerary use is difficult to say. This would imply that it was

150 Roman traveling coach. Relief from *Virunum*, now part of a church wall at Maria Saal, north of Klagenfurt, Austria.

not intended to have been used as a drinking cup during some earthly revelry, but rather to play a role in the funerary ritual, carrying a wish into the beyond.

A more comprehensive account of the inventory of the glassmakers of Cologne during the early fourth century would include descriptions and illustrations of decorated glass drinking horns, tall beakers decorated with colored snake trails and attached trellises of intertwining drawn glass trails and pincer-shaped sea shells, tall bulbous flasks, jugs and bowls ornamented with snake trail patterns as well as vessels of humorous and fanciful shape, the use of which may have been representational rather than functional.[135] It is evident even from these few examples that there was nothing 'provincial' about the glass industry in this northern part of the Empire. The reputation of *Agrippina* as a glassmaking center was such that it attracted the best craftsmen of the Empire to swell the ranks of its resident artists. Its location on a natural trade route gave its glassware, probably also its ground gems and other related enterprises, convenient access to markets in the entire north-west of the Empire. While the first century witnessed perhaps the most inventive phase of the industry, it was during the first half of the fourth century that the glassmakers of the Lower Rhine reached their artistic peak. It is tempting to see in the ornamentations residual aspects of a Celtic sense of style. However, the rich ornamentation is also a characteristic found in Roman art at the time of the late Empire. No doubt the peak of activity reflects the importance which the region acquired under the emperors Constantius and Constantine when, for a short time, the center of power and culture gravitated towards *Treveris* and the north-west. The political relocation to the east during the later fourth century marked the decline of the arts in this region. However, the tradition lived on in the glassmakers' shops of the Franks who combined the old techniques with new ideas.[136]

This brief discussion of the arts and crafts in the Roman provinces of central Europe has not attempted to be all-inclusive. Some significant areas of artistic activity have had to be omitted, such as the cutting of gems and cameos, enameling, the making of jewellery, and the application of wall and ceiling mosaics. A discussion of sculpture in relief and in the round was restricted to the funerary monuments (Fig. 150) while other sculpture was used to illustrate the (religious) syncretism in the northern Roman provinces. The list of omissions is extensive; nevertheless, it is apparent that the arrival of the Romans brought to central Europe the interest in the artistic representation of human activities. Although the Hallstatt and La Tène periods had known anthropomorphic shapes, these generally were used in a fragmented and abstracted fashion.

The Romans showed the northerners that man and his activities were fit subjects for artistic representation. To the natives, used to their curvilinear abstractions, this must have been quite alien at first, unaccustomed as they were to a style which relied so heavily on physical realism. With the establishment of the imperial court at *Treveris* late antique conceptions were introduced to the area. Now representational art was called upon to portray sparkling magnificence, social rank and the abstract notions of the *dominus*, the Divine Emperor. Under Constantine especially, splendid garments were intended to emphasize the radiance of the divine essence incorporated in the highest personage in the Empire, the Emperor by Divine Grace. It was the function of art to express this content symbolically. Thus, the imperial personage was the tallest, the most magnificent, and only members of the imperial family could be shown frontally. All lesser individuals were smaller, less splendid and shown in profile. It will be recalled that the portraits of the ceiling and wall paintings from the imperial residence in *Treveris* hinted subtly at this differentiation. The Christian Church became the heir of this imperial tradition.

Apparently diametrically opposed to one another, the northern curvilinear intertwines and the late Mediterranean representational style actually share an abstract idealism. While the Celtic interlace was to enjoy a brief revival in pre-Carolingian times, ultimately the representational style would assert itself. By means of human and animal forms as well as through the use of architectural elements, art was to orient itself in the physical world. Through stylization it would acquire an abstract and universally valid quality. The artists of Carolingian and early Romanesque times were to find their own points of departure in late Roman art as they too used external appearance as a means of seeking the transcendental ideas behind the physical appearance. Already in late Roman Art a naturalistic representation was no longer the artist's aim but only his starting point. To hint at the idea, the body must be abstracted and transposed from a real into an ideal space. At *Treveris* the radiances which enveloped the heads of the imperial family demonstrated an early approach to the representation of an other-worldly majesty, the *majestas* of Early Christian Art.

4. Provincial Society in Crisis and Transition

At various points in our discussion of the arts it was clear that great individual wealth paid for the extravagant tastes of the Roman citizens of the northern provinces. In addition to some manufacturing and only a little trade, agriculture provided the wealth and main support of the economic base.[1] Owing to a shortage of written sources, archaeology has had to supply much of the evidence about agriculture. With the help of aerial photography ever more Roman farms, *villae rusticae*, are being catalogued, as their outlines are contrasted under the fields. Those located in forested areas remain yet to be discovered.[2]

To supply the needs of the army as well as of the civil and military administrations, in addition to the growing urban populations, a coordinated agricultural system would have been necessary within a very short time to produce a food supply and distribute it effectively. Large areas of agricultural land which originally belonged to the natives were expropriated and assigned to the legions for their exclusive use. On this *territorium legionis* there could be no private ownership.[3] From *Castra Regina* comes an inscription dated AD 178[4] which indicates that soldiers were allowed to rent some of this land administered by the legion. In some instances the soldiers could rent pasture land, the *prata legionum*, and supplement their income through the sale of the harvested fodder to the legion. Pannonian inscriptions indicate that some soldiers were in charge of the cattle and probably of the legion's meat supply.[5] It is evident that the legions made sure that their system of supplies was well secured.[6] Later, when conditions began to deteriorate, Rome made land grants by taking land away from that administered by the legions. Under Septimius Severus these *territoria* were no longer able to guarantee the provisioning of the army.[7]

Thanks to their proximity to Gaul as well as to the large military force stationed along the Rhine, the Rhenish lands soon enjoyed a considerable level of prosperity. By contrast *Raetia* developed more slowly.[8] For the greater part *Noricum* did not, and still does not, offer good agricultural conditions, for climatic as well as for geographical reasons. Throughout the Roman period no great advances could be made there since even the plow could not be used to maximum effectiveness.[9] Then, as now, a pastoral economy with some Alpine farming had to support the population. To varying degrees, but certainly for all the northern provinces, agriculture used most of the available labor.

Generally the land was divided into centuries, 2400 *pedes*,[2] i.e. 710m,[2] nearly 50 hectares subdivided for taxation purposes into parcels of 80 × 40m or what a team of oxen could plow in a day.[10] With time, changing fortunes and the development of large estates, the lines separating such parcels were wiped out. Before these mergers took place surveyors appear to have assessed the land so that each villa was located on 1km² of land.[11] The vastness of the unoccupied lands and the sparsity of villages and towns necessitated the establishment of scattered estates in isolated locations. Such an estate was a *villa rustica*.[12] Within a short time it had to be more than self-sufficient, produce a surplus, maintain maximum independence and show a profit.[13] By rationalization and the maximum use of its human, animal and material resources it could show optimal effectiveness. Utilizing southern experience, the Romans found a three-part structural design to be the most efficient as the building was arranged for occupation, storage and for production.[14] An ideal location would provide access to various soils and moisture levels, near flowing water.[15] Southern exposures swept by refreshing winds were preferred. Access to lines of communication was mandatory to facilitate the distribution of the produce. Approach times for bringing goods to markets would have to be reasonable.[16] Since the army did not build roads everywhere, the landowners had a vested interest in the development and maintenance of roads.

The most common style in *Raetia* was the portico-villa[17] which contained a two-storied central hall, 18 × 9m on the average, in time covered with a large glass skylight. The other rooms were grouped around this central hall.[18] The bath and at least one other room were heated by the hypocaust method.[19] This main part had a portico front, the portico roof being supported by columns *c*. 5m high. In the west, wings projecting like bastions from the portico front are a distinguishing characteristic.[20] Depending on its owner's wealth the basic form of the villa could assume palatial dimensions, decorated with mosaic, wall and ceiling paintings and the many other objects of trade. Especially along the rivers Saar and Moselle and in Rhenish-Hesse, far from any immediate danger, the villas assumed pretentious proportions, such as the villa at Otrang, some 32km north of Trier, which has no fewer than sixty-six rooms, galleries, terraces and other porticoed open–air living areas with wide views of the countryside. Across the Rhine, closer to the *limes*, the types were more uniform and less extravagant in variation, size, design and commodities.[21]

Not all villas were luxury villas. For instance, the farm houses of the small farmer, the *colonus*, or of the veteran whose land belonged to the emperor or to some other private individual were of more modest proportions, between 14 × 10m and 34 × 23m in size and a usual frontage of only 24–28m. Most frequent were the medium-sized estates, two-storied buildings ranging in size from 36 × 28m to 46 × 42m.[22] Buildings with 59m fronts also occur. These villas had up to thirty rooms grouped around the great hall. Such an increase in the living space, the *pars urbana*, was accompanied by a corresponding decrease in the production and storage parts, the *pars rustica*, of the building. Some of these sections were separated from the main building and were hidden behind walls, hedges and fences. The accent in these villas was on living comfort. Rooms were finished with floor mosaics, marble facings, murals on polished plaster, while some rooms were made more comfortable with a hypocaust system. Each had a carefully laid out cellar and almost all of these villas were equipped with a heated bath.[23] On both sides of the Rhine this type of villa was represented widely. The various units were weather-proofed and usually painted brown. A development of this was the *villa urbana*, the residential villa of the independent large estate, for here only the living quarters were housed in the villa, while all other functions were

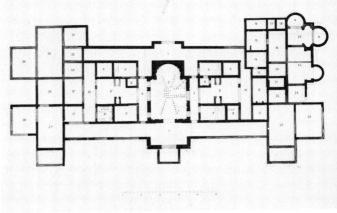

151 Possible appearance of the villa at Konz, near Trier. This villa may have been an imperial summer residence. (Rheinisches Landesmuseum, Trier)

152 Floorplan of the villa at Konz. (Rheinisches Landesmuseum, Trier)

located in the *pars rustica* and the *pars fructuaria*, the sheds and barns. This represents a conclusion to the development started on the medium-sized estates.[24] The residential quarters of the *villa urbana* had a representational function: to display the wealth and status of its owner.[25] These 'stately homes', palatial in appearance, grandiose in layout (Fig. 151), elegant in their tasteful decor, surrounded by gardens with fountains, ponds and parks with columns, statues and sanctuaries, offered their occupants a clear view of the surrounding landscape with its winding rivers and streams, vine covered hillsides, rolling fields and dark green forests. These were the country estates of the wealthy and powerful, the merchants, landowners and administrators of the cultural, mercantile and administrative centers of the provinces. The Alpine lakes of *Germania superior*, *Raetia* or *Noricum*,[26] and the valley of the Moselle and its tributaries offered conditions which allowed the construction of villas in the Italian manner, especially during the late third and most of the fourth century when the emperor's residence was located at *Treveris* and the Court and its officials brought imperial expectations into an already prosperous area (Fig. 152). Such a villa had up to twenty supplementary buildings located over an area of 450 × 700m, all enclosed by a stone wall.[27] The longest perimeter enclosed an enormous estate with a stone wall *c.* 70km in length. These villas with their additional buildings assumed village proportions. Atrium-houses were not usual north of the Alps,[28] since climatic conditions would have discouraged the use of a building plan that left the center of the house open to the sky. The portico plan favored H-shaped houses. However, from northern *Raetia*, at Westerhofen near Ingolstadt, comes evidence of a luxurious country-house built in peristyle fashion, with covered colonnaded sections opening onto an open interior area. The *pars rustica* contained the quarters for servants and field hands, which may have been slaves, the barns and granaries, the stables and workshops and an assortment of other structures. The villa had to be self-sufficient in its food supply but also in its supply of tools, everyday pottery, wooden utensils, and the like.[29] The larger estates will have produced articles for trade as well.

Since the native population did most of the work, one can assume that no fundamental changes in working the land or in the laying out of the fields will have been introduced, except that now sloping areas were terraced.[30] Since the Italian plow was not suited for the northern soils, the Belgian and especially the Raetian two-wheeled plow continued to be used. With it the earth could be turned to greater depth. The land was fertilized with dung and such chemicals as lime.[31] No doubt the rotation of crops was practiced too. On the large western estates harvesting machines were used[32] (see Fig. 111). The grain was threshed through trampling by animals, as documented on an African mosaic,[33] with flails or with sleds on which the runners had been studded with stones. Subsequently the grain and chaff were separated by winnowing, pitching the threshed grain into a strong wind.[34] The archaeological evidence suggests that this was done with great care since grain found was very clean. The grain types cultivated were wheat, such as spelt, emmer and Einkorn, barley but only a little rye.[35] As its dark flour was deemed inferior, rye was held to be only a little better than a weed and not up to standard for human consumption. Oats were grown for fodder. The deliberate control of weeds raised the quality of the crops to high levels. The Romans also practiced the cultivation of such legumes as beans, peas and lentils, of the poppy and of linseed for oil, and of flax and hemp for textile fibers.[36]

Depending on the possibilities offered by the terrain, the raising of livestock may have offered a better return than agriculture. Thus, cattle ranching was practiced in the Main-Taunus and the Rhenish-Hesse and Eifel regions.[37] The extensive beech-oak forests made the raising of pigs a profitable proposition. Cattle were raised for their meat value. Steers and oxen predominated, as steers carried more meat while oxen could perform heavy tasks. Bullocks also had sacrificial value. That cattle were butchered at under three years of age is further evidence that cows were not kept for the sake of giving milk, which in turn accounts for some of the prices in the dairy industry: 24–36 denarii for 1kg of cheese. The Romans introduced longhorn cattle to the north. By crossbreeding they were able to improve the local breeds which now had a shoulder height of 115–140cm.[38] Pigs were grain fattened and butchered once they were a year old. A few sheep and goats were kept to meet the need for wool. Horses bred in *Noricum* and in the Eifel were in particular demand because of their speed. Stud-farms and horse ranches were specialized undertakings necessary in order to meet the demands for remounts of the cavalry and of the circus. Through inter-breeding larger horses were raised. The horse may not have been used in agriculture. By importing peacocks, doves and chickens of the Leghorn type, the Romans complemented the native stocks of chickens, geese, ducks and pigeons. Geese may have been kept only for their feathers. Game was only a very subordinate source of food. From the northern Eifel region comes evidence that the income earned from agriculture was augmented by surface mining, smelting and the making of iron and especially of lead.[39] On the poor soils of that region a mixed economy was necessary. Farther south, the valleys between the Rhine and Moselle offered favorable conditions for the growing of vines. Since the first century AD modest quantities of wine had been produced there.[40] During his short reign from AD 276 to 282 the emperor Probus broke the Italian wine monopoly.[41] This change in policy allowed the northern vineyards to increase their production significantly, thereby contributing greatly to the new prosperity of Trier and the valleys drained by the Moselle and its tributaries.

To the gardens and orchards of the north the Romans brought both enrichment and improvement. Such root vegetables as carrots, beets, celery and radishes, as well as asparagus, lettuce and cucumbers came north with the Romans, as did caraway, parsley, anise, onions, mustard types and coriander. Blackberries, raspberries and strawberries were known locally. The Romans introduced grafting techniques to improve native strains of apples for instance. They also brought pears and plums, sour cherries, apricots and peaches.[42]

The similarity between Germanic designations and the original Latin names indicates quite clearly which of the now common northern fruits and vegetables were introduced by the Romans. No student of the history of Germanic languages can escape the lists of Germanic words borrowed from Latin which deal with such contact areas between natives and Romans as the legal and political spheres, trade and transport, horti- and viticulture and the stone building trades. In all an estimated 550 words entered the Germanic vocabulary at that time, as Germanic and Latin speaking populations came to live side by side, especially during the transition period when Germanic farmers set up their farms near the villas. These farmers could not help but learn new terminologies for the new things they encountered among their established neighbors as all immigrants learn from the resident populations.

The principal urban centers of the northern provinces came into being for various reasons and under diverse conditions. The tribal center of the Treveri had developed into a prospering commercial crossroads before Claudius recognized its merits and raised it to the status of a *colonia* as the *Colonia Augusta Treverorum*.[43] The *Oppidum Ubiorum* was singled out early when the altar to *Augustus et Roma* was established there with the intention that the *Ara Ubiorum* should become the religious focal center of the future province of *Germania*, its altar tended by tribal chiefs, thereby tying the northern tribes to Rome. The *Ara Ubiorum* was a thriving center when Claudius recognized it for the significant cultural and commercial center it had become and named it *Colonia Claudia Ara Agrippinensium*. In neither instance had a military installation preceded the civilian center, although a unit of Spanish cavalry had been posted at *Treverorum*.[44] By contrast *Vetera*, *Bonna*, *Mogontiacum* and *Argentorate* were military fortifications only. The civilian settlements developed at some distance from them, which makes it possible to excavate these fortifications fifteenhundred years later, since the towns have continued to exist on the civilian sites to the present day[45]. Following the conquest of *Raetia* in 15 BC, the *castrum* of the legion at Oberhausen was short-lived.[46] The legion was withdrawn to *Vindonissa* when the Roman administration chose to concentrate its efforts on those parts of the new territory located between the rivers Lech and Rhine.[47] Only towards the end of the reign of Tiberius did *Raetia* experience a change in government policy and receive its own administrative center in what was to become *Augusta Vindelicum*, the northern terminal of the *via Claudia Augusta* among the Celtic Vindelici destined to become an important commercial crossroads.[48] To the east in *Noricum*, the Celtic center on the Magdalensberg was abandoned in favor of the unfortified city of *Virunum*,[49] which was founded expressly as the administrative capital while it continued its earlier function as commercial fulcrum. To the north-east, on the Danube, Tiberius founded *Carnuntum*,[50] a military base and jumping off point for his invasion of Bohemia. The foundations of the Julio-Claudians reflect their aggressive policy. *Vetera*, *Bonna*, *Mogontiacum* and *Carnuntum* were founded by Drusus and Tiberius as strategic military bases from which to launch campaigns of conquest into the interior of central Europe.[51]

During the Batavian Revolt *Vetera I* was destroyed. Under the Flavians *Vetera II* was built nearby,[52] in the vicinity of a local tribal settlement. In direct response to the logistic difficulties experienced during the Batavian Revolt the Romans left the frontier of the upper Rhine in favor of a defensive system further to the east. Its military purpose removed, *Argentorate* was dismantled as a military base. Following

153 Porta Nigra, Roman gate of the late second or early third century, at Trier.

154 Porta Nigra, city view.

the Augustan example, the *Arae Flaviae* were set up—modern Rottweil—across the valley from the military base, in an unsuccessful attempt at providing a religious focus by means of which the native tribes could be tied to Rome in a cultic exercise. That the area would also be a new recruitment area for the army goes without saying. In *Noricum* the Flavians founded *Flavia Solva*. Neither a border city nor a garrison, this unfortified city had neither strategic nor economic significance. It was founded solely as an administrative center and like *Virunum* drew on the population of neighboring Celtic settlements. That this Roman logic did not convince the natives is indicated by the withdrawal of these populations into the mountains when these centers collapsed at the end of the Roman period,[53] giving modern archaeologists unhindered access to these Roman cities. It has proved a boon that the military sites were not always identical with the civilian settlements.

Besides these military bases, established in order to provide offense, administrative and religious centers, there was a fourth type of settlement, the veteran colony. Throughout the Empire these were founded in considerable number. They served a variety of purposes: to reward loyal troops upon their retirement from active service while at the same time shoring up the defensive capabilities of a given military district. The populations of such a *colonia* would reflect the population spectrum of the Empire with Latin as their language of communication.[54] As minority groups in a strange land their individual loyalties would lie with Rome. For such reasons Trajan founded the *Colonia Ulpia Traiana* between AD 98 and 117 just north-west of *Vetera II*, probably incorporating the tribal settlement nearby, near modern Xanten.[55] It is assumed that under Trajan the number of legions in each provincial army corresponded to that of the colonies in the province and since he fixed the number of legions in each province, it follows that he created the new colony probably as a future recruitment area for the army stationed in the vicinity.[56] In every instance extensive grants of agricultural land accompanied the foundation of these communities since commerce and industry were an inadequate economic base.[57]

During the second century the migratory pressure from beyond the northern frontier necessitated defensive measures. In this context *Castra Regina*, modern Regensburg, was built by the *legio III Italica concors* c. AD 179 in the time of Marcus Aurelius to replace an inadequate cohort *castellum*.[58] By then conditions were such that unfortified *Augusta Treverorum*, far to the west, had to be surrounded by a wall of which the *Porta Nigra* (Figs. 153, 154) has remained an impressive reminder.[59] Lastly, the instability of the later Empire has left in imperial *Treveris* important monuments from a century when off and on *Treveris* was the nerve center of the Western Empire, for a time even the imperial capital.

Owing to the organizational principles with which Rome approached all questions of city planning, it follows that all Roman foundations would reflect a basic similarity of layout as a 'pre-fabricated' approach to the major public buildings was combined with a rectangular grid-pattern of intersecting streets.[60] The apparent similarity in layout with the *castra* and *castella* derives from the fact that the military fortifications are in themselves modeled in their organizational efficiency on Hellenistic urban centers.[61] On the other hand, as the various cities were founded in response to different needs, it follows that differences in administrative staffing can be expected. Until the third century provincial communities were subject to different legal considerations as *vici*, villages, as *municipia* or as *coloniae*, the two different types of Roman cities.[62] These latter designations were relatively infrequent; thus, in all of *Germania superior* only *Arae Flaviae* enjoyed the designation *municipium*. In *Raetia* only *Augusta Vindelicum* received the privilege during the second century.[63] *Carnuntum* was given the status of a *municipium* under Hadrian at a time when frontier towns gained in importance,[64] a reflection of military policy rather than of local conditions.[65] That *Mogontiacum* did not develop an independent civilian town is all the more curious as it was the administrative center of *Germania superior*.[66]

As we have seen above, the towns were not limited to the settlement itself but included the agricultural hinterland as well. The wealthy were able to extend the town's influence over this by virtue of their ownership of municipal real estate and of agricultural estates and because the town's *territorium*, usually hundreds of square kilometers, formed part of the administrative unit. It is on this *territorium* that the smaller *vici* were located.[67] It follows that these *vici* stood in a dependent relationship to the larger settlements, the *canabae*, located near the military fortifications and under the authority of the military commanders. These *canabae* were located on the *territorium legionis*, mentioned above.[68] Inhabited by craftsmen and traders who were citizens of other settlements, their legal status differed from that of the purely civilian settlements in that the settlers had no claim on the legion's land and in that the *canabae* were not properly autonomous despite their pseudo-self-governing type of constitution.[69] Among the settlers were the soldiers' families, not recognized by Rome, who had to be members of another community. A *canabae* could not be the place of origin of a Roman citizen. Under Septimius Severus these differentiations began to disappear. During the early third century when Caracalla granted citizenship to the inhabitants of the Empire he also appears to have promoted very many settlements to the rank of *municipium*.[70] The ability to form a town council appears to have been the only criterion. The rank of *colonia* had to be granted. Originally, it was a title that could be claimed only by those settlements whose inhabitants had been Roman citizens and who had left Rome to found a colony. Later, provincial towns had to apply for the rank. With the rank there usually came the grant of the *ius Italicum*.[71] To obtain the privilege the wealthy citizens contributed generously to beautifying their community and towns vied with one another to be recognized as the more worthy.[72] The promotion to *colonia* will have been motivated by power, politics, loyalty to the imperial house of the day and political pay-off. However, to counteract the economic disadvantages, the settlers of the *canabae* tried to secure land in the *territoria* of the civilian settlements and their citizenship. The trend of incorporating *canabae* into the *municipium* or *colonia* in the vicinity became established in order that they might participate in the prosperity and so as to equate the various administrative authorities. In the end all autonomous communities were embraced under the term *civitas*, which led to the abolition of the more cumbersome names as *Colonia Augusta Treverorum* in favor of *Treveris*.[73]

Some of the usual features to be found in these urban centers were the street-grid divided into four more or less equal quarters, each subdivided into *insulae*, the city blocks, which in due course came to be made up of crowded multiple dwellings and rows of houses or private atrium and/or peristyle houses of the wealthy and the shops, stores and warehouses. The Capitol with its official temples and the Forum, as well as assembly halls, council chambers and courtrooms, were located at the center of these cities. In time each city came to have baths, a theater, perhaps even an amphitheater, a circus and an assortment of temples and sanctuaries of the official, native and imported cults, the meeting places of the *collegia*—professional associations and craft guilds. Workshops and factories necessitating the use of fire such as forges, pottery kilns and glassblowers' furnaces had to be located outside of the city walls to reduce the danger of fire to a minimum[74] since initially probably only the public buildings and the houses of the wealthy were built of stone. The cemeteries with their gravestones and monuments lined the main connecting roads, from *Agrippina* to *Bonna*, for instance. Within a short time wooden buildings were replaced by buildings of stone although the half-timbered style will have persisted with private buildings as it still does. That stone architecture had a propagandistic value for the natives not skilled in building with stone was not lost on the Romans. The durable properties of stone served as a ready symbol of Roman power. Emulations of Mediterranean city-scapes, the cities also demonstrated the 'otherness' of Roman civilization. There are indications that Roman Cologne very deliberately presented a forbidding skyline to those looking at it from across the Rhine. In time this skyline was to become a challenge to the Franks beyond the Rhine. In December of AD 355 they succumbed to the temptation and took Cologne, burning down large sections of it.

It has been estimated that the initial administration of *Raetia* from *Augusta Vindelicum* required a staff of about a thousand individuals. Of these about five hundred, the equivalent of a mounted cohort, half cavalry half infantry, provided the personal guard of the governor. The remaining five hundred were the officials who dealt with the internal administration and justice, the financial administration and taxation, secretaries and scribes, court officials, interpreters, such cultic personalities as augurs and sacrificial priests, a corps of police and an extensive range of staff officers of varying rank.[75] To facilitate the art of society and conversation, an equal number of ladies and women-in-waiting would complete the social spectrum, assisted by cooks and kitchen help, servers and diverse entertainers—a miniature court.[76] This admin-

155 Couple, wearing Celtic style of dress. Relief on a gravestone. (Historisches Museum der Pfalz, Speyer)

istration would need to rely on the native social structure of the region, quickly intermingled with the new social realities introduced by the Romans. The local landowning nobility, combined with the foreign merchants, formed the aristocracy while the lower levels consisted of the native peasantry (Fig. 155), craftsmen, traders and slaves.[77] As may be expected the town helped change this pattern as the new prosperity made for cultural assimilation and upwards social mobility.[78] The new citizenry, an urban bourgeoisie (Fig. 156), profited from state appointments,[79] the

156 Gravestone relief of a Roman couple. (Römermuseum, Augst)

ownership of land and a limited degree of industry and commerce. Over the centuries increasing numbers of the city population were constituted by a swelling urban proletariat, the *plebs*, while on the estates the farm population came to be tied to the land so preventing any flight from it.

The civilian communities depended on a curious financial system geared to ameliorate conditions. The communities disposed of very little independent revenue. In no position to pay salaries to their officials, the towns demanded instead not only civic

147

dedication but generous financial contributions as well to help towards the mainten-ance of such public installations as the official temples, roads, sewers, cisterns, viaducts and the like.[80] The remaining financial support came from provincial and imperial funds.[81] It follows that once elected to office, these officials had to have a way of generating an adequate income to recover expenses, especially since they had secured their election to office by means of lavish displays of generosity—costly feasts, festivals and games.[82] Only the most wealthy could aspire to civic office. Having served for one year these officials became members of the municipal council for life.[83]

There was of course a difference between towns. As at other times the granting of a town charter is frequently a challenge rather than a recognition of fact. Many did not live up to the expectations, especially where the requirements for urban life could not be met. This deficiency was most pronounced in centers where the upper social levels owed their social position and ensuing wealth not to their role in the regional economy, agricultural or otherwise, but to their privileges as administrative officials of the Empire. Subject to the uncertainties of the office, their contribution to com-munal life would constitute an element of social and political instability in the com-munity as they were dismissed or as they and their wealth were transferred by the central authority much to the detriment of the local economic and political scene.[84] This raises the general question of the actual participation of the local population in the high culture of Roman provincial life.[85] Inscriptions suggest that native partici-pation in this cultural life was more or less marginal, certainly never a penetrating factor.[86] Civic service was a function of position and ensuing wealth. When not related to political appointments, wealth was based on landownership and its pro-duction.[87] Even merchants and industrialists promptly converted their profits into land. It was, of course, fitting that the individual's wealth be displayed in represen-tative townhouses of the atrium and peristyle types with their spectacular mosaics and paintings and the grandiose villas of the estates in the vicinity.[88] Some held property in several parts of the province. The weakness of this system lay in the potential impoverishment of this class through crop failures, the civil wars of the claimants for the imperial throne, foreign invasion and especially excessive taxation by the central authority.[89] By AD 200 these factors were beginning to make themselves felt.[90] Already during the Marcomannic Wars (AD 165–80) and from AD 233 onward during the Alamannic invasions, the destruction of *Noricum* and *Raetia* and then *Germania superior* was widespread as the population fled to the interior, the inhabitants were decimated, agricultural labor became scarce and fields remained uncultivated.[91] While the resulting shortage of food became an immediate problem as supplies from the south were insufficient and intermittent, the long-term lack of income eroded the prosperity of the communities.[92]

Though the Empire initially did have a sound economic basis in agriculture, industry and trade, it became a habit of the imperial treasury to balance its budgets through military expansion, exploitation and the taking of vast booty.[93] Rome's defensive wars and stationary frontier duties accompanied a stagnating economy. Following the Marcomannic Wars, after AD 165, and the first Alamannic incursions of the Rhineland in AD 233, from which the sparse population of *Raetia* and the Rhine–Danube triangle could not recover,[94] a great regression began to set in. Never too rich in any case, the exodus from the farmland began as the old system of cultivation and the quantity of provisioning became unnecessary.[95] Though the area to the right of the Rhine was abandoned after AD 260 there is now evidence that the villa economy actually persisted there until after AD 400.[96] The rural population had never shared equitably in the material advantages, as the ruling orders were oblivious to their concerns. Their disappearance from the land necessitated the development of a process which converted free men into slaves,[97] tied to the land, to maintain production.[98] Frontier guardianship rather than aggressive war did not, however, provide the vast human resources that earlier times had been able to secure when entire tribes passed into slavery. To cope, extensive tracts of agricultural land were turned into pastures while the large estates, the *latifundia*, parceled out pieces of land to tenant farmers. The reduction of land under cultivation, the steady transformation of independent landowners into tenants of absentee landlords on estates held directly by the emperor, by the imperial aristocracy,[99] by an even smaller provincial and municipal nobility, or by various religious establishments contributed extensively to the gradual impoverishment and enslavement of the rural population. In the end the villas were abandoned rather then destroyed, pointing to a gradual desertion of the estates, caused, at least in part, by a lack of demand for their products as the rich life in the cities and towns faded, the troops were relocated, the populations of the villages and towns decreased and the network of roads deteriorated,[100] in short, by the general reduction of the Roman presence. Some farmers of course remained, especially the *coloni* and the small operators whose limited production had made them less vulnerable to economic fluctuations as they had never been an essential component of the network of distribution. To them it was no longer necessary nor useful, since there was little trade to stimulate marketing. This in turn induced a decrease in market production, recommending to the small farmer a return to self-sufficient levels of production. The fact that the owning of land was tied directly to the prosperity of the cities meant that this flight from the land had an immediate debilitating effect on the cultural and economic vitality of the cities and towns. Neglect, decay and a decrease of personal commitment was accompanied by an increase of the fiscal demands of the provincial and central authorities while the tax base dwindled. Yet the losses had to be made good. Already during the Severan Dynasty, AD 193–235, complaints arose in the Rhineland[101] and elsewhere that the people were being reduced to desperation by excessive taxation, services and requisitions.[102] Eventually such inflationary practices as the debasing of the coinage ruined the bulk of the middle and upper levels of society while it virtually bankrupted the state.[103]

The civil wars between rival imperial claimants were a great aggravation to the economy. They devastated the land as they criss-crossed the provinces, looting as they went, farmer-soldiers holding towns and their *territoriae* to ransom to raise the funds with which to pay off their supporters, bringing famine and disease in their wake.[104] By AD 260 even Alexandria in Egypt had lost 60 per cent of its former population to hunger and disease.[105] Too poor to raise the armies needed to defend the borders and without the requisite manpower for these armies,[106] after AD 260 the emperors bought the services of entire northern tribes to complement the Roman forces depleted by foreign and civil wars and the recurrent epidemics. Romans knew to buy themselves free from serving with these armies.[107]

In an attempt to stem the disintegrating tendencies and increase efficiency, the central authority resorted to increasing its bureaucracy. This attempt at gaining direct control destroyed local self-government without accomplishing its aim.[108] The rapid turn-over of emperors and the accompanying 'spoils system' which swept everyone from office upon the accession of a new ruler led to ruinous practices on all levels

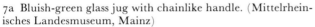

7a Bluish-green glass jug with chainlike handle. (Mittelrhein-isches Landesmuseum, Mainz)

7b Glass amphora, first three centuries AD. (Römisches Museum, Augsburg)

7c 'Snake-trailed' glass, early fourth century AD from Cologne. (Rheinisches Landesmuseum, Bonn)

7d 'Snake-trailed' glass. Ornamental flask from Cologne. (Römisch-Germanisches Museum, Cologne)

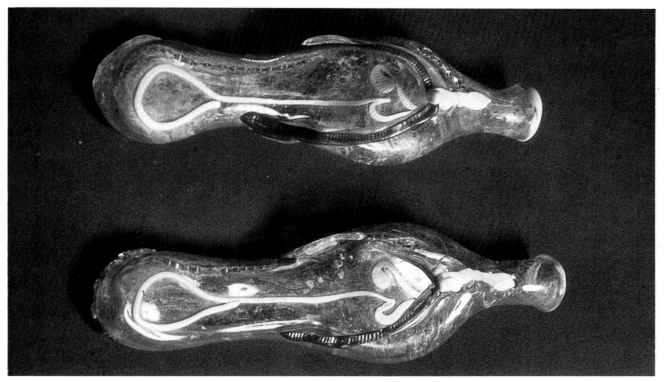

8a Oil flasks in the shape of slippers. Funerary gifts from a woman's grave, AD 259–269. (Römisch-Germanisches Museum, Cologne)

8b Millefiori-glass bowl, from the legion camp at Dangstetten. (Museum für Vor- und Frühgeschichte, Freiburg)

8c 'Cage-cup' from Cologne, a funerary gift. The Greek text wishes that the deceased may live happily always. (Römisch-Germanisches Museum, Cologne)

157 Partly restored Roman tower at the north-west corner of the Roman wall, at Cologne.

as each new official tried to recover his 'election' expenses, knowing his days in office to be numbered. The immense hierarchy of administrative officials, characterized by parasitism, charged with collecting taxes, goods and services, while it imposed the emperor's rule, proved to be less a benefit than a great hindrance.[109] An abrasive aspect of the state, the hierarchy eroded civic liberties as it pauperized the common man, a burden to citizens and farmers, to free-men and slaves alike. Attempts to centralize the government could not be reconciled with the decentralizing trends in the economy and centrifugal tendencies in the social fabric.[110] With the collapse of the supply system the cities became uninhabitable, filthy and perilous deserts, without water supply and sewage disposal as the water conduits caved in and the drainage canals filled with sludge.[111] Without an efficient political organization the cities became a risk to health and life.

The collapse of private enterprise prompted the emperors to establish factories which continued to supply the army with weapons and clothing.[112] A reluctant labor force had to be tied to the jobs in order to maintain the flow of strategic essentials. Such trade and industry as survived in private hands concentrated on luxury items. Long distance trade was discouraged by the fragile system of communications. Life on the roads had become precarious. The countryside swarmed with homeless men, ruined peasants and businessmen, political refugees, victims of the power rivalries, deserters and marauders eking out a hazardous existence in brigandage and revolt.[113] As early as the end of the second century cities far in the interior began to protect themselves with defensive walls (Fig. 157). No doubt to the besieged citizens it was a moot point whether the threat to them came from tax collectors, hordes of brigands, marauding armies or raiding barbarians. By the fourth century districts near *Treveris* which had boasted a thousand settlements during the second and third centuries were reduced to forty.[114] Initially distinct attempts were made to compensate for the losses and rebuild, but the futility of such efforts became apparent to most. After AD 275 the depletion of the Empire's resources could not support the efforts needed to reverse the decline, although emperors of the late fourth century made creditable attempts at shoring up the defenses. Like a nutshell hiding a dried-up kernel, the city walls shielded shriveling populations,[115] insufficient to man the defensive perimeters. Fifty years of private wars waged by the soldier-emperors after AD 235 left an Empire not only too weak to resist invasions from beyond the frontiers but actually extending invitations to foray into a rich and still sparkling realm that was not prepared to take effective countermeasures.[116]

Forced to fight on several fronts at the same time, no single emperor could intervene personally in every crisis. Anyone who tried shortly exhausted both himself and his troops as he marched and countermarched from one part of the Empire to the next, only to be assassinated by his disgruntled subordinates. The short-term political interests of the army were at the expense of the protection of the frontiers of the Empire.[117] As each new emperor first tried to assert and maintain himself, regional needs and dangers slipped to a lesser level of priority. These conditions fostered separatist tendencies. Occasionally emperors tried to deal with the unmanageable size of the Empire by appointing co-emperors. Valerian (AD 253–60) upon being proclaimed emperor, probably in *Raetia*, immediately proclaimed his son Gallienus (AD 253–68) as co-emperor and entrusted him with the defense of the west. While this appointment was a step in the direction of the secession of the Gallic Empire (260–73) under the usurper Postumus,[118] it also brought about the 'Indian Summer' of the Roman Empire in the west, for Gallienus made *Agrippina* his capital, while Postumus located his 'imperial' centers at *Augusta Treverorum* and at *Agrippina*. Largely destroyed by invading Alamanni in AD 275 along with seventy other centers in Gaul,[119] *Augusta Treverorum* became the capital of the western Empire—Spain, Gaul, the two Germanies and later Britain—under Constantius Chlorus. Off and on until AD 390 and the reign of the emperor Valentinian II, *Treveris* was to enjoy the privileged position of imperial capital.

The reigns of Diocletian (AD 284–305) and Constantine (AD 306–37) brought nearly fifty years of uninterrupted stability and peace. However, the political reorganization of the Empire, into two halfs of two parts each, also required a reorganization of the financial structure. For the common man it meant higher taxation to be raised from an economic situation that had not experienced any improvements in the interim. On the contrary, at great cost to the citizen the reforms propped up the Empire once more by regimenting the population, legislating serfdom, tying craftsmen to their occupations for generations[120] and by introducing an outright absolutism which made permanent legislation of all previous temporary emergency measures.

Sponsored by a line of third and fourth century emperors with local interests, sheltered militarily and geographically and enjoying favorable climatic conditions, the valley of the Moselle stands out as a paradisial oasis in a provincial landscape slipping ever deeper into desolation. *Augusta Treverorum*, the financial capital of *Belgica*, rose out of its destruction in AD 275 as *Treveris*, the capital of Constantius Chlorus and for a short time of his son Constantine. During the reign of these two imperial benefactors a building program was launched at *Treveris* which would leave no doubt in the mind of a visitor as he crossed the Moselle bridge,[121] five of its stone piers still

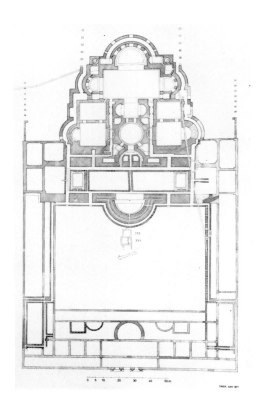

158 Layout of the Constantinian baths at Trier. (Rheinisches Landesmuseum, Trier)

standing today, that he was entering the splendid residence of an Augustus. In our discussion of Roman wall paintings, we have already touched on the brilliance of the private imperial residential quarters.

Visible to all, however, was the monumental palace complex extending over at least seven *insulae*, city blocks. It began in the north with the palace of Helen, the empress-mother. This palace she bestowed on the Christian Church in AD 326. Roman wall fragments are still visible.[122] It was this palace which housed the portrait-ceiling. Seven *insulae* to the south the ruins of the Constantinian *thermae*, the imperial baths, are located.[123] Already in the second century *Augusta Treverorum* could boast the largest baths in the empire, 250 × 170m of actual building; these Barbara Baths[124] ultimately were used to demonstrate the effectiveness of artillery.[125] Designed to complement the larger and older baths, the Constantinian Baths occupied an area of 86,320m², also among the largest in the Empire.[126] Basically cruciform in design (Fig. 158), the plan of the main building shows an intricate system of apses, bays and vaulted rooms surrounded by colonnades. The entrance, located in an arcaded facade, led through a triumphal archway which opened into a vast porticoed exercise court, the *palaestra*. In a setting of marble veneer, columns, frescoes, mosaics and statuary the bathers shivered in the *frigidarium*—the cold bath, lounged in the *tepidarium*—a room of moving warm air, and luxuriated in the *caldarium*—the warm bath.[127] In between they were oiled, scraped and massaged, they conducted business and cultivated contacts, to emerge rested and in harmony with themselves and the world.[128] Under the later emperors Valentinian (AD 364–75) and his son Gratian (AD 367–83) the *thermes* were redesigned to house a palace, the *caldarium* being transformed into a *basilica*. Excavations showed that a *villa urbana* of the first and second

159 Partly
restored ruins
of the
Constantinian
baths at Trier,
early fourth
century AD.

centuries had been located on the terrain of the *palaestra*. The Polydos mosaic was found there[129] (see Fig. 117). Following the departure of the Romans the technology of the bathing installations could not be maintained. Owing to the formidable architecture the baths recommended themselves as fortifications and in the twelfth century were incorporated into the medieval city walls. Even today the remaining walls of the *caldarium* are still 19m high[130] (Fig. 159). Because the decaying Roman buildings offered such a ready supply of building materials, they were used as quarries, thus providing a curious type of continuity into subsequent periods.

Between the palace of the empress-mother and the Constantinian baths there is an extraordinary building, the center of Constantine's palace, the audience hall.[131] After the Pantheon in Rome it is the largest surviving Roman building (Fig. 160). This basilica, the so-called Aula Palatina, was built *c.* AD 310 as the hall of supreme justice. The starkness of its appearance and its isolated setting are misleading. Originally linked to the northern palace by administrative buildings, the 'Aula' was surrounded by porticoed courtyards and a narthex-like colonnade, 60m long, extending across the southern front linking it with the flanking buildings, preceded by a peristyle forecourt. The clean upward sweep with which the building confronts the viewer today helps to confuse him with notions of a 'sense of the Gothic' which does not at all reflect the original Roman intentions. The immaculate brickwork was not visible then, since it was covered with reddish stucco painted with yellow floral motifs. A few fragments of this stucco have survived in the window niches. The upward sweep of the exterior could not affect the viewer because two horizontal galleries which encircled the building at the height of the window ledges interrupted this apparent invitation to optic flight. Nevertheless, optic games are being played here, as it will

155

160 'Aula Palatina' at Trier, built *c.* AD 310 as the basilica of the imperial palace complex.

be noticed that all the window niches, including those of the apse, are at the same height but that the recessed windows of the apse are themselves smaller and those of the upper level are set somewhat lower than those of the long walls (Fig. 161). This is of little significance on the exterior but the optical effect created on the interior, by the smaller windows of the apse, deceives the viewer about the actual length of the interior (Fig. 162). The elevated imperial throne and the tribunal stood under the monumental arch, directly facing the entrance and in approximately the same position as where the altar is located today. The optical trick helped convey the sense of remote aloofness required by the elaborate eastern court ceremonial which was aimed at magnifying the emperor's divine dignity.

The architects[132] and the decorators of this basilica went to great lengths to create in the vastness of this interior the impression of an ideal space. The brilliance, gleam and glitter were not merely vainglorious display.[133] It was mentioned above that art

161 'Aula Palatina', seen from the north-west.

162 'Aula Palatina', interior. (Rheinisches Landesmuseum, Trier)

was called upon to represent supreme magnificence in order to heighten the abstract notions of the *dominus*, the Divine Emperor, to emphasize the transcendental radiance of sublime majesty by means of an abstract idealism. Without columns or pillars to detract from its awesome tectonic massiveness,[134] this flat-roofed basilica cannot have failed to impress upon the visitor the insignificance of his own person. The floor of the audience hall was paved with black and white tiles and mosaic designs. The walls were faced with inlaid polychrome marble in the lower portions while wall paintings decorated the upper portions. Seven niches are recessed into the apse and the legs of the colossal arch. Against a background of sparkling gold and blue mosaic, statuary filled these niches, surrounding the throne with figures taken perhaps from the grandiose mytho-poetic past of gods, demigods, heroes and deified imperial personages, certainly of the imperial household, to provide a setting larger than life. The comfort level of the hall could be controlled by a hypocaust heating system. From five heat sources, ducts heated not only the floor but led under the marble wall veneer to emerge below the windows. Three of these *praefurnia* heated the apse, the imperial space.

In its monumentality this immense structure symbolized the idea of the might and grandeur that was Rome. As architecture this conception enjoyed a long tradition. Elsewhere the basilica, usually the three or five-aisled model, became a suitable prototype of the Christian church building. Where the *praetor's* seat had been located in the semicircular apse of the civic basilica the bishop now took his place, while the seats formerly occupied by the Roman assessors were now used by the members of the church council.[135] It has been suggested that Constantine's own architects,[136] acting under his orders, transformed the civic basilica and created the sacred space in which the ceremonial surrounding the emperor was reflected in the ceremonial service to Christ the King. The imposing arch became the symbol of the victorious church framing the triumphant Christ visible on the vault of the apse. The niches of the apse encrusted with gold mosaic came to portray apostles, saints and church fathers.

In Frankish times, however, the basilica became the seat of the king's deputies, without the imperial idea attached to it. With its windows walled in, the building became a virtually impregnable fortress. During the Middle Ages it passed to the prince-bishops and electors of the Holy Roman Empire who, after the seventeenth century, attached their princely residence to it. Until the nineteenth century it had always been linked with worldly, at best, sacerdotal functions. Only in 1856 was it consecrated as a church by direct intervention of the King of Prussia. It owes its present appearance to the restoration following the extensive damage sustained during World War II.

Since the first century AD the city had an arena (Fig. 163). Located to the east of the Constantinian Baths and partly set into the hillside, it was incorporated into the city wall, the main gates of the arena forming an additional entrance into the city. Its capacity has been estimated at 20,000 spectators, most of the inhabitants of *Treveris*.[137] Following his campaign of devastation directed against the Franks on the right bank of the Rhine, Constantine spent the winter of AD 313/14 at *Treveris*. To celebrate his triumph he sponsored lavish games during which innumerable Franks were thrown to the beasts. Such acts of amusement are not likely to have contributed to the pacification of the frontier.[138] That the Romans were much taken with the realism of the arena has been pointed out already in connection with mosaics. From

163 The amphitheater at Trier, in use from the first to the fourth century AD, had a seating capacity for 20,000 spectators.

164 Roman theater of the former *Augusta Raurica* at Augst, Switzerland.

villas of the Moselle area come many scenes showing human and animal combat. This realism was not restricted to the arena only. The stage demanded it too (Fig. 164). Thus the death scenes in tragedies or in dramatized myths had to be real in that condemned criminals were made to take the place of actors. Where the story demanded burnings, wild beasts, crucifixion, torture, the audience came to insist on real death. Icarus had to die in his fall; if he didn't then wild beasts got him. As in the arena, death had to be faced with style, as taught in the gladiatorial schools. Reluctance to die was a disappointing display of poor style.[139] It may have been little consolation to the condemned that his death at least acquired a picturesque and more mythical significance.[140]

In sharp contrast to these brutalities *Treveris* boasted a reputable institute of higher learning, renowned for paying its faculty the highest salaries in Gaul.[141] The presence of the imperial court brought men of letters to *Treveris*. Constantine the Great, for instance, had surrounded himself with a community of scholars.[142] Valentinian assembled jurists, orators and poets, mainly Gauls, best exemplified by the presence of Ausonius. Ausonius, poet, intellect, most powerful administrator of the western Empire and tutor to the young emperor Gratian, composed his best poem, a description of a journey on the Moselle, in AD 371.[143] In particular, a rhetorical tradition was established in Gaul.

A center of early Christianity, a bishopric since AD 328, *Treveris* hosted such churchmen as the exiled Athanasius of Alexandria (AD 336/7 and 346) who probably began the exultation of the monastic life of St Anthony here, St Jerome who studied here,[144] St Ambrose after AD 330, and St Martin of Tours after AD 370.[145] Christianity was established there already in pre-Constantinian times. It became a center partly because of the support of the imperial house which made extensive secular and religious donations to the Church, such as the palace of Constantine's mother, the graves of martyrs, the location of holy relics and the foundations of important churches on these sites through the efforts of eminent bishops.[146] If the medieval tradition is correct, then the remains of the Apostle Matthias were buried at Trier, brought there by Helena, mother of Constantine, along with such holy Christian objects as the robe which Christ wore during the Passion and the implements of his suffering which Helena found in Jerusalem. The legitimacy of *Treveris* as a center of

159

Christianity would have been established and would have given to *Treveris* great importance as a pilgrimage center. The cultural activity this would have generated there must have been much greater than is apparent in the records. In spite of the temporal decline which came with the departure of the court and the center of administration and the repeated devastations wrought by the Franks during the fifth century, *Treveris* may have maintained considerable spiritual significance.[147] The argument St Augustine applied to Rome in his *De Civitate Dei*, The City of God, that is the transformation of the earthly city of Rome so that the triumph of the heavenly city might be prepared, will have sustained the resolve of the churchmen of *Treveris* as well.

Over a period of more than two hundred years the Roman practice of settling ever new border peoples within the limits of the Empire kept that population in a state of flux. Germanic prisoners of war were no longer enslaved but between AD 297 and 465, as *dediticii*, were assigned to cultivate abandoned farms,[148] while *laeti*,[149] dependents of Germanic origin and close in status to *coloni*, were settled in the *terrae laeticae*, depopulated areas assigned to them by the emperor for which they owed Rome military service.[150] The *laeti* settled across a wide area, especially along the river Maas in *Germania inferior*, in *Belgica* and as far south as central Gaul,[151] frequently straddling the most important invasion routes. Their graves have shown them to represent a mixed culture, where Germanic elements coexisted with late Roman forms.[152] Almost an independent culture in Gaul during the fourth century, their's represents a transition towards the forms reflected in the later invasions. Without really having gained a foothold in these lands, the *laeti* were usually dislodged by the invaders and new inhabitants, obtained by concluding new contracts with tribal remnants, often had to be resettled.[153] That renegade groups would swell the ranks of the *latrones*, brigands, especially in *Germania superior* which became a veritable *latrocinium* is to be expected.[154] Quite different from the *laeti* were the *foederati*, Germanic tribes or tribal units who had been taken into the Empire in return for military service.[155] Again these tribes tended not to be integrated. In *Pannonia* for instance, two hundred years after their first settlement during the sixth century a tribe was still referred to as *antiqui barbari*.

In many areas along the Rhine there is evidence that the tribes settled around villas. Though they did not destroy them, they did not occupy them either, nor did they continue the farming operations.[156] Instead they introduced a new settlement structure. There are, however, some examples of the continued operation of farms into the seventh century where their original owners remained. The evidence is supported by finds from cemeteries which show the coexistence of native and new populations in many areas.[157] In the settled areas the communities can be differentiated in that the natives continued to build in stone while the newcomers used timber. Meadows and fields belonging to villas were distributed along different lines as the Roman parceling system was ignored. The nature of the terrain was the chief criterion. Germanic villages very rarely continued on Roman antecedents. Thanks to the choice of different sites and the return of the land to natural conditions the locations and outlines of these villas are now visible from the air under the cultivated land. The exception to this practice of not occupying the stone houses were those situations, where as *foederati*, tribal chiefs especially had been awarded a specific estate by the Roman administration and the beneficiary took possession of everything pertaining to the operation of the estate—experienced workers, tools, production methods and terminology.[158] This is the context in which the adoption of the pertinent vocabulary took place, when loan words pertaining to the garden and orchard came into Germanic usage. In other instances the isolated estates were replaced by villages as the new population occupied the plains and valleys, the land abandoned by its former owners. Evidently a transformation of conditions was registered as, on the one hand, the settlement patterns changed and Germanic villages were introduced and the Roman *vici* fell into desolation. On the other hand, despite this general rift, a particular break in the continuity was camouflaged by an intensive transmission of tools, Roman methods and concepts and especially by the transmission of Latin terminology.[159] Large sections of cultivated land in the northern provinces had fallen into disuse owing to the desolation brought by civil war, raiding and invading tribes living off the land and the ensuing neglect. Consequently in the last Roman centuries the differences between the highly-cultivated lands of the Empire and the agricultural lands worked by the migratory peasant tribes beyond the Roman frontiers had been largely leveled out. The invading tribes of the fifth century encountered a landscape which had generally regressed to that of an earlier 'State of Nature.'

The clashes which took place along Rome's northern frontiers were not just between attackers and defenders but between a centralized political organization and more simply organized tribal societies whose disorganized and uncoordinated attacks wore down the sophisticated state, to the point that this state had to make use of these societies to protect itself against others following close behind. These northern societies had begun as loosely connected village societies based on close and extended family units scattered along the northern coastlines and along the rivers leading into the interior, sometimes sheltered by impenetrable moors. Over the years differences in social position began to emerge among them, curiously enough associated with evidence of contact with Rome.[160] Towards the south, where contact with the Celtic domains had taken place, notions of socio-political prominence find echoes in the designation *rix—rick—rex* which in the time of Marius, *c.* 103 BC, had taken the form of tribal chieftainships, not to say kingship. By the time Caesar encounters Ariovistus, Caesar clearly dubs him *rex*. While the status of Arminius is evidently that of an aristocrat, his 'royal' position is not at all established. On the other hand, his contemporary Maroboduus of the Marcomanni is designated king. Thereafter, the tribal groups have princely leaders, perhaps only 'warchiefs' at first,[161] many of whom had been hostages demanded by Rome and who had a leadership apprenticeship among the Romans. By the fourth and fifth centuries these leaders attribute their position to their descent from select families descended from mythological ancestors.[162] Though a rudimentary hierarchy of interdependencies is in place among these northern tribes by the fourth century, the bulk of the migratory peasant societies is still assembled on family and clan lines.

It was from these groups that ambitious and adventurous young leaders and their followings had sought service in the Roman *auxilia*, where especially their pronounced sense of personal loyalty singled them out as preferred bodyguards. By the time of Trajan at the beginning of the second century, they were no longer unusual and at the beginning of the third century the emperor Caracalla had surrounded himself with a Germanic bodyguard, while he dressed in Germanic garb. During the third century necessity and expediency saw tribal chiefs and their following offering their services to Rome in which they soon were welcomed by the various factions and in whose services they quickly found themselves to be pitted against one another.[163] Thus Constantine was proclaimed Augustus in *Eboracum* (York) in AD 360 through the machinations of the Alamannic king Erocus[164] and his following who had accompanied Constantius Chlorus, Constantine's father, to Britain. The decisive role played by the Cornuti, a Germanic contingent in the service of Constantine, during the decisive battle of the Milvian Bridge AD 312,[165] which established Constantine's supremacy in the west, was instrumental not only in gaining recognition for these Germanic troops in Roman service but in opening careers for them in the Roman armies thereby affecting the future composition and leadership of these armies. Germanic *gentiles*[166] constituted a rich and heavily romanized tribal upper crust represented in the imperial bodyguards, their various units being designated as *armatura*, *scutarii*[167] and *candidati*,[168] while the *comites* consisted of a Germanic elite troop of young nobles.[169] These units were to provide the officer corps,[170] just as the Praetorian Guard had done during the early Empire.

From Constantine to Theodosius I, from AD 306 to 395, the infrastructure of the army was staffed by Germanic tribesmen when Franks[171] and Alamanni wielded dominant military power as commanders-in-chief in various theaters of the Empire.[172] Thereafter, this power shifted into the hands of Goths[173] and the representatives of other east Germanic tribes. By *c.* AD 400 this caused strong feelings of anti-Germanism in the Empire of the east,[174] especially against favored Goths, culminating in their exclusion from high office. We saw by their Germanic names that these were first generation Germans, born outside of the Empire, who initially had not gained their position through the process of romanization and meritorious service to Rome. Rather than rising through the ranks, they had been entrusted with positions of command from the start owing to the status they had in their own retinues at the time they entered Roman service. Such a process would cause envy and resentment among those passed over for command. Protected by their favored status in the eyes of the emperor, whose stay in power was guaranteed by their loyalty and military pre-eminence, they were natural focal points of hostility. To the historian Ammianus Marcellinus they were the *homines dedicati imperio*, men dedicated to the Empire.[175]

We also saw that the selection of the emperor had become the exclusive prerogative of the army. Before the fourth century the Illyrians had been instrumental in this process. From the fourth century on the Germanic components of the army assumed this role. But while the Illyrians eventually presumed to the imperial purple, being after all quite romanized, the Germans preferred the wielding of power to the possession of the imperial title. In only two instances was the attempt made: by Flavius Magnus Magnentius (AD 350–53), a Briton, perhaps a Frank on his mother's side,[176] who wanted to be considered a Roman, and by Sylvanus (AD 355) who was proclaimed by the Franks.[177] Both times the attempt at usurpation came to nothing. Magnentius committed suicide after his defeats in *Pannonia* and northern Italy by Constantius, son of Constantine, and Sylvanus was murdered after only four months in office. Romanized, neither of them saw himself or his activities as being directed against the Empire. It was more usual for the northern armies to proclaim the emperor, either by themselves or in conjunction with other support, the proclamation of Julian (the Apostate) in AD 360 in Paris, for instance,[178] when his Celto-Germanic troops raised him on the shield and crowned him with the torc, a northern ceremony which was to become Byzantine coronation ritual.[179] The reluctance to assume the title while being in possession of the power of the office provided conditions in which intrigue festered and power struggles took their toll. Nevertheless, as we saw in the first chapter, frequently their military capabilities brought them the recognition of administrative and judicial positions[180] though they never rose to senatorial rank.[181] It would be unfair to suggest that the Empire had now become hostage to its former hostages.[182]

It was pointed out before that these Germanic leaders were not merely power-hungry warlords but individuals who enjoyed the esteem of their contemporaries. In a self-motivated effort at assimilation they made deliberate attempts at establishing links with the Roman aristocracy and becoming a part of the world of the Greco-Roman intellect, to gain the necessary education and thereby assure their contact with Roman society. In the writings of such scholars as the aforementioned Ammianus Marcellinus, a native of Antioch, Eunapios of Sardes, Libanios, who was quite immersed in the Greek concept of the 'barbarian,' Sozombos, Symmachos, Themistios, Zozinus and Zozomos, and the poet Claudius Claudianus the Germanic *Magistri Militum*, Romans by choice, enjoy an image of esteem and favor. Symmachus and Libanios, the height of the intellectual scene of the time, treat the Franks Richomer and Bauto as equals in their correspondence which rings true with sincerity and friendship.[183] Richomer was in demand by Symmachus, Nicomachus and Eugenius not only for his political position but also for his personality, which in their eyes merited respect and friendship. Surely a sign of esteem was the marriage of Stilicho to Theodosius' niece and adopted daughter Serena and the marriage of Bauto's daughter Eudoxia with the young emperor Arcadius. Statues of gratitude were set up for many of these masters of the armies, who in the service of Rome, as *homines dedicati imperio*, rendered what service they could to protect the Empire from the dangers facing it. Augustine, when still a young man, wrote the Panegyric, a laudatory oration, on the occasion of Bauto's accession to the consulship under the emperor Gratian (before AD 383)[184] while Claudius Claudianus had hailed his patron Flavius Stilicho as the outstanding personality of his time.

At the same time much hostility was being generated against these foreigners. Valentinian (AD 364–75),[185] a Pannonian himself, forbade all union between those barbarians already located in Gaul and its Roman citizens while at the same time promoting select Germanic individuals to the higher echelons at the expense of Romans. Invariably expedience had precedence over a consistent policy. Orosius was openly critical of the Germans while Synesios of Cyrene militated actively for the removal of this 'plague of the Roman Empire' from the positions of command in the army and the administration.[186] An especially extreme example of the conflict engendered by the struggle between the pro- and anti-Germanic factions was Eudoxia, daughter of the Frank Bauto, wife of Arcadius and ruling Empress in the east. She actively sponsored the anti-Germanic sentiments which, after an uprising in AD 399, led to a massacre of some 7,000 Goths in Constantinople and to the removal of influential Goths and others from their positions. It may have been a problem for the heathen Germanic elements that they were identified closely with the pagan Romans—scholars as well as aristocrats—who counted among their supporters while the Christian faction was gaining the upper hand. In the Athanasian–Christian 'press' the Germanic masters of the armies, who if they were Christians were practicing the Arian rite, were given a decidedly negative image. The resentment culminated in the execution for treason of Stilicho in AD 408.[187] After Stilicho's death the western Empire became the weaker part, at the mercy of the tensions coiled up within its borders.

Although the Empire of the west may have collapsed with the removal of the last emperor, Romulus Augustulus in AD 476, it was not a shattering event. The Germanic

163

165 Bronze lamp with cross from Augsburg. (Prähistorische Staatssammlung, Munich)

kingdoms which followed in its place saw themselves as representatives of the Empire, especially as they had been charged with vice-regal powers bestowed by Constantinople to dislodge an earlier but now undesirable holder of the title. Whether Ostro-Goths in Italy or Visi-Goths in France and Spain, they considered the Empire to be a whole ruled by a single emperor in Constantinople whose continuing legitimate authority over their occupied lands they did not question. Theodoric the Goth bore the title *patricius*, given him by the emperor in Constantinople. Chlodowegh the Frank was proclaimed *Augustus*, baptized and anointed by the Church and supported by its organizational structure. 'Charged' with the 'deliverance' of other western lands from the Arian heresy, the Franks readily respected the unity of the Empire and came to feel committed to its continuation. In the west the predominance of the Franks throughout the centuries of the Roman decline and their administrative apprentice-ship under Roman tutelage, in what came to be their hereditary lands straddling the Middle and Lower Rhine, put them in a favorable position. It must also be considered that by the time Stilicho's order came to withdraw the military forces from the Rhine frontier the retreat was neither total nor very extensive, as for decades to come Roman field commanders could raise Roman armies in Gaul[188] who, in joint action with Visi-Goths, Burgundians and Franks, could engage in regional warfare or jointly protect the Germano-Roman Christian Empire of the west against the Huns and their heathen Germanic federation.

The concept of the classical Empire as a cohesive, temporal unit survived, manifest in its later, religious period, transposed into a coordinated entity. The western Church survived the transition from universal Empire to regional tribal kingdoms almost intact, held together by the bond of a common faith. The Church had succeeded the imperial administration by establishing units of Church organization parallel with those of the civil service in the administrative centers of the Empire. As the Roman civilian authority faded, the religious centers remained in place to assume and trans-mit as best they could the sense of institutional continuity, giving its members the knowledge of belonging to a larger social entity (Fig. 165). It was to take the north over four centuries before its inhabitants could see beyond family, village and clan to grasp the notion of tribal jurisdiction. Only later still would the possibility of nation as a balanced interlink of tribal units strike them as a functional possibility.

Conclusion

An inquiry into the significance of the Roman Empire for central Europe has access to much archaeological evidence as well as to some historical sources. Even without the benefit of our vast knowledge of Roman history, of its culture and civilization, it would be possible to reconstruct the cultural developments in those parts of central Europe formerly occupied by Rome. In comparison with earlier and later archaeological periods, the material evidence of the Roman presence would stand out sharply and point very clearly to the rather sudden appearance of a brilliant and fully developed material culture, characterized by the use of stone in art and architecture and an emphasis on stylistic elements quite different from the indigenous ones. With such a cultural manifestation it would be natural to link this rather sudden appearance with an upper and ruling social hierarchy which, because of its association with new materials, new forms and new practices, would be deemed to have been foreign. Owing to the wealth of evidence pointing to stylistic changes one would speak of invaders who superimposed themselves on the native populations. Other evidence would point to the continuing presence of a native substratum indicated by a continuity of forms, practices and rituals, demonstrating a fluctuation between impoverishment and enrichment. The appearance of differences would suggest a significant cultural rift. The persistence of certain cultural features, however, would obviously emphasize the continuity of attitudes. Archaeological evidence generally creates the impression that change is very much a function of continuity, of process, assuming the appearance of gently undulating ocean swells. The historical documentary evidence, of ancient Rome for instance, has left a legacy of chronicled critical events which resembles cresting and destructive tidal waves. In dealing with the Roman presence in parts of central Europe the evidence from written sources contributes a dimension which emphasized events and upheavals, expressed points of view and bias, creating the impression of one crisis pursuing another. However, the cultural evidence, much of which has come to light only recently, indicates the existence of a continuum not only during the high culture of the Roman period but of one which extended from Celtic to Germanic times as well. Of course, it cannot be denied that the written and archaeological evidence dealing with the Roman presence north of the Alps has almost completely obliterated the signs of any indigenous culture. This is readily understandable if one considers the spectacular components of the Hellenistic heritage in Roman guise which was being superimposed on what was at that time a lackluster culture succumbing to its own recession.

We have seen that the arrival of the Romans on the western and southern fringes of central Europe created the appearance of a rift in the cultural development of the peoples settled within the newly acquired Roman territories. The material culture within these provinces reflects a very abrupt change in favor of Roman ways which apparently swept all before them. However, native pottery styles, burial practices and some assessable religions point to a modicum of resilience of the indigenous Celtic culture. In general though, we saw that in other aspects, especially those of the external culture, the romanization of the upper levels of native society at least made rapid strides, especially in the urban centers of the newly established provinces. In the countryside, the natural reluctance to change, as well as the reduced emphasis on the part of the superimposed Roman society to integrate this level of the population into the cultural mainstream, meant that the romanization will have proceeded less rapidly and less completely. This is reflected in the term 'pagan', originally applied to the inhabitants of the *pagus*, the countryside, but then applied by the city-dwelling Christians to the country-dwelling non-Christians. Despite the many towns and the villa economy it appears that Roman provincial culture was something alien and insular, not really determined by the native environment, but something aloof, a veneer, in which the natives participated only marginally. Indeed, this level of involvement receded in proportion to the fading of the Roman presence after the third century. In any case, the presence of Italians was limited so that the banners of romanization were carried by other provincials, as we have seen.

It can be argued that the Romans arrived with stereotypes and remained locked within them, while the stereotypes themselves remained an alien quantity in the areas into which they had been transplanted. It was up to the natives to assimilate the stereotypes. In this context the question of the 'Fall of the Roman Empire' takes on something of a sentimental note. It is relevant to those who have adopted these stereotypes as cultural criteria, who identify with them and who even approach them with adulation and determine all quality in terms of the Greco-Roman heritage. To representatives of this sentimental view, the 'Fall of the Roman Empire' was indeed a calamity of cataclysmic proportions to the barbarians within and without, a view with which one could sympathize were it not so overdrawn. The cultural highlights were not the norm and to the downtrodden the spectacular work of the *diatretari* was a matter of great indifference, if not an indication of the very ills. There were people in the early fifth century who thought that life in the lands held by the Germanic tribes was to be preferred to life among the Romans in the areas still occupied by the Empire.[189]

Significant Personalities and Events

58 BC	Caesar defeats Ariovistus and the Suebi.
51 BC	Caesar completes the conquest of Gaul.
15 BC	Drusus and Tiberius annex *Raetia* and *Noricum*.
12 BC–9 AD	Rome attempts the conquest of central Europe.
AD 9	Varus disaster.
AD 13–17	Germanicus resumes the offensive.
AD 63–96	Vespasian and Domitian establish the early *limes* between Rhine and Danube.
AD 98–138	Under Trajan and Hadrian active policy of romanization.
AD 142/3	Antoninus Pius begins to relocate the *limes* further east.
AD 167–80	Marcomannic Wars. Marcus Aurelius conscripts lower social orders.
AD 180	Marcus Aurelius plans to establish new provinces *Marcomania* and *Sarmatia*.
AD 193–211	Septimius Severus democratizes the army and appoints legion commanders not only from the senatorial aristocracy but from the equestrian order as well.
AD 213	Caracalla extends citizenship with the proclamation of the *Constitutio Antoniniana*.
AD 259–68	Postumus proclaims the *Imperium Galliarum* and clears the Franks out of Gaul.
AD 260	'Dry' *limes* ceases to exist.
AD 253–60	Gallienus repels Alamanni in Italy.
AD 271	Aurelian (270–75) defeats Alamanni in Italy. Germani in great numbers are taken into the army.
AD 277	Probus (276–82) repels Franks and Alamanni from Gaul.
AD 286	Diocletian (285–305) divides the Empire into eastern and western parts.
AD 291	Creation of the Rhine-Iller-Danube *limes*.
AD 293	Further subdivision of the Empire.
AD 312	Constantine asserts himself as sole emperor.
AD 364–75	Valentinian resumes offensive along Rhine and Danube.
AD 378	Valens is defeated decisively by the Goths at Adrianople.
AD 379–95	Theodosius, Emperor of the East, restores order.
AD 375–92	Gratian (367–83) and Valentinian II are western co-emperors.
AD 392–94	Eugenius, usurper.
AD 395–423	Honorius, Emperor of the West. Stilicho is executed in AD 408.
AD 395–408	Arcadius, Emperor of the East.

Notes

1. The Military Setting

1 Julius Caesar, *The Gallic War and Other Writings*, transl. by Moses Hadas (New York 1957), p. 5. All further references will be made to this edition and cited as Caesar.
2 Caesar, p. 37.
3 H. Schutz, *The Prehistory of Germanic Europe* (New Haven and London 1983), pp. 338–43.
4 Schutz, p. 339.
5 In Middle High German, Markman still meant protector of the border, inhabitant of the marc—English border march. R. Much, *Die Germania des Tacitus*, dritte, beträchtlich erweiterte Auflage, unter Mitarbeit von H. Jankuhn, herausgegeben von W. Lange (Heidelberg 1967), p. 468.
6 Much, p. 362. See also H.G. Simon, in D. Baatz, F.R. Herrmann, et al., *Die Römer in Hessen* (Stuttgart 1982), p. 53.
7 E. Kornemann, *Römische Geschichte*, in zwei Bänden, 6. Auflage, bearbeitet von H. Bengtson (Stuttgart 1979), II, p. 18.
8 M. Gelzer, *Caesar, der Politiker und Staatsmann* (Wiesbaden 1960), p. 98.
9 Caesar, pp. 26, 32.
10 Caesar, p. 24.
11 Caesar, p. 38.
12 Caesar, pp. 33f.
13 G. Walser, *Caesar und die Germanen, Studien zur politischen Tendenz römischer Feldzugsberichte* (Wiesbaden 1956), p. 21, discusses briefly Caesar's exaggerations.
14 Caesar, pp. 28–31.
15 A. Grenier, *Les Gaulois* (Paris 1970), p. 328.
16 Caesar, pp. 190ff.
17 Caesar, p. 159. That Caesar did not consider them to be Belgae is implied in *Gallic War*, pp. 1, 41f., 127f. Hirtius, who completed the *Gallic War*, however, does seem to take them for Belgae in Bk. VIII.
18 Caesar, pp. 79ff. See also T. Bechert, *Römisches Germanien zwischen Rhein und Maas, Die Provinz Germania Inferior* (Munich 1982),

pp. 28–38, for a summary of Roman activities along the Lower Rhine during the next hundred years.
19 Gelzer, p. 118; also U. Maier, *Caesars Feldzüge in Gallien in ihrem Zusammenhang mit der stadtrömischen Politik* (Bonn 1978), p. 63.
20 Much, p. 394.
21 Caesar, pp. 81ff; also Maier, p. 61.
22 Caesar, pp. 95ff.
23 Maier, p. 71.
24 Caesar, pp. 97, 109ff.
25 Caesar, pp. 111–14; also Gelzer, p. 131.
26 Caesar, pp. 123ff.; also Gelzer, p. 131.
27 Caesar, pp. 146–51; also Maier, pp. 72f.
28 Caesar, p. 75.
29 Caesar, p. 82.
30 Caesar, p. 82.
31 Caesar, p. 81.
32 Caesar, p. 132; F. Behn, *Römertum und Völkerwanderung, Mitteleuropa zwischen Augustus und Karl dem Großen* (Stuttgart 1963), p. 19, suggests that these crossings were strategically worthless and no more than mere attempts at intimidation.
33 Caesar, p. 75.
34 C.M. Wells, *The German Policy of Augustus, An Examination of the Archaeological Evidence* (Oxford 1972), p. 250, suggests Roman acceptance of the status quo in view of the Roman focus elsewhere.
35 Much, p. 363, indicates them to be distinctly Germanic.
36 Velleius Paterculus, *Compendium of Roman History*, transl. by F.W. Shipley, Loeb Classical Library (Cambridge, Mass. and London 1961), II, XCVII, p. 235. *legio V alaudae* seems to have survived this disaster at least in name for it participated in the conquest of Britain and was then stationed at *Vetera* from AD 43–69/70. It was dissolved following its involvement in the Batavian Revolt, see Bechert, p. 68.

37 Velleius, II, XCV, p. 249, for a brief account of the conquest of *Raetia*. See also H.J. Kellner, *Die Römer in Bayern*, 4th ed. 1978 (Munich 1971), pp. 22–4, 96; also A. Johnson, *Roman Forts of the first and second Centuries AD in Britain and the German Provinces* (London 1983), p. 230, and Filtzinger, in Ph. Filtzinger, D. Planck, B. Cämmerer, et al., *Die Römer in Baden-Württemberg*, 2nd ed. (Stuttgart and Aalen 1976), pp. 30f.

38 Ancient sources say little about these campaigns but it must have been the aim to secure the region between the Alps and the Danube to serve as a staging area for future thrusts into the north. For details of these early campaigns, see G. Ulbert, *Die römischen Donau-Castelle Aislingen und Burghöfe, Limesforschungen—Studien zur Organisation der römischen Reichsgrenze an Rhein und Donau*, ed. by H.v. Petrikovits, W. Schleiermacher (Berlin 1959), pp. 78f. Drusus probably fought his campaign with the *legio IX, XIII, XX* and *XXI*, see Filtzinger, in Filtzinger, Planck, Cämmerer, p. 30.

39 G. Alföldy, *Noricum, History of the Provinces of the Roman Empire*, transl. by A. Birley (London and Boston 1974), pp. 52ff., details the dispute about this date.

40 A. Mócsy, *Pannonia and Upper Moesia, A History of the Middle Danube Provinces of the Roman Empire*, transl. ed. by S. Frere (London and Boston 1974), pp. 33f.

41 W. Jobst, *Provinzhauptstadt Carnuntum* (Vienna 1983), makes repeated references to a great N–S amber route passing through Carnuntum. Also M. Henig, ed. *A Handbook of Roman Art, A comprehensive survey of all the arts of the Roman World* (Ithaca, N.Y. 1983), p. 162

42 G. Biegel, in *Kölner Römer Illustrierte* (Cologne 1975), II, p. 103. Hereafter the journal will be cited as *KRI*.

43 G. Webster, *The Roman Imperial Army to Caracalla* (London 1969), p. 43, suggests this Augustan reform to have been a means for the emperor to retain contact with the army and thereby assure its loyalty to him. See also Simon, in Baatz and Herrmann, p. 38. Agrippa planned a strategic road system to form the basis of lasting and effective control. Also Jobst, pp. 34, 42f.

44 J.J. Hatt, *Histoire de la Gaule romaine*, 3rd ed. (Paris 1970), p. 101.

45 Hatt, p. 91. See also Simon, in Baatz, Herrmann, p. 40. Before 12 BC there were no military fortifications along the Rhine. Now forts were established at *Mogontiacum, Vetera, Noviomagus* and a naval base at *Factio* and at least 5 legions and similar numbers of auxiliaries were assembled. These developments point to offensive designs.

46 Kornemann, II, p. 137. See also Filtzinger, in Filtzinger, Planck, Cämmerer, p. 29, who sug-gests that the plan to subjugate *Germania* and to push the frontier of Italy north to the Danube follows from Augustus' reorganization of the administration of Gaul in 16–13 BC.

47 Wells, p. 5. Also Bechert, p. 130, who argues that except during the reign of Augustus, Rome's policy in this sector was always a defensive one. Bechert, p. 30, also suggests that the Elbe frontier may have been Agrippa's idea.

48 Wells, p. 96.

49 Lucius Annaeus Florus, *Epitome of Roman History*, transl. by E.S. Forster, (Cambridge, Mass. and London 1960), LCL II, XXX, pp. 335ff., for an account of the Drusus campaigns into Germania.

50 *Dio's Roman History in Nine Volumes*, with an English transl. by E. Cary, LCL (Cambridge, Mass. and London 1961), III, pp. 379f., VI, pp. 333, 365f., but then Dio always refers to the Germani as Celts.

51 Wells, pp. 93ff., for a detailed discussion.

53 Wells, pp. 154f. Also Simon, in Baatz, Herrmann, p. 41, who suggests that it was a lack of adequate planning which forced the campaign to be broken off.

53 Velleius, II, XCVII, p. 253, indicates Drusus to have reduced *Germania* almost to the status of a tributary province, and Florus, p. 337, claims that Drusus had opened the way through the Hercynian Forest.

54 Wells, p. 156. Tiberius was at *Ticinium*/Pavia when he received the news of his brother's accident. Bechert, p. 178, suggests that he travelled 350 km. At the time the imperial couriers travelled up to 90 km per day and twice that far if the message was urgent.

55 Hatt, p. 106.

56 Kornemann, II, p. 141.

57 Wells, p. 157. Also Simon, in Baatz, Herrmann, p. 51, who questions the generally accepted theory that it was Rome's intention from the start to establish a province reaching from the Rhine to the Elbe. That the large fortresses at Oberaden and Dangstetten and the supply base at Rödgen were abandoned c. 8/9 BC is taken to suggest that Rome considered its goals to have been reached, namely that a large buffer zone to protect Gaul had been secured by treaties. This plan did not require large scale military operations bent on dominating such a large area as *Germania* and that it was later unrest in the interior which caused Rome to reconsider this policy.

58 Velleius, II, CV, CVI, pp. 269ff.

59 Wells, p. 158. Simon, in Baatz, Herrmann, p. 49, argues that Ahenobarbus did not undertake this campaign from the Danube when still governor of *Illyria*, but from *Mogontiacum*, when he was in command on the Rhine.

60 Kellner, p. 73, states that no noteworthy Germanic finds dating to the first and second centuries AD have been made in the Oberpfalz. See also Simon, in Baatz, Herrmann, p. 49. Kellner, p. 29, dates Ahenobarbus' campaign to the Elbe to AD 7.

61 Kornemann, II, p. 142. Simon, in Baatz, Herrmann, pp. 49f., places this uprising into AD 1 when the revolt of most of the tribes between Rhine and Elbe caused Rome to reconsider its buffer-zone-policy for *Germania*.

62 Ph. Filtzinger, 'Römische Provinzen auf deutschem Boden', in *KRI*, II, p. 105. Also Filtzinger, Planck, Cämmerer, p. 36, where Filtzinger sees in the *Oppidum Ubiorum* the capital of the new province of *Germania*.

62 Filtzinger, *KRI*, II, p. 105, as well as in Filtzinger, Planck, Cämmerer, p. 34.

64 W. Pflug, *Media in Germania, Die Römer mitten in Germanien, Eine Darstellung der römischen Expansion in Germanien* (Giessen 1956). p. 15.

65 Velleius, II, CVI, pp. 273f., suggests that nothing remained to be conquered except the Marcomanni. However, Simon, in Baatz, Herrmann, pp. 46f., relativizes Velleius' statement that Tiberius had transformed *Germania* into a tribute paying province. Simon suggests that Tiberius arrived at contractual dependency arrangements with the tribes.

66 Pflug, p. 14. Bechert, p. 59, sees in the military service a deliberate attempt to dissolve the old tribal order.

67 Dio, VII, LVI, 18, p. 39.

68 Grenier, pp. 78f. Arminius had attained the rank of tribune, see Bechert, p. 30.

69 Wells, p. 10.

70 Schutz, pp. 159, 251, 261, 294. Also Jobst, pp. 31, 37, 44, among many references to this amber route. Jobst, p. 32 points out that Augustus, Ahenobarbus, Tiberius, Drusus are all documented to have spent some time in this area.

71 Velleius, II, CVIII, pp. 275ff., sketches their power and the threat they were seen to pose to Italy as the motive for Tiberius' resolve to attack them. Also Simon, in Baatz, Herrmann, p. 50, and Kellner, p. 29, who sees in the Cherusci and the Marcomanni two centers of Germanic power which would have to be overcome if the Elbe was to become a tenable boundary. Jobst, p. 32, points to a speech which Tiberius gave before the Roman Senate in AD 19, 13 years after the aborted campaign, in which he still points to the real danger to Rome fermenting in the area. During that same year intrigue forces Maroboduus to seek the protection of Rome. See note 104 below.

72 Pflug, p. 52. Jobst, pp. 44f., argues that when the sources, Velleius and the elder Pliny, refer to the winter camps of Tiberius, the references can only mean temporary military

bases since no permanent camps were erected before Claudius.

73 Velleius, II, CVIII, pp. 275ff. Simon suggests that it was the task of the army led by Saturninus to check Maroboduus' allies to the north, Baatz, Herrmann, p. 50.

74 Velleius, II, CV, p. 267. He served as prefect of cavalry in *Germania*.

75 Velleius, II, CX, p. 277.

76 Mócsy, pp. 37ff.

77 Wells, p. 161.

78 Velleius, II, CXVII–CXXI, pp. 297–307.

79 Filtzinger, in Filtzinger, Planck, Cämmerer, p. 36, claims that Arminius roused the tribes to follow the Pannonian example.

80 Wells, pp. 156f.

81 Wells, p. 239.

82 Dio, VII, LVI, pp. 39-53.

83 Florus, II, XXX, p. 339.

94 K. Lindemann, *Der Hildesheimer Silberfund, Varus und Germanien* (Hildesheim 1967), p. 14, doubts the length of the battle and sees it as an example of the Roman desire to be seen as heroic.

85 Tacitus, *Histories and Annals*, transl. by C. H. Moore and J. Jackson, (Cambridge, Mass. and London), I, LX, p. 347.

86 Florus, II, XXX, p. 341.

87 Tacitus, *Annals*, I, LX, p. 346.

88 Pflug, pp. 58f.; also Kornemann, II, p. 143, who suggests that it was Philipp Melanchton who first applied the name to the area.

89 Hatt, p. 108.

90 Wells, p. 239.

91 Suetonius, *Life of Augustus*, transl. by J. C. Rolfe, Loeb Classical Library (Cambridge, Mass. and London), XXIII, p. 155.

82 Dio, VII, LVI, pp. 51f.

93 R. E. Smith, *Service in the Post-Marian Army*, reprint of the 1958 edition (Manchester 1961), p. 71, n 2. The three legions had to be replaced, but volunteer recruits barely kept the existing legions at strength. To raise three new legions was virtually impossible.

94 Wells, p. 249, points to poetic references of Roman "manifest destiny".

95 *Res Gestae Divi Augusti*, Loeb Classical Library (Cambridge, Mass. and London), V, 26, vol. 39, pp. 387f.

96 After AD 9 the legions under the command of Tiberius were: at *Vetera*, *legio V alaudae* from Spain, *legio XXI rapax* from *Vindonissa*; at *Oppidum Ubiorum*, *legio I Germanica*, *legio XX Valeria victrix* from *Pannonia*, at *Mogontiacum*, *legio XIV gemina*, *legio XVI Gallica* from *Vindelicum*, *legio II Augusta* from Spain and in the Alpine lowlands *legio XIII gemina*. See Simon, in Baatz, Herrmann, p. 54. Filtzinger, in Filtzinger, Planck, Cämmerer, p. 37, claims that *legio I* had been raised hurriedly from among the population of Rome.

97 Wells, p. 241.

98 Kornemann, II, pp. 172f., also Hatt,

99 pp. 110f,; see also Webster, p. 267, who indicates that the popularity of Germanicus was such that his birthday was still celebrated by the army in the third century.

99 Simon, in Baatz, Herrmann, p. 55, argues that Germanicus' campaign in AD 15 may have had the purpose of demonstrating the glory of the imperial family through the increasing reputation of the heir.

100 Webster, p. 159. Also Filtzinger, in Filtzinger, Planck, Cämmerer, p. 39.

101 E. A. Thompson, *The Early Germans* (Oxford 1965), pp. 72–108, for a detailed discussion of Roman diplomacy.

102 Tacitus, *Annals*, II, XLVI, p. 459.

103 Thompson, p. 91, for Roman rationale.

104 Tacitus, *Annals*, II, LXII, p. 479. Also R. E. M. Wheeler, *Rome beyond the Imperial Frontiers* (London 1954), p. 20, for a brief account of Maroboduus' fate.

105 Simon, in Baatz, Herrmann, p. 59, states that Arminius was murdered when he tried to impose a more strictly organized kingdom on the Cherusci.

106 In AD 28 the Frisian uprising caused Rome considerable losses, yet Rome did not insist on retribution, nor on the re-establishment of the old dependency agreement.

107 M. Cary, *A History of Rome, Down to the Reign of Constantine* (London 1957), p. 626, note 21. Also Tacitus, *Germania*, XXXIII, XXXVII. Baatz, in Baatz, Herrmann, p. 71, states that Vespasian's expansion to the Upper Danube was a tenacious effort rather than the result of battles and of campaigns of conquest, though the legate in command was awarded battle honors. Simon, in Baatz, Herrmann, pp. 53f, 65, also suggests that in Claudio-Neronian times, from c. AD 50 onward, there is only little evidence of a Germanic population east of the Roman lines, perhaps because Rome had cleared the land of tribes as a protective measure. Such settlements as there were must have existed with Roman approval, perhaps in return for strategic support. Filtzinger, in Filtzinger, Planck, Cämmerer, pp. 49ff., points out that no Germanic finds have so far been made in south-western Germany that can be dated to before AD 260. There was continuity of settlement from the Pre-Roman La Tène period even if the Celtic population assimilated quickly.

108 Already Tiberius had divided the command of the army of the Rhine into two military districts, with four legions each—the district of the army of the Upper Rhine, of the *exercitus Germanici superioris*, and the district of the army of the Lower Rhine, of the *exercitus Germanici inferioris*, see Filtzinger, in Filtzinger, Planck, Cämmerer, p. 37. See also M. E. Wightman, *Roman Trier and the Treveri* (New York, Washington 1971), p. 127, who suggests that the creation of these two provinces was a regularization of the existing division between districts that by then were already self-governing *civitates* and those territories administered directly. W. Meyers, *L'Administration de la province romaine de Belgique* (Bruge 1964), p. 12, argues that the late creation of the two Germanic provinces had symbolic rather than administrative significance and that in this fashion the emperors delayed as long as possible the admission to have lost definitely transrhenish *Germania*. See Bechert, pp. 26f., for the boundaries of *Germania inferior*.

109 Filtzinger, "Limites in Deutschland", *KRI*, II, p. 107.

110 Pflug, p. 5, rejects the Varus defeat as one of those "decisive" battles which changed the face of Europe. Not so J. F. C. Fuller, *Decisive Battles of the Western World* (Frogmore, St. Albans 1975), I, pp. 162–81.

111 Smith, p. 71, note 2.

112 Kornemann, II, p. 223, argues that the Gallic populations which were settled by the Flavian emperors to the east of the Rhine were intended to balance the Germanic elements in the area, but see note 107 above.

113 R. MacMullen, *Soldier and Civilian in the Later Roman Empire* (Cambridge, Mass. 1963), pp. 15–17, depicts the legions and auxiliaries as builders, also G. R. Watson, *The Roman Soldier* (London 1969), pp. 143f., who states that building and similar activities were a means of preventing idleness and boredom and potential unrest in the ranks. Only indirectly were the soldiers the vanguard of Roman civilization. See Planck, in Filtzinger, Planck, Cämmerer, pp. 121–61; Baatz, in Baatz, Herrmann, pp. 84–156, and Kellner, pp. 21–167.

114 See Simon, Planck, in Filtzinger, Planck, Cämmerer, pp. 56, 202 respectively for details.

115 Webster, pp. 109–14, for details about the various legions. See Bechert, pp. 67f., for a list of the legions stationed in *Germania inferior*. Also Filtzinger, in Filtzinger, Planck, Cämmerer, p. 61; Baatz, in Baatz, Herrmann, p. 219; Johnson, p. 336, note 104, and Jobst, p. 108.

116 D. Baatz, *Der Römische Limes, Archäologische Ausflüge zwischen Rhein und Donau* (Berlin 1974), p. 17; also Baatz, in Baatz, Herrmann,, p. 135; Filtzinger, in Filtzinger, Planck, Cämmerer, pp. 6of.; see also Webster, pp. 114–21, about the organization of the legions; also Watson, pp. 13, 21–4. Caesar's *legio V alaudae* was formed of Gauls who received their citizenship upon entry into the legion. After the reforms of Augustus this was no longer possible. See Bechert, p. 65 and note 96 above.

117 Webster, p. 119, tells of one centurion who had served with thirteen legions without

promotion. Normally centurions died in the service. See also Watson, pp. 75–88, for a detailed analysis of the rank structure. Also Baatz, in Baatz, Herrmann, p. 135; Filtzinger, in Filtzinger, Planck, Cämmerer, p. 23; Kellner, p. 68; and Jobst, pp. 55ff. For the careers of military commanders, see Johnson, pp. 140–2. During the early Empire all the *cohortes* were of equal size. Then, during Flavian times the first cohort was increased in size and reorganized to contain 5 centuries of 160 men, giving it a total strength of 800 men. Johnson, p. 17, also suggests that the 120 men of cavalry were distributed throughout the individual centuries. Bechert, p. 65, projects a legion's strength at 6,400 men, of whom about 1,500 were employed as administrative and supply personnel.

118 G.L. Cheesman, *The Auxilia of the Roman Imperial Army* (Oxford 1914, reprinted Hildesheim 1971) is still the accepted standard work on the subject; see also Webster, pp. 142–55, on the nature, organization and equipment of the *auxilia;* also Watson, pp. 15f., 24f., also Johnson, pp. 19–26, and Baatz, in Baatz, Herrmann, pp. 134f., and Filtzinger, in Filtzinger, Planck, Cämmerer, pp. 63–7.

119 Cheesman, pp. 22f., for a discussion of designations.

120 Cheesman, pp. 25ff., 36–45, for size and organization. Johnson, pp. 20f., indicates that the military units may have come into being during the Flavian army reforms which also saw the doubling of the first cohort and that the term *miliaria* probably meant not 1,000 men, but 1½ times the size of the quingenary units. Bechert, p. 66, proposes that the 400 men who were on seconded duty in various offices of the province and elsewhere were carried on the lists of the first cohort and that this accounted for the larger size of this cohort, on paper at least.

121 Baatz, *Limes,* p. 19, as well as in Baatz, Herrmann, p. 135.

122 Cheesman, pp. 28f.; also Webster, p. 149, who emphasizes their poorer physique, poorer training and lower pay. See Johnson, p. 20, who states that the *alae* were most prestigious in status and received the highest pay. See Kellner, p. 67, for auxiliary formations and actual units stationed in *Raetia* in the early 2nd century AD. Filtzinger, in Filtzinger, Planck, Cämmerer, pp. 78f., for units and their locations and pp. 99ff., for units and their location in southern Germany, c. AD 400.

123 Baatz, *Limes,* pp. 19f.; Cheesman, pp. 85ff. The *numeri* enjoyed a looser organization as they retained their native characteristics and commanders. They were less romanized since they came from more remote regions of the Empire.

124 Cheesman, p. 57, on the recruitment and distribution. Irregular units, the *exercitus tumultuarius,* could be called up as emergency levies. There were also units of provincial militia, Filtzinger, in Filtzinger, Planck, Cämmerer, pp. 62f.

125 G. Alföldy, *Die Hilfstruppen der römischen Provinz Germania Inferior* (Düsseldorf 1968), pp. 97f.

126 Ibid. pp. 96–8. Alföldy gives a detailed picture of enlistment ages: during the Julio-Claudian period recruits in the west varied in age between 20 to 28 years, in *Danubia* between 20 to 23 years; during the Flavian period in the west between 20 to 36 years, along the Rhine and Danube between 15 to 20 years. One Remus of the *ala Noricum* was 15, another 18.

127 Cheesman, p. 117. By the second century AD the auxiliary units were largely romanized.

128 Smith, p. 72, points out that in 13 BC Augustus required all recruits to swear to serve 16 years. In AD 6 the length of service was increased to 20 years. Pay scales ranged as follows: legionaries received 1,200 sesterces per annum, auxiliaries 1,000, *decurio* of an *ala* 6,000, *centurio* 10–14,000, *tribunus* up to 80,000, *praefectus* of an *ala* 60,000 and a *legatus legionis* far over 100,000.

129 Smith, pp. 51ff. Marius had set the precedent of making land grants available as a means of social reintegration for veterans. The practice created a pool of human resources in the provinces on which the army could call for young recruits.

130 Kellner, pp. 69f. Between 200 BC and AD 200 the *gladius* was used, thereafter the *spatha.* Webster, pp. 122–32, for details of the legionary's equipment. Also Baatz, in Baatz, Herrmann, pp. 135–39; and Filtzinger, in Filtzinger, Planck, Cämmerer, p. 62; and Bechert, pp. 70ff.

131 J. Garbsch, *Der spätrömische Donau-Iller-Rhein-Limes* (Stuttgart 1970), p. 17.

132 Alföldy, *Hilfstruppen,* see note 125 above, also pp. 90f.; also Cheesman, pp. 70, 89. With Trajan and especially after Hadrian these units were encouraged to maintain native methods and characteristics, such as their war cries, which in the late Empire were adopted by all units of the Roman army.

133 Alföldy, *Hilfstruppen,* pp. 107f.; also Watson, pp. 133–7, for a discussion of marriages, unofficial marriages, the diploma and the *conubium* in terms of citizenship and inheritance; also Filtzinger, in Filtzinger, Planck, Cämmerer, p. 86 and Johnson, pp. 9f.

134 Alföldy, *Hilfstruppen,* p. 110.

135 For details of the revolt, see Tacitus, *Histories,* IV, V. See also Alföldy, *Hilfstruppen,* pp. 101ff.; also Webster, pp. 67ff., for a summary of the Batavian Revolt.

136 S. Katz, *The Decline of Rome and the Rise of Medieval Europe* (Ithaca, N.Y. 1961), p. 29.

137 K. Genser, *Die Entwicklung des römischen Limes an der Donau in Österreich* (Salzburg 1975).

138 Katz, p. 45; according to Webster, p. 108, Italy provided next to no troops. Funerary inscriptions point mainly to *Africa* and *Pannonia* as recruiting areas.

139 Webster, p. 264, points out that the body guard came to be drawn from the *auxilia*. Tacitus, *Annals*, I, XXIV, p. 287, states that Germani belonged to the imperial body guard already under Tiberius.

140 Genser, also Cheesman, p. 120, points to the increasing tendency towards matrimony as early as the 2nd century AD as life along the frontiers became ever more settled.

141 Kornemann, II, p. 307; also Cheesman, p. 114, who suggests that from Hadrian's time onward the posting along the borders became permanent.

142 M. Cary, pp. 707f.

143 Webster, p. 89 indicates that Hadrian's permanent attachment of *numeri*, the native levies, to auxiliary fortifications, led to almost hereditary garrison troops recruited from among the frontier peoples. Also Filtzinger, in Filtzinger, Planck, Cämmerer, p. 86; and Kellner, p. 142.

144 Smith, pp. 27–43, illustrates that already during the Civil Wars of the Republic the oath of loyalty had been given to the person of the general and not to the state represented in the general.

145 Katz, pp. 47f.

146 Garbsch, pp. 6f., for an enumeration of the waves of invasions.

147 Cheesman, pp. 138f., suggests that since the border areas, the normal recruiting grounds for the army, were the first to suffer from the invasions and raids and since the imperial hinterland was loath to provide even reluctant recruits, the administration had no choice but to recruit from among prisoners of war and finally hire entire tribes from beyond the frontiers.

148 Cheesman, pp. 100f., points out that the increased reliance on barbarian forces for defence may have been a failure but was not a mistake in principle.

149 Watson, p. 67, for details of camp construction; see also Webster, pp. 166ff., on the development of encampments from leather tent cities to permanent fortifications, pp. 176f., on the construction of the defences. See Johnson, for all aspects of Roman fort construction: p. 1, Roman marching camps; pp. 27–30, classical sources concerning Roman fort plans: p. 228, Johnson points out that hardly anything is known about the form and internal arrangements of Roman camps during the 1st century BC.

150 Wells, pp. 150f.; Johnson, pp. 222–34, deals with structural developments to the time of Augustus.

151 Wells, p. 230; also Johnson, p. 232, concerning the supply base at Rödgen.

152 Wells, p. 217; also Johnson, p. 231.

153 Baatz, *Limes*, p. 27. Johnson, pp. 31, 230, 234–46, indicates that during the times of Augustus and Tiberius the forts were polygonal in shape and tended to follow the contours of the site and that only from the time of Claudius onward did a regular shape become the characteristic feature. *Carnuntum*, however, retained its very irregular shape throughout, see Jobst, pp. 46f.

154 Baatz, *Limes*, pp. 27ff., for details of the disposition of buildings; also Wells, pp. 130ff.; and Webster, pp. 188–201, for buildings located within the fortifications. See also Baatz, in Baatz, Herrmann, p. 142; also Filtzinger, in Filtzinger, Planck, Cämmerer, pp. 66–70.

155 See especially Johnson for detailed discussion of all aspects. Jobst, pp. 45–75, gives a good analysis of the legion fort *Carnuntum*.

156 Wells, p. 87. See Bechert, pp. 86–90, for details of the camp at Haltern.

157 Webster, pp. 203f., for details of the *canabae* and *vici*. Also Cheesman, p. 117, for the *canabae* as veteran settlements. See Johnson, p. 239, who states that the *vicus* at Burghöfe may be the earliest example of a Roman civilian settlement in Western Europe, datable to the first half of the 1st century AD.

158 Cheesman, p. 30; also Johnson, p. 17; Filtzinger, in Filtzinger, Planck, Cämmerer, pp. 70ff. and Jobst, pp. 55–62.

159 Wells, p. 186.

160 See especially Watson, pp. 31–74, for details of daily routines, such as weapons training and conditioning for endurance.

161 Webster, p. 179, points out that extensive campaigning would lead to rapid deterioration of the timber and earth fortifications, so that in the earlier period considerable time would be spent on the maintenance of the fortified encampments.

162 Baatz, *Limes*, pp. 45f., and Watson, pp. 72f., for details of barracks duties.

163 Webster, pp. 266f., Johnson, p. 111; and Watson, pp. 127–30f., provide details of religious and cultic practices as unifying elements.

164 Troops of the legion could expect to be on detached duty. For a discussion of such functions, Webster, pp. 263–66.

165 Baatz, *Die Saalburg, Ein Führer durch das römische Kastell und seine Geschichte* (Bad Homburg 1976), for details on this *castellum*. Also Johnson, p. 273 and elsewhere. See Baatz, in Baatz, Herrmann, pp. 469–74.

166 Cheesman, pp. 65f., for a discussion of the *cohortes civium romanorum*.

167 Baatz, *Limes*, pp. 13–16, for historical details pertaining to this sector (see note 116 above). Kellner, p. 48, suggests that Domi-

tian marched against the Chatti because he had been called by the Cherusci to help in their constant strife with the Chatti. Baatz, in Baatz, Herrmann, p. 74, is of the opinion that in AD 84 Domitian tried to have the Cherusci attack the Chatti in the rear, probably as part of the Roman policy of divide and rule.

168 Baatz, *Limes*, p. 15. Also Baatz, in Baatz, Herrmann, p. 73.

169 Domitian employed legions I, VIII, XI, XIV, XXI and troops from Britain in legion strength, plus auxiliaries to a total of c. 30,000 men. See Baatz, in Baatz, Herrmann, p. 73.

170 M. Cary, pp. 614ff.; also Kornemann, II, p. 221.

171 Hatt, p. 160, speaks of 5 legions and numerous auxiliaries which annexed all the territory between *Argentorate* and Lake Constance.

172 Tacitus, *Germania*, p. 176, note 2, 'ten cantons'. This move marked the emergence of a concept of linear borders with frontier defences, Kellner, pp. 47f.

173 Hatt, p. 160, speaks of 'proletaires gaulois'; M. Hutton, translator of the LCL edition of Tacitus' *Germania*, speaks of the "wastrels of Gaul", LCL, p. 177.

174 Kornemann, II, p. 278, indicates that Britons came to be deployed along this line as builders and border guards. Webster, p. 95, points to the *numeri* of Britons stationed in the Odenwald. Webster, p. 97, also argues that this relocation of the frontier was rather a part of the Antonine agrarian reform, a means of including good farm land to help support a growing population. Moving the border eastward reduced the significance of *Arae Flaviae*, Filtzinger, in Filtzinger, Planck, Cämmerer, p. 49.

175 For details of the *limes* see Baatz, *Limes*, 39–45 and in Baatz, Herrmann, pp. 374–423; Filtzinger, in Filtzinger, Planck, Cämmerer, pp. 57, 72–81; Kellner, pp. 49, 59. See also Johnson, p. 269.

176 Baatz, *Limes*, p. 7. In all, over 200 *castella* are known in Germany, see Johnson, p. 14. Baatz, in Baatz, Herrmann, p. 211, argues that pushing the *limes* forward reflects anticipatory measures in reaction to population movements and shifts of power in *Germania*. Also Kellner, p. 134, concerning the Raetian *limes*.

177 Baatz, 'Zur Grenzpolitik Hadrians in Obergermanien', in E. Birley, et al., *Roman Frontier Studies* (Cardiff 1974). However, see Baatz, in Baatz, Herrmann, pp. 469f.; also Johnson, p. 273.

178 Baatz, in Baatz, Herrmann, pp. 139f., divides the Roman troops supporting the Upper German limes during the 2nd and early 3rd century into 2 legions of c. 11,000 men, 22

auxiliary cohorts and 3 *alae*—a total of c. 13,000 men, as well as units of *numeri* of some 4–6,000 men, fluctuating between a total strength of 28–30,000 men, the 2 legions forming a strategic reserve in their *castra* at *Argentorate* and *Mogontiacum* on the Rhine, Baatz states, however, that only about 4 or 5 men guarded every 300 to 1000 m.

179 H. v. Petrikovits, 'Beiträge zur Geschichte des Niedergermanischen Limes', in J. E. Bogaers, C. B. Rüger, *Der Niedergermanische Limes* (Cologne 1974). Also Bechert, pp. 78ff.

180 G. Precht, 'Köln-Deutz, spätrömische Festung', in *KRI*, II, pp. 129f. See Bechert on all aspects relating to *Germania inferior*.

181 F. Křížek, 'Die römischen Stationen im Vorland des norisch-pannonischen Limes bis zu den Markomannenkriegen', in Birley, et al., *Studien zu den Militärgrenzen Roms, Vorträge des 6. Internationalen Limeskongresses in Süddeutschland* (Colonge, Graz 1967).

182 Baatz, *Limes*, pp. 43f.; also Kellner, p. 51.

183 Behn, p. 46, claims that they were frequent visitors to the markets at *Augusta Vindelicum*. Tacitus, *Germania*, 71, p. 202, does not mention the city.

184 Thompson, pp. 79ff., gives a detailed discussion of Roman methods.

185 Thompson, p. 86.

186 Thompson, p. 91, note 1.

187 Thompson, pp. 93ff., suggests that it was the deliberate policy of the imperial government to bestow coercive, personal power on individuals who had not previously wielded it.

188 Thompson, pp. 99f.

189 M. Cary, p. 656.

190 Thompson, pp. 102f.

191 Kellner, pp. 71f., sees not only Germanic but also Ponto-Scythian, Dacian and even Celtic tribal units on the move looking for land.

192 Kellner, pp. 71f.

193 Filtzinger, in Filtzinger, Planck, Cämmerer, pp. 81f.; also Kellner, pp. 72ff., who indicates that with the stationing of the 2 legions in *Raetia* and *Noricum* the status of these provinces was changed from proconsular to praetorian provinces and with it the civilian administration came under the commander of the legion, a senatorial *legatus Augusti pro praetore*.

194 Kellner, p. 73.

195 Kellner, pp. 74f., for details concerning *Castra Regina*. The inscription proclaiming the foundation of *Castra Regina* in AD 179/80 represents a good example of imperial propaganda. The inscription on the *porta principalis* names Marcus Helvius Clemens Dextrianus as legion commander and governor—*legatus Augusti pro praetore*. His seat was in the provincial capital at *Augusta Vindelicum*.

196 Baatz, *Limes*, p. 63.

197 Garbsch, pp. 6f., provides an extensive list of invasions from the north. Also Baatz, in

Baatz, Herrmann, p. 214; Filtzinger, in *KRI*, II, p. 108 and in Filtzinger, Planck, Cämmerer, pp. 91, 95 and 84f. Here Filtzinger argues that the pressure of the Goths forced the Burgundians upon the Semnones who in turn penetrated the territory of the Hermunduri, perhaps absorbing many of them, and reached the *limes* in AD 213. There the Romans reported for the first time the presence of a mixed people, the *Alamanni homines*. These tribal units, the Alamanni, were Suebian peoples belonging to the West-Germanic group of peoples. Against this Alamannic concentration the emperor Caracalla launched a massive offensive with troops drawn from all the legions stationed in Europe. Even the *legio II Traiana* stationed in Egypt and the *legio II adiutrix* from *Aquincum* on the Middle Danube received marching orders for *Raetia*. For his victory over the Alamanni Caracalla assumed the title *Germanicus maximus*—greatest victor over the Germani. His campaign may have been effective, since in AD 215 units of the *legio III Italica concors* were transferred from the Danube to the East, to be used in the Parthian campaign. See Kellner, p. 132.

198 Kellner, p. 138.

199 Kellner, pp. 149, 154.

200 G.C. Brauer, *The Age of the Soldier Emperors, Imperial Rome AD 244–284* (Park Ridge, N.J. 1975), pp. 181–5.

201 Brauer, especially pp. 121–4, 141–3, 244–346.

202 Kellner, pp. 147ff.

203 Brauer, p. 180.

204 Brauer, pp. 194f., for descriptive detail.

205 Kellner, p. 153; also Brauer, p. 246.

206 Kornemann, II, pp. 357ff.; also M. Cary, p. 730; Kellner, p. 157; also Filtzinger, in Filtzinger, Planck, Cämmerer, p. 102, for details of Diocletians organization of the Empire.

207 Kornemann, II, pp. 366ff. Also Filtzinger, in Filtzinger, Planck, Cämmerer, p. 97.

208 Kornemann, II, p. 369. Also Filtzinger, in Filtzinger, Planck, Cämmerer, pp. 98, 101. As part of the refortification of this border watchtowers, *burgi*, with room for 15–20 men were located 1–4 kilometers apart. The *castella* housed an administrative core and a mobile reserve. The remainder of the garrison was posted to about 12–15 *burgi* along the *limes*.

209 Kornemann, II, p. 370.

210 R.I. Frank, *Scholae Palatinae, The Palace Guards of the Later Roman Empire* (American Academy in Rome 1969), p. 64. The decisive role played by the Cornuti, a Germanic contingent, in the final battle at the Milvian Bridge was recognized by Constantine. This recognition led to a general inclusion of Germani in the elite units and opened the door for further advancement to positions of command.

211 Hatt, p. 295.

212 Kellner, pp. 173, 181. Ammianus Marcellinus, *The Surviving Books of the History of*, in Three Volumes, with an English translation by J.C. Rolfe, LCL, XXVIII, 5, 10–11, p. 167, makes the curious suggestion that the Burgundians were descendants of Romans, perhaps left there by Drusus and Tiberius.

213 Frank, pp. 64ff., details the position played by Franks at the court during the 2nd century AD.

214 Hatt, p. 293, indicates that the battle of Mursa, AD 351, cost the Empire 54,000 casualties which could not be replaced.

215 Frank, p. 79, points out that the core of the new military nobility created for the 4th century army was trained in the *scholae palatinae*, its troops recruited from Germanic tribes, its officers non-Roman and Roman aristocrats, tied personally to the person of the emperor. It is worth remembering that the concept "Roman" was not an ethnological term in any case, but rather a judicial consideration.

216 M. Waas, *Germanen in römischem Dienst im 4.Jahrhundert nach Christus* (Bonn 1965), pp. 91ff.

217 This was an extraordinary event in view of the decree that intermarriages were expressly forbidden, a crime which under Valentinian (AD 370) bore the death penalty, see Frank, p. 66.

218 Waas, pp. 110–16.

219 Waas, pp. 119–22.

220 Waas, pp. 83–6; J.B. Bury, *A History of the Roman Empire from Arcadius to Irene* (AD 395 to AD 800) (Amsterdam 1966, reprint of the 1889 ed.), p. 61, note 1, credits Bauto and Arbogast with the pacification of the Goths.

221 W. Seyfarth, ed. of Ammianus Marcellinus, *Römische Geschichte*, mit einem Kommentar, übersehen von Wolfgang Seyfarth, in vier Teilen (Berlin 1971), IV, p. 362, note 74, indicates that Flavius Richomer protected Eugenius, the aspirant to the purple put forward by the pagan faction in AD 392.

222 J.B. Bury, *History of the Later Roman Empire from the Death of Theodosius I to the Death of Justinian* (New York 1958), I, pp. 106f., details Stilicho's position at court and his military leadership.

223 Bury, *History*, pp. 119, 165. Claudian was the unofficial poet-laureate at the court of Honorius where he was retained by Stilicho and acted as his propagandist.

224 Seyfarth, IV, p. 350, shows that one Mallobaudes, who had served as *comes domesticorum* in the imperial service, returned to his tribe. He is also referred to as *rex Francorum*, a title he probably received after his return, while one Malarichus, when named *magister armorum*, declined the office and returned home, p. 279, note 74.

225 Bury, *History*, pp. 170–75, details the fall of Stilicho and the murder of his family.

2. Roman Religious Culture along the Rhine and the Danube

1 A. Grenier, *Les Gaulois* (Paris 1970), p. 347.
2 Grenier, p. 348.
3 J.J. Hatt, *Histoire de la Gaule romaine*, 3e édition (Paris 1970), pp. 139ff. T. Bechert, *Römisches Germanien zwischen Rhein und Maas, Die Provinz Germania Inferior* (Munich 1982), p. 36, points to the repeated revolts in Gaul and left-rhenish *Germania* as signs of superficial romanization—*romanitas*.
4 5. Katz, *The Decline of Rome and the Rise of Medieval Europe* (Ithaca, N.Y. 1961), p.16.
5 H. Schoppa, *Die Kunst der Römerzeit in Gallien, Germanien und Britannien* (Munich 1957), p. 21.
6 Schoppa, p. 22.
7 G. Alföldy, *Noricum, History of the Provinces of the Roman Empire*, transl. by A. Birley (London and Boston 1974), pp. 136f.; also H.J. Kellner, *Die Römer in Bayern* (Munich 1971, 2nd ed. 1978), p. 108, who suggests that it was the Romans' conscientiousness towards the gods which caused them to accept and venerate the gods of other peoples.
8 G. Ristow, *Kölner Römer Illustrierte*, 1, ed. by M. Wellershoff (Cologne 1974), p. 140. Hereafter the journal will be cited as *KRI*. Bechert, p. 217, indicates that *religio* was a concern for precise cultic procedures and not a deep religious feeling. Through ritual one tried to tie the unknown forces.
9 Kellner, p. 108, believes that the religious center at *Cambodunum*/Kempten may have been a fourth religious focus, its name having been lost.
10 Tacitus uses this expression in his *Germania*, transl. by M. Hutton, Loeb Classical Library (Cambridge, Mass. London 1970), 43, p. 203. This could be done easily by merely placing *dea* or *deus* before the name of a local god. See Bechert, p. 230.
11 Alföldy, p. 137.
12 Alföldy, p. 142.
13 Alföldy, p. 135.
14 Alföldy, pp. 135f.; also Kellner, p. 107 who points to Jupiter having been linked with the native gods Arubianus or Poeninus in *Raetia*. Generally Jupiter was revered in his own right.
15 A. Mócsy, *Pannonia and Upper Moesia, A History of the Middle Danube Provinces of the Roman Empire*, transl. by S. Frere (London and Boston 1974), p. 191.
16 J. de Vries, *Kelten und Germanen* (Berlin and Munich 1960), p. 18.
17 G. C. Picard, 'César et les Druides', in *Hommage à la mémoire de Jerome Carcopino* (Paris 1977), pp. 230f., points out that Caesar did not use the word 'Druid' but only spoke of '*sacerdotus*'.
18 de Vries, 'Die Druiden', in *Kairos, Zeitschrift für Religionswissenschaft und Theologie*, 11 (Salzburg 1959), p. 68, asserts that Caesar's comments on the Druids are reliable.
19 Grenier, p. 312; see de Vries, in *Kairos*, 11, p. 75; see also H. Schutz, *The Prehistory of Germanic Europe* (New Haven and London 1983), pp. 270ff.
20 Grenier, p. 311.
21 Julius Caesar, *The Gallic War and Other Writings*, transl. by M. Hadas (New York 1957), pp. 135f.
22 de Vries, in *Kairos*, 11, p. 79, interprets this to mean that Druidic teaching was most purely preserved in Britain, while it was already showing signs of decay in Gaul.
23 de Vries, *Kelten und Germanen*, p. 83, points to similar practices in ancient India.
24 Caesar, p. 137.
25 Caesar, p. 136.
26 Grenier, p. 311.
27 Caesar, p. 135.
28 Caesar, p. 135.
29 Grenier, p. 311.
30 Caesar, p. 136.
31 Pliny, *Natural History in 10 Volumes*, vol. VIII, transl. by W.H.S. Jones, Loeb Classical Library (Cambridge, Mass. London), pp. 549f.
32 de Vries, in *Kairos*, 11, pp. 71f.
33 de Vries, in *Kairos*, 11, pp. 71f., for a more detailed discussion.
34 de Vries, in *Kairos*, 11, pp. 73–76, points to the existence of a political structure.
35 Grenier, p. 316.
36 Grenier, p. 316; see also A.D. Booth, *A Study of Ausonius' "Professores"*, unpublished dissertation (McMaster University, Hamilton, Canada 1974), p. 379.
37 Booth, p. 378, argues that it was probably not until romanization was in progress that the Druids emerged as a central force to protect and maintain Gallic traditions.
38 F. Leroux, *Introduction générale à l'étude de la tradition celtique I* (Rennes 1967).
39 F. Schlette, *Kelten zwischen Alesia und Pergamon, Eine Kulturgeschichte der Kelten* (Leipzig, Jena, Berlin 1979), p. 125.
40 Leroux, p. 29, argues that polytheism and anthropomorphism are in essence derivations of Greco-Roman religious thought, reflecting an enforced specialization of divine function which as distinguishing features lay claim to superior intellectual capacity. See also J.V.S. Megaw, *Art of the European Iron Age, A Study of the Elusive Image* (Bath 1970), p. 20.
41 Megaw, p. 20.
42 Grenier, p. 292.
43 de Vries, *Kelten und Germanen*, p. 100, note 79, believes that the animal representations were never more than symbolic representations of the gods and not divine objects of worship in themselves, though he admits that they may derive from earlier times.

44 de Vries, *Keltische Religion* (Stuttgart 1961), pp. 91–6, 181; see also G. Mahr, *Die Jüngere Latènekultur des Trierer Landes, Eine stilkundliche und chronologische Untersuchung auf Grund der Keramik und des Bestattungswesens* (Berlin 1967), pp. 159–64, who cannot point to such practices in the core area of the tribe of the Germani.

45 de Vries, *Keltische Religion*, pp. 172–5.

46 de Vries, *Keltische Religion*, pp. 176–80.

47 Grenier, p. 301.

48 Megaw, p. 20.

49 Grenier, p. 291.

50 K.M. Linduff, "Epona: a Celt among the Romans", in *Latomus, Revue d'études latines* (Berchem-Bruxelles 1979), pp. 812–37.

51 P.-M. Duval, *La vie quotidienne en Gaule pendant la paix romaine* (Paris 1967), p. 309.

52 Leroux, p. 33.

53 de Vries, *Keltische Religion*, p. 18, suggests that the pre-eminence of Mercury in Caesar's summary may mean no more than that merchants, for whom Mercury was the patron divinity, were the source of his information.

54 de Vries, *Keltische Religion*, p. 22.

55 de Vries, *Kelten und Germanen*, p. 96.

58 Caesar, p. 137; also Grenier, pp. 287, 292.

57 de Vries, *Keltische Religion*, p. 81.

58 Alföldy, p. 150.

59 G. Ristow, "Zwei keltische Götter in Köln, Rad- und Hammergott", in *KRI*, I, p. 87.

60 Duval, p. 304; also Grenier, p. 187; also de Vries, *Keltische Religion*, pp. 91–6.

61 Schutz, pp. 17of.

62 Lucan, *Pharsalia*, I, lines 444f. Dramatic Episodes of the Civil War. A new translation by R. Graves (Harmondsworth 1956), p. 38.

63 It was Herodotus who suggested the essential nature of all divinities was only apparently differentiated by local names.

64 Grenier, p. 294.

65 Duval, p. 308.

66 de Vries, *Keltische Religion*, pp. 45–50.

67 Grenier, p. 294.

68 Caesar, p. 137; also de Vries, *Keltische Religion*, p. 50, who suggests that the 'drowning scene' on the Gundestrup Cauldron represents a sacrifice to Teutates.

69 de Vries, *Keltische Religion*, pp. 63f.; also Grenier, p. 293.

70 Duval, p. 309; also Grenier, p. 293.

71 See also E. Will in H.J. Eggers, E. Will, R. Joffroy, W. Holmquist, *Kelten und Germanen in heidnischer Zeit* (Baden-Baden 1964), p. 99; also Ph. Filtzinger, 'Die Jupitergigantensäule von Wahlheim,' in *Fundberichte aus Baden-Württemberg*, I (Stuttgart 1974), pp. 437ff.

72 Grenier, p. 294.

73 Leroux, pp. 59–70, discusses the sacred nature of the sacrifice. She insists that this question has always been misunderstood and been approached from a moral rather than a metaphysical point of view. She maintains that animal substitution will have been possible in most instances, so that human sacrifice will have been rare and certainly there were no bloodbaths.

74 Caesar, p. 137.

75 Tacitus, *Germania*, IX, pp. 144f. See Kellner, pp. 110f. for the importance of Mercury in *Raetia*.

76 de Vries, *Keltische Religion*, pp. 71–8.

77 Grenier, p. 288.

78 Kellner, pp. 111f., points out that Apollo was not prominent in *Raetia*, but that he was revered in his Celtic guise as Apollo Grannus, alone as well as in the company of other gods.

79 Alföldy, pp. 194, 239.

80 de Vries, *Keltische Religion*, pp. 104–7, suggests that the stag god bears the name Cernunnos only once and that on an altar dedicated to Esus, found under the choir of Notre Dame in Paris. de Vries also argues that gods with animal attributes are not of Indo-European origin but belong to an earlier time.

81 Grenier, p. 295.

82 M. Dillon and N.K. Chadwick, *The Celtic Realms* (London 1967), p. 13; also de Vries, *Keltische Religion*, pp. 50–5.

83 Dillon and Chadwick, p. 13; also de Vries, *Keltische Religion*, p. 54.

84 Leroux, p. 33.

85 Duval, pp. 309ff., provides a select list.

86 Caesar, p. 137.

87 de Vries, *Keltische Religion*, pp. 78f.

88 Grenier, p. 198.

88 de Vries, *Keltische Religion*, pp. 114–16. *Germania inferior* was the center of the cult around the *matrones*. See Bechert, p. 228.

90 G. Ristow, 'Die Matronengöttinen' in *KRI*, I, p. 90; also Ristow, 'Boudennehische Matronen,' in *KRI*, I, p. 91; Ristow, 'Der Matronentempel bei Zinsheim,' in *KRI*, II, p. 194; also H.G. Horn, 'Matronenaltare aus Morken-Harff,' *KRI*, II, pp. 194f.

91 P. La Baume, *The Romans on the Rhine* (Bonn 1966), pp. 51ff.

92 H. Birkhan, *Germanen und Kelten bis zum Ausgang der Römerzeit, Der Aussagewert von Wörtern und Sachen für die frühesten Keltisch-Germanischen Kulturbeziehungen* (Vienna, Cologne, Graz 1970), pp. 518–44, argues for Germanic familiarity with these figures and a confluence in the Ubian area with Celtic notions of fertility, assistance at birth, the fates and warlike functions, the latter accounting for their popularity with the military.

93 W. Heiligendorff, *Der Keltische Matronenkultus und seine Fortentwicklung im Deutschen Mythos* (Leipzig 1934); also Wightman, *Roman Trier and the Treveri* (New York, Washington 1971), p. 242, who identifies them with such

names as Faith, Hope and Charity, or Les Trois Vierges in northern Luxembourg.

94 Heiligendorff, p. 20.

95 de Vries, *Keltische Religion*, pp. 123–7; for a detailed discussion see especially Linduff, 'Epona,' in *Latomus*, pp. 817–37.

96 Linduff, p. 819, note 9, argues that Epona was not Celtic alone but Indo-European.

97 Linduff, p. 823.

98 See B. Cämmerer, 'Römische Religion', in Ph. Filtzinger, D. Planck, B. Cämmerer, et al., *Die Römer in Baden-Württemberg* (Stuttgart, Aalen 1976), pp. 163–98, as well as E. Künzl in D. Baatz, F.-R. Herrmann, et al., *Die Römer in Hessen* (Stuttgart 1982), pp. 178–203, for a detailed discussion of Roman religion as it pertains to the provinces along the *limes*.

99 de Vries, *Keltische Religion*, pp. 31–4. See also Künzl, in Baatz, Herrmann, pp. 187, 191, who sees in these columns a synthesis of Celtic and Italic elements of the late first century AD but especially of the period AD 160/70–240.

100 G. Ristow, 'Jupitersäulen und Jupiterpfeiler—eine Darstellung der Römischen Götterherrschaft,' in *KRI*, I, pp. 140f; also P. Noelke, 'Säulen- und Pfeilerweihungen für Jupiter,' in *KRI*, II, p. 188; also Filtzinger, 'Die Jupitergigantensäule von Wahlheim,' in *Fundberichte aus Baden-Württemberg*, I (Stuttgart 1974), pp. 437ff; also Filtzinger, 'Jupitergigantensäule von Wahlheim, Kreis Ludwigsburg,' in *KRI*, II, pp. 189f., and Filtzinger, 'Jupitergigantensäule,' in *KRI*, II, pp. 190f.

101 Noelke, *KRI*, II, p. 188; also Birkhan, pp. 290–303.

102 Birkhan, p. 292, points out that they enjoyed particular popularity between the rivers Moselle and Neckar. Künzl, in Baatz, Herrmann, p. 184, holds the opinion that it was the native, Celtic and later oriental cults and not the Greco-Roman divinities which dominated the religious life in the Rhine-Main area.

103 See especially Birkhan, pp. 296ff.; also Künzl in Baatz, Herrmann, pp. 162, 187–94.

104 Hatt, p. 137, suggests the column was raised to commemorate this very event.

105 B. Cämmerer, in Filtzinger, Planck, Cämmerer, pp. 169ff., indicates that antique mythology saw in the triumph of the gods over the titans the symbolic victory of order and culture over chaos and the boundless forces of darkness; see also J. von Elbe, *Roman Germany, A Guide to Sites and Museums* (Mainz 1975), pp. 169, 258. Birkhan, pp. 296ff., suggests that the very presence of the other gods reinforces the claim to identity with the *cosmocrator*, who performs the symbolic conquest over a barbarian enemy as represented in the giant. H. J. Kellner, *Die Römer in Bayern* (Munich 1971, 1978), pp.

109f, has noticed that these columns were especially popular during the second century AD, a time when the oriental cults were making their presence felt in the west.

106 Filtzinger, *KRI*, II, p. 191.

107 von Elbe, p. 399.

108 A. and R. Schmid, *Die Römer an Rhein und Main. Das Leben in der Oberrheinischen Provinz* (Frankfurt 1972), p. 213. Kellner, p. 136; proposes that the increasing influence of oriental families in the west paved the way for the oriental cults.

109 S. F. G. Brandon, 'The idea of the Judgement of the Dead in the Ancient Near East,' in J. R. Hinnels, ed., *Mithraic Studies* (Manchester 1975), pp. 470ff.

110 R. MacMullen, *The Roman Government's Response to Crisis, AD 235–337* (New Haven and London 1976), p. 13, suggests a tendency to rely upon revelation and mystical communication rather than upon rational analysis to meet the crisis of the third century.

111 W. Tarn and G. T. Griffith, *Hellenistic Civilization* (London 1953), p. 343.

112 G. Ristow, 'Jupiter Dolichenus—der siegende Gott', in *KRI*, I, p. 146. Bechert, pp. 233f., claims an appeal to Dolichenus once led Roman arms to victory which accounted for his popularity with the army.

113 M. P. Speidel, *The Religion of Iuppiter Dolichenus in the Roman Army* (Leiden 1978), p. 1.

114 Tarn and Griffith, p. 343.

115 Speidel, p. 2.

116 Speidel, p. 3.

117 Speidel, p. 4.

118 Speidel, p. 10.

119 Speidel, pp. 11, 38f.

120 Speidel, pp. 38f.

121 Speidel, p. 41.

122 Speidel, pp. 21–4, engages in a more detailed discussion of the pair in the context of the cult of Dolichenus.

123 Alföldy, p. 195.

124 Speidel, pp. 25f.

125 Speidel, p. 26.

126 Speidel, p. 27, quotes F. Cumont.

127 Speidel, p. 29.

128 Speidel, p. 28.

129 Speidel, p. 43.

130 Speidel, p. 44.

131 Speidel, pp. 64ff.

132 M. Wellershoff, 'Aurelianus,' in *KRI*, I, pp. 268f.

133 Mócsy, pp. 258f.

134 Speidel, p. 72.

135 Speidel, pp. 74f.

136 See also E. Schwertheim, *Die Denkmäler orientalischer Gottheiten im römischen Deutschland* (Leiden 1974), pp. 305–15. Kellner, p. 117, points to the sites in *Raetia* where the cults of Dolichenus—Sol and Mithras had merged to become almost one.

137 Ristow, 'Die große Göttermutter der Cybele

und der Götterjüngling Attis,' in *KRI*, I, p. 144. Bechert, pp. 232f.

138 H. Jens, *Mythologisches Lexikon* (Munich 1958), p. 11.

139 See also Schwertheim, pp. 290–305.

140 Tarn and Griffith, pp. 353f.

141 Tarn and Griffith, pp. 355ff.

142 Tarn and Griffith, p. 358.

143 Tarn and Griffith, p. 359f.

144 Ristow, 'Das ägyptische Himmelsgötterpaar Isis und Osiris,' in *KRI*, I, p. 149.

145 von Elbe, p. 196.

146 Schwertheim, pp. 267ff., indicates that the greatest number of monuments dedicated to this cult has been found in Germany, dating from the end of the 2nd and from the 3rd centuries AD and of which eighteen were military and forty-six were civilian dedications.

147 C. M. Daniels, 'The role of the Roman Army in the spread and practice of Mithraism,' in *Mithraic Studies*, p. 251.

148 Mócsy, p. 255.

149 Daniels, in *Mithraic Studies*, p. 263.

150 Mócsy, p. 255.

151 Mócsy, p. 256.

152 Alföldy, p. 195.

153 According to Schwertheim, p. 284, the finds from Germany offer something of an artistic 'resumé' of the cult. See G. Webster, *The Roman Imperial Army to Caracalla* (London 1969), pp. 270f., for Mithraic rituals and the location of Mithraic sanctuaries.

154 Daniels, in *Mithraic Studies*, pp. 249–74.

155 Ibid.

156 Mócsy, pp. 276, 324; MacMullen, *Crisis*, p. 42, indicates that the Celtic god Belenus, along with Mithras and Dolichenus were Diocletian's favorite divinities.

157 S. Katz, *The Decline of Rome and the Rise of Medieval Europe* (Ithaca, New York 1961), p. 68; see also Webster, p. 271, according to whom Christianity had little effect in the military areas.

158 Daniels, in *Mithraic Studies*, p. 267; also von Elbe, p. 369.

159 Mócsy, pp. 258f.

160 P. Thieme, 'The concept of Mitra in Aryan belief,' in *Mithraic Studies*, p. 30.

161 R. L. R. Gordon, 'Franz Cumont and the doctrines of Mithraism,' in *Mithraic Studies*, pp. 215–48. Cumont finds himself opposed by most of the authors in *Mithraic Studies*, especially on p. 225.

162 J. R. Hinnels, 'Reflections on the bull-slaying scene,' in *Mithraic Studies*, pp. 291f.

163 Hinnels, in *Mithraic Studies*, pp. 290f.

164 M. Schwarz, 'Cautes and Cautopates, the Mithraic torchbearers,' in *Mithraic Studies*, p. 406.

165 Schwarz, in *Mithraic Studies*, p. 414.

166 L. A. Campbell, *Mithraic Iconography and Ideology* (Leiden 1968), p. 377.

167 M. J. Vermaseren, *Mithras, The Secret God* (London 1963), p. 77.

168 Campbell, p. 378.

169 Campbell, p. 373.

170 Vermaseren, p. 79.

171 Campbell, p. 389.

172 Vermaseren, p. 67.

173 A. and R. Schmid, p. 211.

174 Cämmerer, in Filtzinger, Planck, Cämmerer, p. 198. It is suggested here that the bull's meat and blood were consumed in the form of bread and wine.

175 Vermaseren, p. 138.

176 Vermaseren, p. 140.

177 Vermaseren, pp. 141–53, offers details.

178 Mócsy, pp. 254, 259.

179 R. G. A. Carson, 'From Tiber's seven hills to world dominion,' in Michael Grant, ed., *The Birth of Western Civilization, Greece and Rome* (London, New York, Toronto 1964), p. 237.

180 Hatt, pp. 273–9, for pagan and Christian interpretations of Constantine's vision. See also MacMullen, *Crisis*, p. 37, who suggests that by such phenomena as divine signs in critical situations the ruler fulfilled the hopes of his subjects for the advent of better times, of a Golden Age.

181 C. Colpe, 'Mithras-Verehrung, Mithras-Kult und die Existenz iranischer Mysterien,' in *Mithraic Studies*, pp. 397ff.

182 R. E. Witt, 'Some thoughts on Isis in relation to Mithras,' in *Mithraic Studies*, p. 490.

183 Witt, in *Mithraic Studies*, p. 491.

184 von Elbe, pp. 110f. This scene is carved on a rotating disc. On the reverse it shows the Phaeton myth. An inscription names one Silvestrius Silvinus of the tribe of the Bituriges from western Gaul, evidently one of the great master stone carvers of his day, see F. Behn, *Römertum und Völkerwanderung, Mitteleuropa zwischen Augustus und Karl dem Großen* (Stuttgart 1963), p. 39.

185 von Elbe, pp. 168f.

186 Campbell, p. 169; see also B. Heukemes, in Filtzinger, Planck, Cämmerer, p. 282, who points to a possible link with a Jupiter-Giant column nearby.

187 von Elbe, p. 237.

188 F. Cumont, 'The Dura Mithraeum,' in *Mithraic Studies*, p. 188.

189 Gordon, in *Mithraic Studies*, pp. 224f.

190 Schwertheim, pp. 285–9, argues that the cultic monuments are evidence which allows the conclusion that Mithraism was developing along independent cultic and pictorial lines. Thus the reversible relief of the tauroctony, turned at some time during the cultic exercise to show the meal between Mithras and Sol and the coexistence of oriental, native and Roman gods in the relief, is a unique feature, characteristic for the rhenish areas of *Germania superior*.

191 Filtzinger, in *KRI*, II, pp. 189f.

192   For greater detail, see Cämmerer, in Filtzinger, Planck, Cämmerer, pp. 169ff., 520, but especially pp. 210ff., for mystical terminology and the degrees of initiation.

193   Witt, in *Mithraic Studies*, pp. 486f.

194   Witt, in *Mithraic Studies*, p. 493.

195   Witt, in *Mithraic Studies*, p. 489.

196   K. Wilvonseder, *Keltische Kunst in Salzburg, Schriftenreihe des Salzburger Museums, Carolino Augusteum*, Nr. 2 (Salzburg 1960), p. 33, sees the ready acceptance of the oriental religions, with their emphasis on the transcendental, not only by the military but by the native population as well, to be a characteristic of the native Celtic population seeking to complement the worldly aspects of life with the other-worldly.

3.   Arts and Crafts

1   M.E. Wightman, *Roman Trier and the Treveri* (New York, Washington 1971), pp. 242–49, claims continuity of La Tène funerary customs into the 1st century AD. However, see H. Schutz, *The Prehistory of Germanic Europe* (New Haven and London 1983), pp. 305f.

2   Schutz, pp. 272–91.

3   Will, in Eggers, Will, Joffroy, Helmquist, *Kelten und Germanen in heidnischer Zeit* (Baden-Baden 1964), p. 90.

4   See also N.K. Sanders, *Prehistoric Art in Europe* (Harmondsworth 1968), p. 38.

5   H. Schoppa, *Die Kunst der Römerzeit in Gallien, Germanien und Britannien* (Munich 1957), p. 9.

6   Schoppa, p. 38.

7   Will, in Eggers, Will, Joffrey, Helmquist, p. 115.

8   L. Weber, *Als die Römer kamen … Augusta Vindelicorum und die Besiedlung Raetiens* (Landsberg am Lech 1973), p. 145, claims the area to have been depopulated during the conquest.

9   Schutz, pp. 230f., 281–4.

10   G. Webster, *The Roman Imperial Army to Caracalla* (London 1969), pp. 273f., points out that civilization was not an explicit objective of the military, but came with the spread of the Roman Way as the only way, the way of the urban center. See T. Bechert, *Römisches Germanien zwischen Rhein und Maas, Die Provinz Germania Inferior* (Munich 1982), pp. 58f., who stresses the civilizing role of the military.

11   Künzl, in Baatz, Herrmann, *Die Römer in Hessen* (Stuttgart 1982), pp. 157, 173, points out that the imported art of the upper class is almost completely lost. As such most of the works of 'art' have an official and political intention. As public works it is their function to display the majesty of the Empire. The 'art' is secondary. See Bechert, pp. 206ff.

12   See illustrations in *KRI*, I (Cologne 1974), p. 39.

13   Webster, p. 272, indicates that proper burial practice was viewed as a solemn contract with the dead. As member of a club, the *collegium funeraticium*, to which a soldier had to make regular contributions, his funerary feast and burial were assured. It was the duty of his heirs to erect the monument.

14   B. und H. Galsterer, 'Römische Inschriften,' in *KRI*, I, pp. 31f. Also Künzl, in Baatz, Herrmann, pp. 160ff.

15   Will, in Eggers, Will, Joffroy, Helmquist, p. 92.

16   Schoppa, p. 14.

17   Webster, p. 272, claims this motif to symbolize the victory over death.

18   In the museum of the Kerameikos, the ancient cemetery of Athens, the prototype of this relief is still on view. It is the funerary monument of one Dexileos, who fell in 396 BC during the Corinthian War.

19   H. Borger, et al., in *KRI*, I, p. 232.

20   Galsterer, in *KRI*, I, p. 31.

21   P. Noelke, 'Quader von der Koblenzer Moselbrücke,' in *KRI*, II, p. 169.

22   Schoppa, p. 15. Künzl, in Baatz, Herrmann, pp. 159f., points out that this characteristic love of detail, besides being of great help to historians of weaponry, serves as a means of social representation, a matter of considerable importance to the heirs and the executors of the deceased's last will and testament.

23   *KRI*, I, p. 236.

24   *KRI*, I, p. 202, Künzl, in Baatz, Herrmann, p. 161, dates the increase of popularity of this type of monument following the death of Nero in AD 68.

25   Künzl, in Baatz, Herrmann, p. 167, suggests that the horse and servant could be omitted to reduce the price of the monument. Künzl points to the implied mystical symbolism of the funerary meal.

26   H. Schoppa, *Der römische Steinsaal, Schriften des Städtischen Museums Wiesbaden*, Nr. 3 (Wiesbaden 1965), pp. 8f.

27   Künzl, in Baatz, Herrmann, p. 167, places his death into the wars of Domitian against the Chatti (AD 83–5) and consequently terms the execution of the relief 'conservative', though he admits that the style is that of the workshops of *Mogontiacum* of the first half of the 1st century AD. From the middle of the first century AD onward the figures begin to detach themselves from their background and gain greater expression. See Bechert, p. 209.

28   A. Mócsy, *Pannonia and Upper Moesia, A History of the Middle Danube Provinces of the Roman Empire*, transl. by S. Frere (London and Boston 1974), plates 11c, 12b. Mócsy, pp. 124f., takes these to be products under rhenish influence. Along the Rhine, from the beginning of the 2nd century AD, the martial

themes of the funerary monuments of the military give way to the tastes of the civilian population.

29 See Mócsy, p. 179, for a more detailed discussion of sculpture in *Pannonia*.

30 G. Alföldy, *Noricum, History of the Provinces of the Roman Empire*, transl. by A. Birley (London and Boston 1974), p. 332, note 77.

31 E. Dietz, 'Portraitkunst in Noricum,' *Gymnasium, Zeitschrift für Kultur der Antike und Humanistische Bildung*, Beiheft, 5, ed. by F. Bömer and L. Voit, *Germania Romana, II. Kunst und Kunstgewerbe im Römischen Deutschland* (Heidelberg 1965), pp. 93–101.

32 Alföldy, p. 140.

33 Alföldy, p. 175, also plates 27, 28.

34 U. Bracker-Wester, 'Das Grabmonument des Poblicius,' in *KRI*, I, pp. 51ff. Throughout our area fragments of such monuments continue to be found which indicate that the population erected many more than the few surviving ones would indicate.

35 H. Galsterer, in *KRI*, I, p. 53.

36 Wightman, p. 37, suggests that the economic opportunism during the period following the conquest would have brought economic difficulties to the inexperienced natives, rich and poor alike. The city was also the financial capital of *Gallia, Germania superior* and *inferior*.

37 H. Schoppa, *Kunst der Römerzeit*, p. 24.

38 Will, in Eggers, Will, Joffroy, Helmquist, pp. 106ff.

39 W. Schleiermacher, 'Augusta Vindelicum,' in *Gymnasium, Beiheft 1, Germania Romana I: Römerstädte in Deutschland* (Heidelberg 1960), plate XII.

40 P. Noelke, 'Baukalk für eine ganze Provinz', in *KRI*, II, p. 136f.

41 P. Pratt, 'Wall painting', in D. Strong and D. Brown, *Roman Crafts* (London 1976), pp. 223–9. Also Bechert, pp. 189f.

42 H.J. Kellner, *Die Römer in Bayern* (Munich 1971, 2nd. ed 1978), p. 100, claims that the Romans used mainly al-secco techniques for their wall paintings.

43 Pratt, in Strong, Brown, pp. 224f.

44 Pratt, p. 228.

45 Pratt, p. 229.

46 J. Hock, in G.H. Leute, J. Hock, *Das Landesmuseum für Kärnten und seine Sammlungen* (Klagenfurt 1976), p. 85.

47 Alföldy, p. 45.

48 A. Linfert, 'Aus dem Musterbuch einer Malerfirma,' in *KRI*, I, p. 113. Only certain rooms, such as the dining room were painted. See Bechert, pp. 129f.

49 Th. K. Kempf, 'Bild einer kaiserlichen Braut. Von konstantinischen Deckenmalereien aus dem Trierer Dom,' in *KRI*, II, pp. 175f. Also Kempf, 'Das Haus der heiligen Helena,' *Neues Trierisches Jahrbuch*, Beiheft (Trier 1978). Especially W. Weber, *Con-*

stantinische Deckengemälde aus dem römischen Palast unter dem Trierer Dom (Trier 1984).

50 Wightman, p. 59, supposes such a power struggle to have taken place in AD 326.

51 J.G. Deckers, 'Die Decke des Trierer Prunksaals,' in *KRI*, II, p. 179. See W. Weber, p. 28, who summarizes the discussion which argues that the 'portraits' are of symbolic and allegorical nature.

52 Deckers, in *KRI*, II, p. 176. Also Kempf, in *Trierisches Jahrbuch*, p. 4. But see W. Weber, p. 26.

53 Deckers, in *KRI*, II, p. 177. Also W. Weber, p. 28.

54 One of the male figures, dressed in the garb of a philosopher, is perhaps Lactantius; another wears the wreath of a rhetor and is probably Nazarius. See Kempf, in *Trierisches Jahrbuch*, pp. 5f. One of the figures is shown dedicating his work to the personage at the center of the ceiling. See also W. Weber, pp. 22f.

55 Deckers and Kempf have different views, as is evident in *KRI*, II, pp. 175ff. See W. Weber, pp. 28f.

56 Deckers, in *KRI*, II, pp. 176f. Kempf, in *KRI*, II, pp. 175f. and in *Trierisches Jahrbuch*, p. 4, interprets her to be the empress-mother, Flavia Julia Helena, the first lady of the court. See also W. Weber, pp. 26f.

57 Kempf, *Trierisches Jahrbuch*, p. 5, interprets her to be Constantine's sister, Flavia Julia Constantia. W. Weber, p. 27, corrects this to 'step-sister'.

58 Deckers, in *KRI*, II, pp. 178f., takes her to be the ruling empress Maxima Fausta.

59 Kempf, in *KRI*, II, p. 176, and in *Trierisches Jahrbuch*, p. 5, takes the 'flower girl' to be the imperial bride. Also W. Weber, p. 27.

60 Kempf, in *Trierisches Jahrbuch*, p. 13.

61 O.S. Neal, 'Floor Mosaics,' in Strong, Brown, pp. 241–52. Bechert, p. 212, indicates that in *Germania inferior* the mosaics were found mainly in the provincial capital, *Agrippina*.

62 Alföldy, p. 118.

63 Illustrations, *KRI*, I, p. 201.

64 Illustrations, *KRI*, I, p. 239.

65 M. Grant, 'Poetry, Prose and Rhetoric', in M. Grant (ed.), *The Birth of Western Civilization, Greece and Rome* (London, New York, Toronto 1964), p. 242.

66 Illustration, 'Philosopher's Mosaic,' in *KRI*, I, p. 102.

67 This mosaic, located in the Römisch-Germanisches Museum in Cologne, has been used to argue in favor of a Platonic 'renaissance' in Cologne under the emperor Gallienus, but that the Diogenes portrait had been altered to represent the cynical philosopher in his barrel, when Postumus, a cynic himself, usurped the purple. See J. Bracker, 'Das Philosophenmosaik,' in *KRI*, I, pp. 100ff., 222.

R. MacMullen, *The Roman Government's Response to Crisis, AD 235–337* (New Haven and London), p. 19, argues that this 'renaissance' does not stand up to careful analysis.

68 U. Bracker-Wester, 'Dramatischer Höhepunkt in der Arena,' in *KRI*, I, pp. 137, 157.

69 For details concerning the mosaics found at Trier, see Wightman, pp. 89ff.

70 U. Bracker-Wester, 'Das Dionysosmosaik,' in *KRI*, I, p. 50. This mosaic consists of about 1.5 million *tesserae*. Bechert, p. 213.

71 Alföldy, p. 89.

72 Alföldy, p. 183.

73 Neal, in Strong, Brown, p. 244.

74 Neal, p. 245.

75 D. Brown, 'Pottery', in Strong, Brown, pp. 75–91.

76 H. Schoppa, *Die Römische Kaiserzeit, Schriften des Städtischen Museums Wiesbaden* (Wiesbaden 1963), p. 12; see also F. Behn, *Römertum und Völkerwanderung* (Stuttgart 1963), p. 31, who agrees that Arretine ware was more artistic in its ornamentation but that the *terra sigillata* from southern Gaul was made of better clay, was fired to greater hardness and was therefore more durable, artistry ceding to technology.

77 Alföldy, p. 73.

78 A.H.M. Jones, *The Roman Economy, Studies in Ancient Economic and Administrative History*, ed. by P.A. Brunt (Oxford 1974), pp. 38f., argues that it was the prohibitive cost of land transport which led to the location of factories in the provinces.

79 Will, in Eggers, Will, Joffroy, Helmquist, p. 118.

80 Schoppa, *Kaiserzeit*, p. 12; Wightman, p. 199, indicates that the wares produced at this center captured the British market.

81 Alföldy, p. 178.

82 Schoppa, *Kunst der Römerzeit*, p. 35.

83 Schoppa, *Kaiserzeit*, pp. 11f.

84 Brown, in Strong, Brown, pp. 78ff.

85 Brown, p. 83.

86 Brown, p. 86.

87 Brown, p. 78; also Schoppa, *Kunst der Römerzeit*, p. 35; also Will, in Eggers, Will, Joffroy, Helmquist, p. 118.

88 Brown, pp. 90f.

89 Schoppa, *Kaiserzeit*, p. 13.

90 Will, in Eggers, Will, Joffroy, Helmquist, p. 119.

91 Brown, p. 86

92 For details, see R. Higgins, 'Terracottas', in Strong, Brown, pp. 105–9.

93 Higgins, p. 109.

94 D. Linfert-Reich, 'Kleiner Beleuchtungsluxus,' in *KRI*, I, pp. 168f.

95 D.M. Bailey, 'Pottery lamps,' in Strong, Brown, pp. 93–103.

96 Bailey, p. 94.

97 Bailey, pp. 99f.

98 D. Brown, 'Bronze and Pewter', in Strong, Brown, pp. 25–41.

99 Alföldy, p. 112.

100 Alföldy, p. 46.

101 Alföldy, p. 46, also p. 297, note 41.

102 Will, in Eggers, Will, Joffroy, Helmquist, p. 109.

103 Brown, in Strong, Brown, p. 25.

104 *Der Schatzfund von Straubing*, Gäubodenmuseum–Römische Abteilung, without name of author, place or date of publication, pp. 25–33; also H.G. Horn, 'Der Schatzfund von Straubing,' in *KRI*, II, pp. 124-7.

105 Horn, in *KRI*, II, p. 126.

106 *Schatzfund*, p. 25; also Horn, in *KRI*, II, pp. 124ff.

107 Behn, pp. 17f, suggests these helmets to be deathmasks placed on the face of the deceased and then preserved in the family sanctuary.

108 *The Praeger Picture Encyclopedia of Art* (New York 1965), p. 159.

109 Horn, in *KRI*, II, p. 125.

110 R. Roerer, *Kleine Vor- und Frühgeschichte Württembergs* (Stuttgart 1963), p. 42; also Webster, p. 155.

111 Webster, p. 155, claims that the celebration was occasioned by the anniversary of the founding of Rome. Kellner, p. 70, suggests that these games were either based on Thracian examples or were a continuation of Etruscan traditions.

112 P. MacKendrick, *Romans on the Rhine, Archaeology in Germany* (New York 1970), p. 81, still subscribes to this view.

113 U. Gehrig, 'Der Hildesheimer Silberfund,' Staatliche Museen, Preußischer Kulturbesitz (Berlin 1976).

114 D. Sherlock, 'Silver and Silversmithing,' in Strong, Brown, p. 20.

115 Sherlock, p. 23.

116 Gehrig, 'Hildesheimer Silberfund.'

117 Schutz, p. 186, as well as many other references indexed under 'depots.'

118 A. Linfert, 'Römischer Tafelluxus—Das Silbergeschirr von Manching,' in *KRI*, II, pp. 132f.

119 J. Price, 'Glass,' in Strong, Brown, pp. 111–25. Also Bechert, pp. 197ff.

120 B. Döhle, 'Die Glasproduktion,' in R. Günther, H. Köpstein, *Die Römer an Rhein und Donau* (Berlin 1975), p. 272.

121 Döhle, p. 273.

122 P. La Baume, 'Römisches Prunkglas,' in *KRI*, I, pp. 114–19.

123 Döhle, p. 273.

124 A. und R. Schmid, *Die Römer an Rhein und Main* (Frankfurt 1972), pp. 87f.

125 Price, p. 116.

126 Schmid, p. 88.

127 Price, p. 122.

128 Döhle, p. 292.

129 J. Bracker, 'Schwebende Gläser,' in *KRI*, I, p. 108.

130 Price, p. 123.

131 Döhle, p. 290.
132 La Baume, in *KRI*, I, p. 116.
133 Döhle, p. 293.
134 La Baume, in *KRI*, I, p. 116.
135 Of such inventories the museums of Cologne, Mainz, Bonn, Frankfurt, Trier, to name only a few, give ample evidence.
136 Behn, p. 44.

4. Provincial Society in Crisis and Transition

1 A.H.M. Jones, *The Roman Economy, Studies in Ancient Economic and Administrative History*, ad. by P.A. Brunt (Oxford 1974), p. 30 and especially p. 37, where Jones outlines the prohibitive cost of land transport, so that trade focussed mainly on luxury goods and the needs of a wealthy minority, p. 129; also Baatz, in D. Baatz, F.R. Herrmann, *Die Römer in Hessen* (Stuttgart 1982), pp. 91f., concerning taxes and tolls, pp. 93–103, for agriculture and industry, pp. 110–14, for transportation, roads and river systems. See Also T. Bechert, *Römisches Germanien zwischen Rhein und Maas, Die Provinz Germania Inferior* (Munich 1982), p. 179, for the cost of land transport.

2 M.E. Wightman, *Roman Trier and the Treveri* (New York and Washington 1971), p. 139. To Wightman the term *villa* denotes farms and country-houses built at least partly of stone. See Baatz, Herrmann, p. 139, for a map showing the distribution of *villae rusticae* in S-W central Europe. For a review of aerial photography, geophysical and magnetometric procedures as search methods, see Bechert, pp. 14–19.

3 R. MacMullan, *Soldier and Civilian in the Later Roman Empire* (Cambridge, Mass. 1963), pp. 7–12, for a more detailed discussion.

4 P. Oliva, *Pannonia and the Onset of Crisis in the Roman Empire* (Prague 1962), p. 312, note 3.

5 Oliva, p. 314,

6 MacMullen, *Soldier*, pp. 43, 78f., claims that commanding officers kept villas inside or outside the camps.

7 A. Mócsy, *Pannonia and Upper Moesia, A History of the Middle Danube Provinces of the Roman Empire*, transl. by S. Frere (London and Boston 1974), p. 218. Filtzinger, D. Planck, B. Cämmerer, *Die Römer in Baden-Württemberg* (Stuttgart 1971, 2nd. ed. 1976), pp. 86f., points out, that c. AD 230 the emperor Severus Alexander extended the privileges of the border army by allowing the hereditary transfer of land, provided that the heirs assumed military service. The emperor hoped to link personal interests with those of the Empire.

8 B. Böttger, in R. Günther, H. Köpstein, *Die Römer an Rhein und Donau* (Berlin 1975),

p. 138; H.J. Kellner, *Die Römer in Bayern* (Munich 1971, 2nd. ed. 1978), treats *Raetia* in great detail. Kellner, pp. 52f., points out that with the establishment of the *limes* most of the traffic passed north of the Danube so that this area experienced more rapid growth, while most of *Raetia* became something of a backwater, see especially Kellner, p. 53.

9 G. Alföldy, *Noricum, History of the Provinces of the Roman Empire*, transl. by A. Birley (London and Boston 1974), p. 107.

10 Böttger, in Günther, Köpstein, p. 139; see also M. Müller-Wille, 'Die landwirtschaftliche Grundlage der villae rusticae,' in *Gymnasium, Beiheft 7, Germania Romana III. Römisches Leben auf Germanischem Boden* (Heidelberg 1970), p. 28; also Kellner, p. 85.

11 Böttger, in Günther, Köpstein, p. 141.

12 J. Percival, *The Roman Villa, An Historical Introduction* (Berkeley and Los Angeles 1976); also H. Hinz, 'Zur Bauweise der villa rustica'', in *Gymnasium*, 7, pp. 16–25; also Bechert, pp. 157–69 and Kellner, pp. 85–91.

13 Percival, p. 120.

14 Böttger, in Günther, Köpstein, p. 147.

15 Böttger, in Günther, Köpstein, p. 148; also P. MacKenrick, *Romans on the Rhine, Archaeology in Germany* (New York 1970), p. 135.

16 Percival, p. 159, stresses the importance for the villa economy. About the road system see Filtzinger, in Filtzinger, Planck, Cämmerer, pp. 42, 75ff., as well as Kellner, pp. 55–8.

17 Percival, pp. 51–105, for regional types and their distribution, especially pp. 81–7; see also Hinz, in *Gymnasium*, 7, p. 16, and Kellner, p. 54.

18 Percival argues that the use of the hall in Pre- and Post-Roman Celtic and Germanic society and its use in the hall-villas raises the question of the depth of Roman influence, so that the social structure may not have been Roman at all, but native with Roman trappings. Wightman, p. 151, dealing with Treveris and environs suggests that the majority of villa owners were natives of the region.

19 Böttger, in Günther, Köpstein, p. 149.

20 MacMullen, *Soldier*, pp. 41f., suggests that this feature is an expression of the military influence.

21 Percival, p. 84, indicates that in the more precarious regions of *Germania inferior* and *superior*, *Raetia* and *Noricum* the buildings were less luxurious, placing greater emphasis on defence and efficiency of production, yet the villa at Westerhofen, perhaps the hunting villa of the governor of *Raetia*, was as impressive as any, see Kellner, p. 88, for details.

22 Böttger, in Günther, Köpstein, pp. 151f.

23 Böttger, in Günther, Köpstein, pp. 150–4. Also Kellner, pp. 85–91.

24 Percival, p. 36, interprets villas to be an indicator of advancing romanization, the villa at Mayen for instance, serving as an example of the developing stages from small wattle hut to complex structure, see pp. 134ff.; also Wightman, p. 139, who stresses the continuity of occupation of certain sites from La Tène to Roman times evident in the foundations of buildings in which the transition from wooden to stone construction can be read. See also Hinz, in *Gymnasium*, 7, pp. 16–19. Baatz, in Baatz, Herrmann, p. 80, stresses that these villas did not continue older settlements even though there was continuity of population elements; and Kellner, p. 84, points out that while on the one hand rich Celts made the transition to Roman citizenship and with their large estates shaped the landscape, on the other hand the majority of the population continued to settle on isolated farmsteads, but without Roman veneer.

25 Böttger, in Günther, Köpstein, p. 155.

26 According to Percival, p. 87, Switzerland and Austria have yielded evidence of particularly immense and prosperous villas characterized by corridor houses up to 100 m long. See also Hinz, in *Gymnasium*, 7, pp. 22f. For a treatment of the Roman presence in the Swiss highlands, see G. T. Schwarz, 'Die Römer im Bergland der Schweiz', in *Gymnasium*, 7, pp. 115–19. See also W. Modrijan, 'Römische Bauern und Gutsbesitzer in Noricum', in *Gymnasium*, 7, pp. 120–37. For a detailed discussion of the villas in *Germania inferior*, see W. C. Braat, 'Die Besiedlund des römischen Reichsgebietes in den heutigen nördlichen Niederlanden', in *Gymnasium*, 7, pp. 52–61; also H. Hinz, 'Zur römischen Besiedlung in der Kölner Bucht', *Gymnasium*, 7, pp. 62–9.

27 Böttger, in Günther, Köpstein, p. 156; also MacKendrick, p. 153. The suggestion that this wall enclosed an imperial horse farm is disputed by MacMullen, *Soldier*, p. 149, note 104, who suggests that it belongs into the 4th century. Wightman, pp. 170f., proposes that it was a property boundary enclosing other villas thereby constituting an example of the concentration of land ownership, containing up to 200 individual farms.

28 Hinz, in *Gymnasium*, 7, p. 23; Modrijan, in *Gymnasium*, 7, p. 128, credits this style to Roman city architecture, derived from Hellenistic examples. In *Noricum* it was the preferred style.

29 In the west, during the critical times of the late Empire, the villas became fortified towns, supported by private armies, see MacMullen, *Soldier*, p. 151; concerning self-sufficiency, see Percival, pp. 160f.; also Böttger, in Günther, Köpstein, pp. 159f. For a complete treatment of the Roman inventory of tools, implements and other utensils and their functions, mills, presses, types of fencing, rope making, measuring instruments, water raising devices, basketry and earthenware, see K. D. White, *Farm Equipment of the Roman World* (Cambridge 1975). A late Roman grave at Rodenkirchen near Cologne contained an extensive inventory of agricultural equipment in the form of bronze copies, see Müller-Wille, in *Gymnasium*, 7, pp. 35ff.

30 Böttger, in Günther, Köpstein, pp. 167f.

31 Müller-Wille, in *Gymnasium*, 7, p. 37; also Böttger, in Günther, Köpstein, p. 170.

32 For details, see Müller-Wille, in *Gymnasium*, 7, pp. 37f. Palladius, writing in the 4th century AD, describes such a machine. See Bechert, pp. 166f.

33 Illustrations, in M. Grant, *Birth of Western Civilization, Greece and Rome* (London, New York, Toronto 1964), p. 293.

34 Müller-Wille, in *Gymnasium*, 7, p. 39.

35 Müller-Wille, in *Gymnasium*, 7, p. 32. Also Baatz, in Baatz, Herrmann, pp. 95f.

36 Müller-Wille, in *Gymnasium*, 7, p. 34; also Böttger, in Günther, Köpstein, p. 173.

37 Böttger, in Günther, Köpstein, pp. 174ff. Bechert, p. 168, indicates that in parts of *Germania inferior* bone finds point to a predominance of beef of over 60%.

38 Kellner, p. 93.

39 Hinz, in *Gymnasium*, 7, p. 68; also P. Noelke, 'Nideggen/Nordeifel, Römischer Gutshof'', in *KRI*, II, pp. 182f. Wightman, p. 163, argues that Roman emphasis on agriculture caused the population of this region to decrease as the soil could not support a farming population, allowing at best the pasturing of livestock and of horses.

40 H. Cüppers, 'Wein und Weinbau zur Römerzeit im Rheinland', in *Gymnasium*, 7, pp. 138–45. The emperor Probus broke the Italian wine monopoly as a means of restoring the economy of the Mosel region, see Wightman, p. 55. However, F. Behn, *Römertum und Völkerwanderung* (Stuttgart 1963), p. 35, suggests that Probus is to be credited only with the legalization of an ongoing illegal practice. See also Cüppers, in *Gymnasium*, 7, p, 145, note 22.

41 Oliva, p. 316, for details concerning the provinces on the Middle Danube.

42 Böttger, in Günther, Köpstein, p. 177. The application of southern knowledge to northern agriculture led to an increase in productivity per worker, per area and to a greater variety of produce than had been known in Pre-Roman times, see Baatz, in Baatz, Herrmann, p. 95.

43 See Wightman, pp. 4of., for the circumstances leading to the naming of Trier, its identification as a *colonia* and its status.

44 The evidence for the presence of such a unit consists of the tombstones of two Spanish

cavalry men which do not seem to have been found on the site of an early fortification. Wightman, p. 36, doubts the existence of such a fortification.

45 That the name *Mogontiacum* contains the name of the Celtic god (of light?) Mogo or Mogon equated with Apollo, makes the existence of an earlier Celtic settlement in the area conceivable. Perhaps the Celts recognized the same strategic reasons which led to the founding of the Roman *castrum*, D. Baatz, 'Die Topographie des römischen Mainz', in *Gymnasium*, I, p. 54. Behn, p. 13 suggests that the military considerations pertaining to the site hindered the economic and social development of the civilian settlement.

46 The number of finds at Oberhausen is so extensive that a large Roman force, possibly two legions, *legio XVI Gallica* and *legio XXI rapax*, as well as other auxiliary units, such as the *cohors Trumplinorum* from the eastern Alps and the *ala Pansiana* from Gaul, was stationed there. Caius Vibius Pansa had raised the *ala* in 15 BC. He is documented to have been the first legate of the area, *legatus Augusti pro praetore in Vindolicis*. See Kellner, p. 28; also Filtzinger, in Filtzinger, Planck, Cämmerer, pp. 32, 34, 40. *Legio XIII gemina* may also have been under his command.

47 Kellner, p. 20, suggests that after AD 17, when the policy of further conquest in central Europe had been abandoned, the stationing of strong forces in *Raetia* became unnecessary. With the withdrawal to *Vindonissa*, *Raetia* ceased to be a staging area. Filtzinger, in Filtzinger, Planck, Cämmerer, pp. 39ff., supposes that after AD 9, Oberhausen had been garrisoned by only a detachment, after AD 14 perhaps by veterans who had participated in the revolt at *Oppidum Ubiorum* when under the command of Germanicus they objected to the accession of Tiberius to the throne that year. It was *legio XIII gemina* which was stationed at *Vindonissa* after AD 16/17 to protect the road system to *Germania, Gallia, Italia* and *Noricum*. Very little is known about the Roman forces in *Raetia* during the 1st century AD. The army of *Raetia*, the *exercitus Raeticus*, is first mentioned on coins minted in the time of Hadrian. Only from the 2nd century on are units known through diplomas and then only auxiliary *alae* and *cohortes*. Only with the stationing of *legio III Italica concors* at *Castra Regina* in AD 179 does the province receive a resident legion. Its commander is also provincial governor. See Kellner, pp. 66ff.

48 L. Weber, *Als die Römer kamen ... Augusta Vindelicorum und die Besiedlung Raetiens* (Landsberg am Lech 1973), p. 49, attributes the name of this road not to Claudius, who had merely had the road restored in AD 46/47,

but to Drusus of the Claudian family. Filtzinger, in Filtzinger, Planck, Cämmerer, p. 42, shares the view that the *Via Claudia Augusta* had been conceived by Drusus as a link between northern Italy and the Danube.

49 Alföldy, p. 78. Bechert, p. 100, argues that the Romans established new cities to realize their own ideas concerning the layout of cities in the conquered territories.

50 Alföldy, p. 19, sees in the name *Carnuntum* a reflection of the Celtic tribal name of the Carni, which may point to the existence of a settlement on the site already during the *Regnum Noricum*. See also W. Jobst, *Provinzhauptstadt Carnuntum* (Vienna 1983), p. 43. For Jobst, pp. 33, 43ff., the sources, Velleius Paterculus and the elder Pliny, indicate that the camp erected by Tiberius was only a marching camp set up for the winter.

51 C. M. Wells, *The German Policy of Augustus, An Examination of the Archaeological Evidence* (Oxford 1972), Bechert, p. 85, points out that the *castra* also protected such installations as canals and other waterworks and supervised tribal concentrations.

52 Vespasian abolished the double legionary fortresses after the unrest of AD 69/70, since they represented too large a military concentration in case of dissension. Those *castra* which had burnt down were rebuilt in stone as one-legion-fortresses. See A. Johnson, *Roman Forts of the 1st and 2nd Centuries AD in Britain and the German Provinces* (London 1983), p. 250.

53 Alföldy, p. 214. An excellent example is modern Xanten, a corruption of *Ad Sanctos*, a name derived from the Christian cemetery on and around which the Post-Roman settlement grew up. It was built with the stones of *Colonia Ulpia Traiana*. In its final stage *Traiana* had shrunk from 83 hectares to 16. See Bechert, pp. 106–13, 261.

54 G. Webster, *The Roman Imperial Army to Caracalla* (London 1969), p. 277, sees the *coloniae* to have been a means of romanization. The demobilization of troops in veteran settlements turned retired soldiers into respectable citizens.

55 For details concerning the *Colonia Ulpia Traiana*, see H. Hinz, 'Die Colonia Ulpia Trajana bei Xanten', in *Gymnasium*, I, pp. 29–50. It is curious that the tribal name of the local settlement was not incorporated in the Roman name.

56 Mócsy, p. 118; also Webster, p. 278.

57 With Hadrian the founding of veteran colonies came to an end, see G. R. Watson, *The Roman Soldier* (London 1969), p. 148.

58 T. Becher, 'Regensburg—Castra Regina, Legionslager und Lagerturm', in *Kölnez Römer Illustrierte* (Cologne 1975), II, p. 122; see also G. Ulbert, 'Das römische Regensburg', in *Gymnasium*, I, pp. 64–77.

59 For details of the city fortifications and their construction, see Wightman, pp. 92–8. She suggests that the *Porta Nigra* had a defensive as well as a representational purpose. Concerning the *Porta Praetoria* at Regensburg, she suggests it to be a 3rd century rebuilding of a 2nd century structure. See also E. Zahn, 'Trier, Porta Nigra, ein Stadttor,' in *KRI*, II, pp. 170f.

60 See MacMullen, *Soldier*, p. 175, concerning the practice of Roman standardization of town planning. See also Jones, p. 5, who indicates that the trend towards urbanization was sometimes actively encouraged through official building programs, thereby complementing a spontaneous desire of the population to join the Greco-Roman World.

62 R.E.M. Wheeler, *Roman Art and Architecture* (New York, Washington 1964) pp. 32f., argues against the derivation of Roman cities from Greek precedents. Bechert, p. 100, supports the view that Roman cities derived from Greek precedents as illustrated in the Greek cities of southern Italy and Sicily.

62 W. Schleiermacher, 'Municipium Arae Flaviae,' in *Gymnasium*, 1, p. 60; see also Jones, pp. 6ff., and Bechert, pp. 46f. A *colonia* was more significant than a *municipium*, see Baatz, in Baatz, Herrmann, p. 84.

63 Weber, pp. 157, 225, states that Augsburg is documented to have been a *municipium* since the time of Hadrian. Kellner, pp. 44, 58, suggests that Hadrian, of the family of the Aelians, was so impressed with the splendour of *Agusta Vindelicum* that he gave it his name so that after AD 122/23 the center was known as *Municipium Aelium Augustum*. Kellner, p. 81, thinks it possible that the religious centers *Cambodunum/*Kempten and *Brigantium/*Bregenz may also have been promoted to the rank of *municipium*. Kellner details the administrative organization. Beside *Agrippina*, a *colonia* since AD 50 and *Traiana*, a *colonia* since c. AD 98, *Germania inferior* had only two other colonies, later promoted to *municipium*: *Batavorum*, c. AD 200 and the *Municipium Aelium Cannanefatium*, elevated c. AD 162. See Bechert, p. 47.

64 According to Behn, p. 27, it was Septimius Severus who raised *Carnuntum* to the level of *colonia*. It was at *Carnuntum* that Septimius Severus was proclaimed emperor by his legion, the *legio XIV gemina*. See also Oliva, p. 242.

65 Mócsy, p. 119, Kellner, p. 37, points out that in *Noricum* five settlements had been raised to the level of *municipium* already under Claudius: *Virunum, Celeia, Aguntum, Teurnia* and *Juvavum*. With all but *Teurnia* the change in status coincided with the relocation to a more favorable site. *Noricum* had different constitutional arrangements: its governor bore the title *procurator Augusti regni Norici*. Fewer auxiliaries were raised in *Noricum*.

66 Baatz, 'Topographie,' in *Gympasium*, 1, p. 56. The settlement did not rise in legal status to the level of a *municipium*.

67 In the west self-governing tribal political units were arranged as *civitates* and *pagi*. For a detailed discussion, see Wightman, pp. 124–8; see also Jones, p. 4, on the composition and judicial nature of the *civitas*; also Kellner, p. 82; Baatz, in Baatz, Herrmann, pp. 87–90. Most of the territory was occupied by the cities and the *civitates*. See Bechert, p. 50, for the differences in their relationship to Rome. The cities of antiquity had an extensive territory to supply its agricultural needs. *Civitates* embraced geographic regions or tribal communities, subdivided into *pagi*, the agricultural area cultivated by *villae rusticae*. *Vici* were tribal, economic and administrative centers. Bechert, pp. 50, 143f., details the differentiations. The *territorium legionis* was under military administration. Its function was to guarantee the supplies of the camp. The area was probably worked by tenant farmers. Considering that a legion of 6000 men required 6000 kg of wheat per day, or 1500 tons per year and since it could not live on wheat alone, it is evident that the supply question was of foremost importance. See Kellner, pp. 82f.

68 See also MacMullen, *Soldier*, pp. 119–25, for details concerning *canabae*. The *canabae legionis* surrounded the *castrum* and are distinct from other civilian settlements such as *vici*, *municipia* or *coloniae* which were subject to the civilian administration. See Filtzinger, in Filtzinger, Planck, Cämmerer, pp. 74f. Also Bechert, p. 153.

69 Mócsy, p. 219.

70 Mócsy, p. 221.

71 Under the *ius Italicum* the land was legally assimilated with the tax-free land of Italy. See Jones, p. 8.

72 For the social structure, see Baatz, in Baatz, Herrmann, pp. 86–90; also Kellner, pp. 81f.

73 Here the *colonia* and the *civitates* existed side by side, each with its own officials. Bechert, pp. 113–16, points out that already during the 2nd century AD the concept *civitas* assumed the meaning of city or town until it had the same significance as *municipium*. See Wightman, p. 41f. She points to W. Mayers, *L'Administration de la province romaine de Belgique* (Bruge 1964), p. 115, who, however, was unable to discover any functionaries of the *colonia* among the inscriptions which he examined.

74 H. Hellenkemper, 'Colonia Claudia Ara Agrippinensium, Stadtraum und Umland:, in *KRI*, II, p. 175.

75 W. Schleiermacher, 'Augusta Vindelicum,'

in *Gymnasium*, 1, pp. 79ff. For *Germania inferior*, Bechert, pp. 41–4, suggests an administrative staff of only 200.

76 F. Millar, et al., *The Roman Empire and its Neighbours* (London 1967), p. 62, indicates that the governor's entourage of friends, learned men and advisors brought from 'home', hoped to share in the privileges, benefits and opportunities.

77 Alföldy, pp. 117f.

78 See MacMullen, *Soldier*, pp. 97–110, on the local aristocracies of the Empire, the upward mobility of veterans and on business interests. Bechert, p. 58, points out that the new Roman order allowed the native populations to loosen old dependency arrangements and to take advantage of the new social opportunities which urbanization presented. He also argues, p. 62, that Roman society was not a class society and that upward mobility was possible.

79 MacMullen, p. 160, points out that military as well as political patronage were a means acquiring social position. Jones, p. 136, points out that politics, administration and the practice of law were the sources of great wealth drawn from booty, governmental extorsion and corruption and government contracts, but seldom from official salaries.

80 See Jones, pp. 11f., on the organization of civic government. It was Rome's objective to place power in the hands of the propertied class and thereby bring stability and submission to local government. Jones, p. 29, illustrates that this system was based on endowments freely given rather than on taxation which was considered to be an emergency measure. The maintenance of public buildings and installations was the duty of the *civitas*. See Baatz, in Baatz, Herrmann, p. 89.

81 Jones, p. 29, states that by the fourth century the cities came to depend on imperial transfer payments.

82 See Jones, pp. 14–19, on the deterioration of the practice. It was seen initially to be an honor for which successful candidates had to be willing to pay, see Jones, p. 13. W. Goffart, *Caput and Colonate, Towards a History of Late Roman Taxation* (Toronto 1974), p. 29, note 26, suggests that costly offices were regarded precisely as a tax on the rich.

83 Galsterer, 'Köln wird Stadt,' in *KRI*, I, p. 48. According to Goffart, pp. 102f., communities counted on the public-spirited commitment of the municipality. Initially a *civitas* was composed of all freemen whether citizens of Rome or provincials. Wealth was a prerequisite for participation in the administration and this wealth was based on agriculture. At the top of the social scale stood members of the equestrian and senatorial nobility which could include members of the native nobility. This was a closed society, the

ordo decurionum. From the privileged ranks came the councillors. Social rise was possible through service in magisterial functions, generally into the *secundo ordo*, composed of freed-men and others who through their acquired wealth had gained status and could be charged with the performance of certain social functions, such as the administration of the games and the organization of the imperial cult, at their own expense of course. See Kellner, pp. 8off.; also Filtzinger in Filtzinger, Planck, Cämmerer, pp. 121ff. in the end the civic officials became an hereditary caste. See Jones, p. 16.

84 Mócsy, p. 226.

85 Wightman, p. 42, indicates that for Trier there is no evidence of a veteran settlement, nor of a large body of civilian Roman citizens. Kellner, p. 103, supports the idea that the native population made a serious attempt to play an active part in the cultural processes of the Empire. Bechert, p. 123, suggests that even such large cities as *Agrippina* were characterized by a petit bourgeoisie and its concerns for the self, the family and the immediate neighborhood.

86 Mócsy, pp. 226f. Kellner, p. 102, points to evidence of literacy and numeracy among the native Celts and among the slaves.

87 This led to the ruinous institution of the large plantation designed to bring profit not through the increase in productivity but through cheap labor, to make possible a life of luxury for the landowner in the city of his choice. See A. E. R. Boak, *Manpower Shortage and the Fall of the Roman Empire in the West* (Ann Arbor, Mich. 1955), p. 31.

88 Wightman, p. 60, states that members of the local council were forced to live in the towns as a guarantee that their civic duties and payments would not fall in arrears.

89 Jones, p. 83, calculates that 90% of taxation was based on agriculture; p. 138, that trade and industry contributed only 5% of the overall income during the late Empire. In the 2nd century the popular election faded for lack of willing candidates, see Jones, p. 13.

90 At the same time landowners seeking exemption from service on council could try to disqualify themselves by putting some of their holdings in shipping, as merchants were not eligible for public office, see Jones, p. 58.

91 Alföldy, pp. 174f.; see also Boak, pp. 22–8.

92 According to Jones, p. 37, in case of famine, inland towns had to draw on stockpiles, as transport from afar could not assure supplies.

93 See Jones, p. 135, on the profitability of waging war during periods of expansion.

94 Böttger, in Günther, Köpstein, pp. 182f.; Boak, p. 63, points out that *Raetia* was never extensively urbanized.

95 See Percival, pp. 48-51, on the decline of agriculture and the accompanying economic ills.

96 Böttger, in Günther, Köpstein, p. 185.

97 See Boak, pp. 48-51; also Percival, p. 119, on the *coloni* and their changing status; also Jones, p. 87. Inheritance had reduced parcels of land below subsistence levels, while over-assessments and crop failures forced small landowners into dependency. Also H.J. Diesner, *Die Völkerwanderung* (Leipzig 1976, 2nd ed. Gütersloh 1980), pp. 1off. Bechert, p. 61, on the other hand suggests that although the colonate bore traits of enslavement, a picture of exploitation and oppression is difficult to develop.

98 Jones, pp. 293-307; Goffart, p. 71f., points to the Constantinian Law of AD 332 which decreed that if a *colonus* tried to flee from his land he be chained like a slave in order to retain taxpayers for the communities rather than to increase the landowner's capital. A law of AD 357 required that land retain its cultivators when sold to prevent depopulation thereby decreasing the fiscal strength of a given area, see Goffart, pp. 78f. For purposes of taxation this became bondage to the land on which one was born, Goffart, p. 87.

99 Jones, p. 137, argues that the imperial aristocracy, concentrated in Italy, absorbed in rent perhaps a larger share of the wealth of the Empire, than the state absorbed in taxation.

100 Insecurity furthered the breakdown of whatever long-distance trade and transport there was and in turn contributed to the decline of urban prosperity. See Boak, p. 57.

101 Katz, p. 31.

102 G.C. Brauer, *The Soldier Emperors, Imperial Rome AD 244-284* (Park Ridge, N.J. 1975), pp. 8f., and Boak, p. 79, point out that Septimius Severus imposed on the councils the responsibility of collecting taxes owed to the state by the citizens and the territories administered by the cities. Any shortfall had to be met from their personal wealth. Such a practice could not but sap the economic strength of this group and ultimately reduce their number. Forced to serve in every position of the council coupled with the hereditary nature of the offices, this 'caste' of municipal officials was doomed to ruin. See Boak, pp. 82ff.

103 Neither Diocletian's attempt to grant the privileges of paying taxes to those not previously included in the lists, nor the compulsory taxation imposed by his successors could reverse the trend. Demand for payment in money discouraged payment in the form of services, see Goffart, pp. 47f.

104 MacMullen, *Soldier*, pp. 84f., points out that even under peaceful conditions the billeting of soldiers in the towns had a negative effect on civilian morale.

105 Katz, p. 35; according to R.E. Smith, *Service in the Post-Marian Army* (Manchester 1961), p. 71, when Augustus set up the peace-time army on a war-time footing he saddled the Empire with too heavy a burden for its resources. As Boak, p. 94, points out, to meet a replacement rate of 48,000 men in the west, during the late 4th century AD, the emperor Honorius asked slaves to volunteer. Such methods reduced the physical qualifications of the troops. By the 5th century the army had only strength on paper, see Boak, pp. 97-100.

106 Katz, p. 35; according to Boak, p. 92, the emperor Probus (AD 276-82) was the first to enlist troops directly from across the frontier.

107 According to Boak, pp. 28f., the settlement of barbarians within the frontiers was the only recourse. See Millar, pp. 119-26, on the changing composition of the army before the end of the 3rd century. Webster, p. 279, states that in the end the increasing number of unassimilated foreigners in the army gradually diluted the value of citizenship.

108 Increasing illiteracy and innumeracy, a general decline in education aided by actual hostility towards 'pagan' learning, and the impoverishment of the municipal senatorial groups, disqualified many from holding public office, see R. MacMullen, *The Roman Government's Response to Crisis, AD 235-337* (New Haven and London 1976), p. 67. An imperial officialdom had to fill the gap, see Wightman, p. 68. According to Jones, pp. 9f., already in the 2nd century were imperial supervisors appointed to scrutinize municipal finances. Goffart, p. 94, sees the local balance of power threatened by economic conditions and taxation, as the representatives of imperial authority pursued the interests of the central authority at the expense of local interests.

109 In the absence of any census, the emperor's men knew the location of local personal wealth, see Goffart, p. 94.

110 Goffart, p. 108, indicates that the introduction of shares of assessment, uniform for large areas, without regard to economic differences, furthered imperial centralization while at the same time inducing communities to put on an air of poverty, to qualify for tax relief. Within a short time spectacular building programs were replaced by more modest projects.

111 MacMullen, *Soldier*, p. 129, states that civic buildings were wrecked to provide building materials for the walls. The cities were dying.

112 From the time of Diocletian the army, the civil service and the population of Rome

were supported by taxes in kind. Clothes for the army and the civil service were supplied partly from levies in kind, partly from state factories, while weapons were produced in public armament works. These institutions left little commercial manoeuvrability for middlemen and merchants, see Jones, p. 38. At *Treveris* the factories producing shields, war engines and embroidered cloth drew on the large imperial estates for raw materials, see Wightman, p. 67.

113 Boak, p. 27; also Wightman, p. 172.

114 MacKendrick, p. 153.

115 Boak, p. 57.

116 Wightman, p. 57, suggests that the sad state of the frontier was not so much the result of series of invasions as of a long period of disorganization and moral collapse.

117 Hatt, pp. 222–30.

118 Wightman, p. 53, sees in the usurpation of Posthumus a means of establishing an effective defence against the invasions from across the Rhine and not a 'national' uprising.

119 Wightman, p. 55, cautions that not all traces of fire need point to this invasion.

120 Boak, p. 103.

121 See Wightman, pp. 78f., for details concerning this bridge.

122 Wightmann, pp. 100–13: also R. Schindler, 'Trier, Kaiserliche Residenzstadt im 4. Jahrhundert n. Chr.,' in *KRI*, II, pp. 171f.

124 For details see Wightman, pp. 82ff. The name derives from a later church dedicated to St. Barbara.

125 H. Cüppers, 'Trier, städtische Thermen—Kaiserliche Thermen,' in *KRI*, II, pp. 172f.

126 Ibid.

127 The bather followed the sequence hot to cold.

128 Wightman, p. 102, suggests that the Constantinian baths were reserved exclusively for imperial use.

129 Cüppers, in *KRI*, II, p. 173.

130 Ibid.

131 See Wightman, pp. 103–9, for discussions, also W. Binsfeld, 'Trier, "Basilika", Kaiserlicher Audienzsaal,' in *KRI*, II, pp. 173f.

132 The use of the tile-like bricks for the entire building suggests the presence of an architect from the eastern provinces of the Empire, see Wightman, p. 107.

133 Wheeler, p. 12, suggests that the Roman aim was above all the creation and adornment of interiors to reflect imperial pride and growing self-awareness and the importance of the individual.

134 According to Wightman, p. 104, the zone below the windows was sectioned by pilasters with Corinthian capitals.

135 *The Praeger Picture Encyclopedia of Art*, p. 40.

136 M. Gough, 'From the ancient to the medieval world, a bridge of faith', in M. Grant, (ed.) *The Birth of Western Civilization, Greece*

and Rome (London, New York, Toronto 1964), p. 333.

137 See Wightman, pp. 79f., 93f., for details of this amphitheater. Also Schindler, in *KRI*, II, p. 166. Bechert, p. 112, states that in the north no or only few gladiatorial combats were staged.

138 Hatt, p. 280; also Bracker-Wester, 'Dramatischer Höhepunkt in der Arena', in *KRI*, I, p. 137, who dates such an event to AD 306 and refers to the death of only the royal prisoners. K.K. Stroheker, *Germanentum und Spätantike* (Zürich, Stuttgart 1965), p. 15, claims that after AD 310 such spectacles were frequent.

139 A. and R. Schmid, *Die Römer an Rhein und Donau, Das Leben in der Obergermanischen Provinz* (Frankfurt 1973).

140 Wightman, p. 82, points out that theater north of the Alps was often linked with the ritual of temples and sacred sites and not with performances of the classical repertoire. Bechert, pp. 138–41, indicates that by the end of the 2nd century AD one third of the days of the year were designated holidays and although not all of these were celebrated away from Rome, the need for amusement was great. It generally took the form of animal baiting, horse racing and gladiatorial shows. A gladiatorial school is documented in *Agrippina*.

141 For this stipulation in the *Codex Theodosianus*, see Wightman, p. 65.

142 M. Cary, p. 757; see Hatt, p. 320.

143 J. Matthews, *Western Aristocracies and the Imperial Court, AD 364–425* (Oxford 1975), pp. 69–87, details the role played by Ausonius under Gratian. In AD 368 Decimus Magnus Ausonius accompanied the emperor Valentinian on an Alamannic campaign, to tutor the latter's son Gratian. As share of his booty he received Bissula, a young Alamannic girl, about whom he was to write in his poems. Soon afterwards he wrote the poem 'Mosella'. Filtzinger, in Filtzinger, Planck, Cämmerer, p. 113.

144 Matthews, p. 47, tells us that St. Jerome studied the writings of Hilarius of Poiters while at *Treveris*.

145 Th. K. Kempf, 'Das Haus der heiligen Helena', *Neues Trierisches Jahrbuch, Beiheft* (Trier 1978), p. 11. On the growth of Christianity in the Treveran area, see Wightman, pp. 227–37.

146 According to Wightman, p. 241, many pagan sites took on a Christian guise during this period. See also Diesner, pp. 10–34.

147 Wightman, pp. 205f., suggests that in spite of the decline and depopulation, all churches continued in use and that there was no complete disruption during the 5th century as there is no break evident in the list of bishops with names of the Roman provincial type.

148 See Millar, pp. 89f., on the *dediticci*.

149 R.I. Frank, *Scholae Palatinae, The Palace Guards of the Later Roman Empire* (American Academy in Rome 1969), p. 60, points out that *laeti* were tribes settled on allocated land, separate in that they kept their tribal organization and culture and did not become a part of the city-state culture of the Empire.

150 That these peoples could occupy land without any serious displacement of the existing populations implies that it was a question of only small groups of foreigners, see Boak, p. 42, note 54. It hardly needs stating that there was much vacated land by this time.

151 See Hatt, p. 357, for locations in Gaul.

152 Wightman, p. 251, suggests that these elements in the population buffered the violence of later arrivals.

153 Günther, Köpstein, p. 346.

154 Ibid.

155 Mócsy, p. 341.

156 Böttger, in Günther, Köpstein, pp. 186ff.; Percival, pp. 169f., argues for partial re-occupation during the 5th century, the making of repairs from the available debris and the continuation of rural life.

157 See also Percival, pp. 183–93, who points to the ruins of villas continuing as burial sites and early churches.

158 Böttger, in Günther, Köpstein, p. 188.

159 Ibid.

160 H. Schutz, *The Prehistory of Germanic Europe* (New Haven and London 1983), pp. 309–22. Also H. Krüger, *Die Jastorfkultur in den Kreisen Lüchow-Dannenberg, Lüneberg, Uelzen und Soltau, Göttinger Schriften zur Vor- und Frühgeschichte*, ed. Herbert Jankuhn (Neumünster 1961), p. 19, argues for a decrease in princely power and the dormancy of the aristocratic social order during this early Iron Age in the north which was not to be reawakened until the contact with Rome was made.

161 Millar, pp. 311ff.

162 J.B. Bury, *History of the Later Roman Empire from the Death of Theodosius I to the Death of Justinian* (New York 1958), I, p. 109, states that the Visi-Goths had hitherto not had a king and that Alaric was the first to be elected king by the assembly of his people.

163 M. Waas, *Germanen im römischen Dienst im 4. Jahrhundert nach Christus* (Bonn 1965), pp. 10ff., gives a summary of high ranking barbarians in Rome's service.

164 See also Stroheker, p. 42.

165 Frank, p. 64.

166 Günther, Köpstein, p. 350; see also Frank, pp. 53f., who identifies gentiles as barbarian tribes allied to the Empire and obliged to provide troops.

167 Frank, pp. 53f. defined an *armatura* as a unit of men picked for parade purposes. *Scutari* are shield bearers, as their name suggests.

168 W. Seyfarth, ed. Ammianus Marcellinus (Berlin 1971), p. 280, note 88, sees in the name the suggestion that they were dressed in white, stationed close to the emperor when in the field.

169 Günther, Köpstein, p. 350. According to Frank, p. 59, most of the *scholares* were Germani.

170 Frank, p. 63, identifies the *scholae* as the officers' corps.

171 See Frank, pp. 67f.; also Stroheker, pp. 11–29, for the preferred status enjoyed by the Franks; Frank, pp. 68ff.; also Stroheker, pp. 33–50, for the status of the Alamanni in Roman service.

172 About AD 370 the Alaman Vadomar was appointed *dux Phonices* in the east, supported by Alamannic troops, see Stroheker, p. 37. The Alamanni held lower ranks, see Frank, p. 68.

173 Stroheker, p. 11.

174 Frank, p. 64, suggests that already the assassination of Sylvanus (AD 355) had an 'anti-Frankish' aspect to it.

175 Waas, p. 35; also Ammianus, XV, 5, 6, '*homines dedicatos imperio*', in Seyfarth, I, p. 122.

176 Wightman, p. 60.

177 It appears that falsified documents forced him to take the step towards usurpation, Ammianus, XV, 5, , in Seyfarth, I, pp. 121–31. Also Filtzinger, in Filtzinger, Planck, Cämmerer, pp. 108f.

178 Waas, p. 18.

179 G.R. Watson, *The Roman Soldier* (London 1969), p. 115, states that torcs were an early form of decoration, as evident on gravestones of the 1st century AD, and not a sign of the barbarization of the army.

180 Waas, pp. 28–32, for their role in the civic administration.

181 Waas, p. 74.

182 G. Webster, *The Roman Imperial Army to Caracalla* (London 1969), p. 280, suggests that the influx of new blood was the reason for the lasting cohesion of the Empire.

183 Libanios was the panegyrist for Richomer when the latter acceded to the consulship in Constantinople in AD 384, see Stroheker, p. 25.

184 Waas, p. 42.

185 Hatt, p. 326.

186 Waas, p. 49, also p. 74, note 222; also Bury, p. 129, who indicates that the anti-Germanic movement in the east centered around Synesius.

187 See Matthews, pp. 253–83, for a detailed account of Stilicho's regime; see Bury, pp. 170–5, for an account of the death of Stilicho's family and the massacre of Germanic auxiliaries stationed in Italy. Hatt,

p. 355, proposes intrigue and conspiracy as the reason for Stilicho's execution for treason and the extensive ensuing massacres.

188 Wightman, pp. 250–9, indicates that entire Roman provincial communities continued to exist and that descendants of the Roman provincial population began to use Germanic names.

189 R.M. Haywood, *The Myth of Rome's Fall* (New York 1962), p. 169.

Bibliography

Geza Alföldy, *Die Hilfstruppen der römischen Provinz Germania Inferior* (Düsseldorf 1968).

Geza Alföldy, *Noricum, History of the Provinces of the Roman Empire*, transl. by A. Birley (London and Boston 1974).

Ammianus Marcellinus, *The Surviving Books of the History*, in three vols, with an English transl. by J.C. Rolfe, Loeb Classical Library (Cambridge, Mass. and London 1964).

Ammianus Marcellinus, *Römische Geschichte*, Lateinisch und Deutsch mit einem Kommentar, übersehen, von Wolfgang Seyfarth, in 4 Teilen (Berlin 1971).

Res Gestae Divi Augusti, The Acts of Augustus, transl. by F.W. Shipley, Loeb Classical Library (Cambridge, Mass. and London).

Dietwulf Baatz, 'Zur Grenzpolitik Hadrians in Obergermanien', in E. Birley, B. Dobson, M. Jarrett, eds. *Roman Frontier Studies* (Cardiff 1974).

Dietwulf Baatz, *Der römische Limes, Archäologische Ausflüge zwischen Rhein und Donau* (Berlin 1974).

Dietwulf Baatz, *Die Saalburg, Ein Führer durch das römische Kastell und seine Geschichte* (Bad Homburg 1976).

Dietwulf Baatz, Fritz-Rudolf Herrmann, et al., *Die Römer in Hessen* (Stuttgart 1982).

Tilmann Bechert, *Römisches Germanien zwischen Rhein und Maas, Die Provinz Germania Inferior* (Munich 1982).

Friedrich Behn, *Römertum und Völkerwanderung, Mitteleuropa zwischen Augustus und Karl dem Großen* (Stuttgart 1963).

Helmut Birkhan, *Germanen und Kelten bis zum Ausgang der Römerzeit, Der Aussagewert von Wörtern und Sachen für die frühesten Keltisch-Germanischen Kulturbeziehungen* (Vienna, Cologne, Graz 1970).

Arthur E.R. Boak, *Manpower Shortage and the Fall of the Roman Empire in the West* (Ann Arbor, Mich. 1955).

J.E. Bogaers, C.B. Rüger, *Der Niedergermanische Limes* (Cologne 1974).

A.D. Booth, *A Study of Ausonius' 'Professores'*, unpublished dissertation (Hamilton, Canada 1974).

George C. Brauer, *The Age of the Soldier Emperors, Imperial Rome AD 244-284* (Park Ridge, N.J. 1975).

J.B. Bury, *A History of the Roman Empire from Arcadius to Irene (AD 359-AD 800)*, reprint of the 1889 edition (Amsterdam 1966).

J.B. Bury, *History of the Later Roman Empire from the Death of Theodosius I to the Death of Justinian*, I, reprint of an earlier edition (New York 1958).

Leroy A. Campbell, *Mithraic Iconography and Ideology* (Leiden 1968).

Franz Cumont, *The Mysteries of Mithra*, transl. from the 2nd revised edition by T.J. McCormack (New York 1956).

Max Cary, *A History of Rome, Down to the Reign of Constantine* (London 1957).

George Leonard Cheesman, *The Auxilia of the Roman Imperial Army* (Oxford 1914, Hildesheim 1971).

Emilienne Demongeot, *La Formation de l'Europe et les invasions barbares, Des origines germaniques à l'avènement de Dioclétien* (Paris 1969).

Hans-Joachim Diesner, *Die Völkerwanderung* (Leipzig 1976, Gütersloh 1980).

Myles Dillon and Nora K. Chadwick, *The Celtic Realms* (London 1967).

Dio's Roman History in Nine Vols., with an English transl. by Ernest Cary, (Cambridge, Mass. and London 1961).

Paul-Marie Duval, *La vie quotidienne en Gaule pendant la paix romaine* (Paris 1967).

H.J. Eggers, E. Will, R. Joffroy, W. Holmquist, *Kelten und Germanen in heidnischer Zeit* (Baden-Baden 1964).

Joachim von Elbe, *Roman Germany, A Guide to Sites and Museums* (Mainz 1975).

Philipp Filtzinger, 'Die Jupitergigantensäule von Wahlheim', *Fundberichte aus Baden-Württemberg*, I (Stuttgart 1974).

Philipp Filtzinger, Dieter Planck, Bernhard Cämmerer, et at., *Die Römer in Baden-Württemberg* (Stuttgart and Aalen 1976).

Lucius Annaeus Florus, *Epitome of Roman History*, transl. by E.S. Forster (Cambridge, Mass. and London 1960).

R.I. Frank, *Scholae Palatinae, The Palace Guard of the Later Roman Empire* (Am. Ac. in Rome 1969).

J.F.C. Fuller, *Decisive Battles of the Western World*, I (Frogmore, St. Albans, 1975).

Jochen Garbsch, *Der spätrömische Donau-Rhein-Iller-Limes* (Stuttgart 1970).

U. Gehrig, *Der Hildesheimer Silberfund, Veröffentlichungen des Museums für Vor- und Frühgeschichte, Staatliche Museen Preussischer Kulturbesitz* (Berlin 1976).

Matthias Gelzer, *Caesar, der Politiker und Staatsmann* (Wiesbaden 1960).

Matthias Gelzer, *Caesar, Politician and Statesman*, transl. by Peter Needham (Cambridge, Mass. 1968).

Kurt Genser, *Die Entwicklung des römischen Limes an der Donau in Osterreich* (Salzburg 1975).

Walter Goffart, *Caput and Colonate, Towards a History of Late Roman Taxation* (Toronto 1974).

Michael Grant, ed. *The Birth of Western Civilization, Greece and Rome* (London, New York, Toronto 1964).

Albert Grenier, *Les Gaulois* (Paris 1970).

R. Günther, H. Köpstein, *Die Römer an Rhein und Donau* (Berlin 1975).

Gymnasium, Zeitschrift für Kultur der Antike und Humanistische Bildung, Beihefte, herausgegeben von Franz Bomer und Ludwig Voit, Heft 1, *Germania Romana I: Römerstädte in Deutschland* (Heidelberg 1960); Heft 5, *Germania Romana II: Kunst und Kunstgewerbe im römischen Deutschland* (Heidelberg 1965); Heft 7, *Germania Romana III: Römisches Leben auf Germanischem Boden* (Heidelberg 1970).

J.J. Hatt, *Histoire de la Gaule Romaine*, 3e édition (Paris 1970).

C. and S. Hawks, eds. *Greeks, Celts and Romans, Studies in Venture and Resistance, Archaeology in History I.* (London 1973).

R.M. Haywood, *The Myth of Rome's Fall* (New York 1962).

W. Heiligendorff, *Der Keltische Matronenkultus und seine Fortentwicklung im Deutschen Mythos* (Leipzig 1934).

Martin Henig, ed. *A Handbook of Roman Art, A comprehensive survey of all the arts of the Roman world* (Ithaca, N.Y. 1983).

J.R. Hinnels, ed. *Mithraic Studies, Proceedings of the First International Congress of Mithraic Studies*, vols. I, II (Manchester 1975).

H. Jens, *Mythologisches Lexikon* (Munich 1958).

Werner Jobst, *Provinzhauptstadt Carnuntum* (Vienna 1983).

Anne Johnson, *Roman Forts of the 1st and 2nd Centuries AD in Britain and the German Provinces* (London 1983).

A.H.M. Jones, *The Roman Economy, Studies in Ancient Economic and Administrative History*, ed. by P.A. Brunt (Oxford 1974).

Julius Caesar, *The Gallic War and Other Writings*, transl. with an introduction by Moses Hadas (New York 1957).

S. Katz, *The Decline of Rome and the Rise of Medieval Europe* (Ithaca, N.Y. 1961).

Hans-Jörg Kellner, *Die Römer in Bayern* (Munich 1971, 1978).

Kölner Römer Illustrierte, I, ed. M. Wellershoff (Historische Museen der Stadt Köln 1974).

Kölner Römer Illustrierte, II, ed. G. Biegel (Historische Museen der Stadt Köln 1975).

Ernst Kornemann, *Römische Geschichte*, in zwei Bänden, 6. Auflage, bearbeitet von Hermann Bengtson (Stuttgart 1970).

Frantisek Křižek, 'Die Römischen Stationen im Vorland des norisch-pannonischen Limes bis zu den Markomannenkriegen', in Birley, et al., *Studien zu den Militärgrenzen Roms, Vorträge des 6. Internationalen Limeskongresses in Süddeutschland* (Cologne, Graz 1967).

Heinrich Krüger, *Die Jastorfkultur in den Kreisen Lüchow-Dannenberg, Lüneburg, Uelzen und Soltau*, in Herbert Jankuhn, ed. *Göttinger Schriften zur Vor- und Frühgeschichte*, Neumünster 1961).

Peter La Baume, *The Romans on the Rhine*, transl. from the German *Die Römer am Rhein*, by B. Jones, Sammlung 'Rheinisches Land' (Bonn 1966).

Françoise Le Roux, *Introduction générale à l'étude de la tradition celtique I* (Rennes 1967).

G.H. Leute, J. Hock, *Das Landesmuseum für Kärnten und seine Sammlungen* (Klagenfurt 1976).

Kurt Lindemann, *Der Hildesheimer Silberfund, Varus und Germanien* (Hildesheim 1967).

K.M. Linduff, 'Epona: a Celt among the Romans', *Latomus, Revue d'études latines* (Berchem-Bruxelles 1979).

Lucan, *Pharsalia, Dramatic Episodes of the Civil War.* A new translation by Robert Graves (Harmondsworth 1956).

Paul MacKendrick, *Romans on the Rhine, Archaeology in Germany* (New York 1970).

Ramsey MacMullen, *Soldier and Civilian in the Later Roman Empire* (Cambridge, Mass. 1963).

Ramsey MacMullen, *The Roman Government's Response to Crisis, AD 235-337* (New Haven and London 1976).

Ulrich Maier, *Caesars Feldzüge in Gallien (58–51 v. Chr.) in ihrem Zusammenhang mit der stadtrömischen Politik, Saarbrücker Beiträge zur Altertumskunde*, Band 29 (Bonn 1978).

John Matthews, *Western Aristocracies and the Imperial Court, AD 364-435* (Oxford 1975).

J.V.S. Megaw, *Art of the European Iron Age, A Study of the Elusive Image* (Bath 1970).

W. Meyers, *L'Aministration de la province romaine de Belgique* (Bruge 1964).

Fergus Millar, et al., *The Roman Empire and its Neighbours*, English edition (London 1967).

Andras Mócsy, *Pannonia and Upper Moesia, A History of the Middle Danube Provinces of the Roman Empire*, transl. by S. Frere (London and Boston 1974).

Rudolf Much, *Die Germania des Tacitus*, Dritte, beträchtlich erweiterte Auflage, unter Mitarbeit von Herbert Jankuhn, herausgegeben von W. Lange (Heidelberg 1967).

Pavel Oliva, *Pannonia and the Onset of Crisis in the Roman Empire* (Prague 1962).

John Percival, *The Roman Villa, An Historical Introduction* (Berkely and Los Angeles 1976).

Walter Pflug, *Media in Germania, Die Römer mitten in Germanien, Eine Darstellung der römischen Expansion in Germanien* (Giessen 1956).

G.P. Picard, 'César et les Druides', in *Hommage à la mémoire de Jerome Carcopino* (Paris 1977).

Dieter Planck, ed. *Archäologische Ausgrabungen in Baden-Württemberg 1982* (Stuttgart 1983).

Dieter Planck, *Das Freilichtmuseum am rätischen Limes im Ostalbkreis*, Serie: *Führer zu archäologischen Denkmälern in Baden-Württemberg*, Nr. 9 (Stuttgart 1983).

Pliny, *Natural History*, Vol. VIII, translated by W.H.S. Jones, XCV (Cambridge, Mass. and London).

Praeger Picture Encyclopedia of Art (New York 1965).

R. Roerer, *Kleine Vor- und Frühgeschichte Württembergs* (Stuttgart 1963).

N.K. Sandars, *Prehistoric Art in Europe* (Harmondsworth 1968).

Der Schatzfund von Straubing, Römische Abteilung—Gäubodenmuseum (Straubing).

Friedrich Schlette, *Kelten zwischen Alesia und Pergamon, Eine Kulturgeschichte der Kelten* (Leipzig, Jena, Berlin 1979).

Armin and Renate Schmid, *Die Römer an Rhein und Main, Das Leben in der Obergermanischen Provinz* (Frankfurt 1972).

Helmut Schoppa, *Die Kunst der Römerzeit in Gallien, Germanien und Britannien* (Munich 1957).

Helmut Schoppa, *Der Römische Steinsaal, Sammlung Nassauischer Altertümer, Schriften des Städtischen Museums Wiesbaden* (Wiesbaden 1965).

Herbert Schutz, *The Prehistory of Germanic Europe* (New Haven and London 1983).

Alfred Schütze, *Mithras, Mysterien und Urchristentum* (Stuttgart 1972).

Elmar Schwertheim, *Die Denkmäler orientalischer Gottheiten im Römischen Deutschland* (Leiden 1974).

R.E. Smith, *Service in the Post-Marian Roman Army* (Manchester 1961).

Michael P. Speidel, *The Religion of Iuppiter Dolichenus in the Roman Army* (Leiden 1978).

Karl F. Stroheker, *Germanentum und Spätantike* (Zürich, Stuttgart 1965).

Suetonius, *Life of Augustus*, translated by J.C. Rolfe (Cambridge, Mass. and London 1970).

Tacitus, *Germania*, translated by M. Hutton (Cambridge, Mass. and London 1970).

Tacitus, *Histories and Annals*, translated by C.H. Moore and J. Jackson, (Cambridge, Mass. and London).

W. Tarn and G.T. Griffith, *Hellenistic Civilization* (London 1953).

E.A. Thompson, *The Early Germans* (Oxford 1965).

Günther Ulbert, *Die römischen Donau-Kastelle Aislingen und Burghöfe, Limesforschungen, Studien zur Organisation der römischen Reichsgrenze an Rhein und Donau*, herausgegeben von H. von Petrikovitz und W. Schleiermacher (Berlin 1959).

Velleius Paterculus, *Compendium of Roman History*, transl. by Frederick W. Shipley (Cambridge, Mass. London 1961).

M.J. Vermaseren, *Mithras, The Secret God* (London 1963).

Jan de Vries, 'Die Druiden', in *Kairos, Zeitschrift für Religionswissenschaft und Theologie*, 11 (Salzburg 1959).

Jan de Vries, *Kelten und Germanen* (Berlin and Munich 1960).

Jan de Vries, *Keltische Religion* (Stuttgart 1961).

Manfred Waas, *Germanen im römischen Dienst im 4. Jahrhundert nach Christus* (Bonn 1965).

Gerold Walser, *Caesar und die Germanen, Studien zur politischen Tendenz römischer Feldzugsberichte* (Wiesbaden 1956).

G.R. Watson, *The Roman Soldier* (London 1969).

Leo Weber, *Als die Römer kamen . . . Augusta Vindelicorum und die Besiedlung Raetiens* (Landsberg am Lech, 1973).

Winfried Weber, *Constantinische Deckengemälde aus dem römischen Palast unter dem Trierer Dom*, Bischöfliches Dom- und Diözesanmuseum Trier, Museumsführer Nr. 1 (Trier 1984).

Graham Webster, *The Roman Imperial Army to Caracalla* (London 1969).

C.M. Wells, *The German Policy of Augustus, An examination of the Archaeological Evidence* (Oxford 1972).

Robert E.R. Wheeler, *Roman Art and Architecture* (New York, Washington 1964).

K.D. White, *Farm Equipment of the Roman World* (Cambridge 1975).

Mary Edith Wightman, *Roman Trier and the Treveri* (New York, Washington 1971).

Kurt Willvonseder, *Keltische Kunst in Salzburg, Schriftenreihe des Salzburger Museums Carolino Augusteum*, 2 (Salzburg 1960).

194

Index